IMAGES
of America

California, Pennsylvania

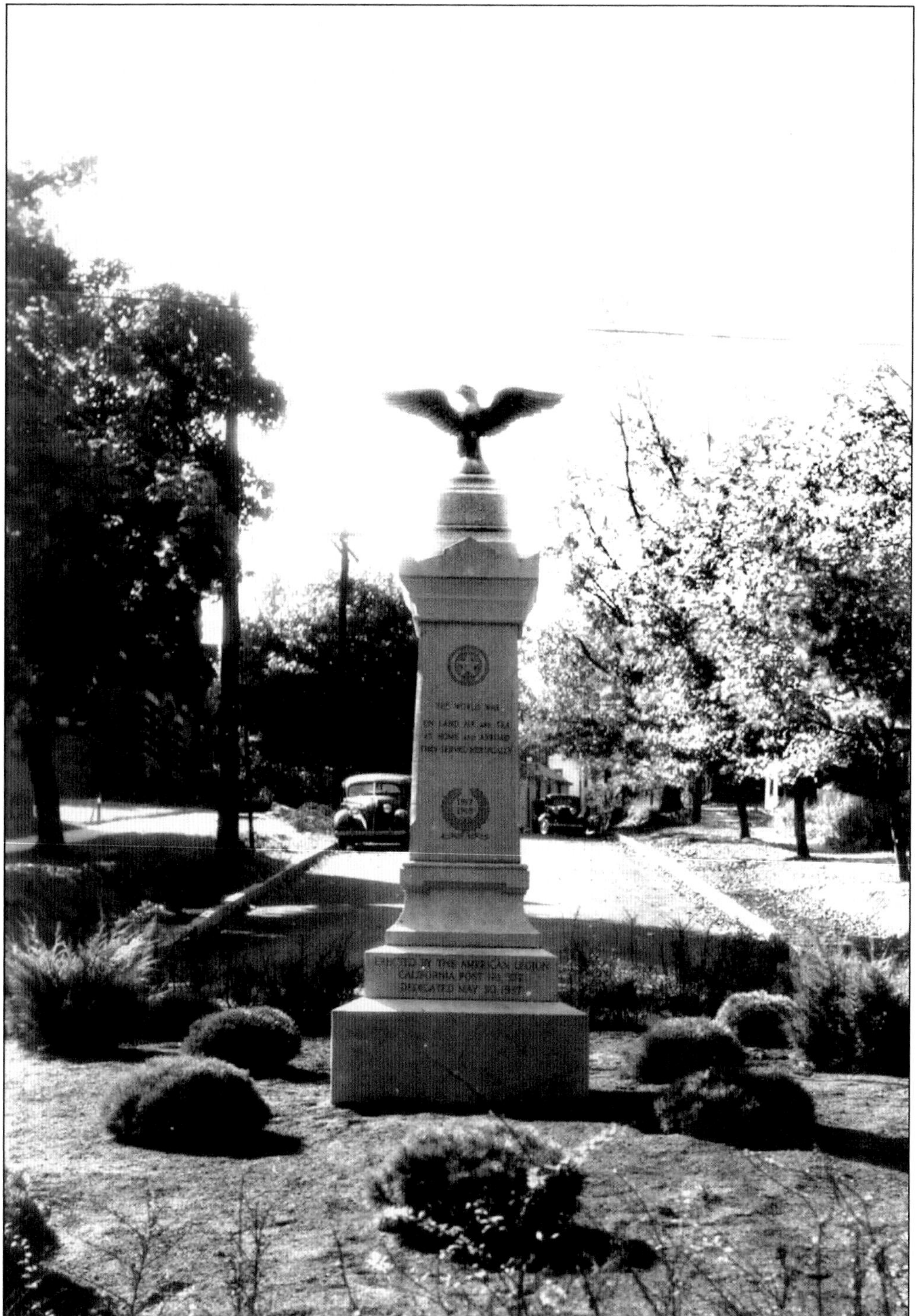

TAYLOR SQUARE. The square named for Earl and Hallie Taylor is located at the center of Fourth and Liberty Streets. Originally intended to honor World War I veterans, it now honors all veterans.

IMAGES
of America

CALIFORNIA, PENNSYLVANIA

California Area Historical Society

ARCADIA
PUBLISHING

ISBN 978-0-7385-1154-2

Published by Arcadia Publishing
Charleston, South Carolina

Printed in the United States of America

Library of Congress Catalog Card Number: 2002113747

For all general information, contact Arcadia Publishing:
Telephone 843-853-2070
Fax 843-853-0044
E-mail sales@arcadiapublishing.com
For customer service and orders:
Toll-free 1-888-313-2665

Visit us on the Internet at www.arcadiapublishing.com

Author's note: The mission of the California Area Historical Society is to preserve the history of the California area and the significance of its settlers. The society has compiled this publication in conjunction with the celebration of its 10th anniversary. Readers who wish to share photographs or other historical materials related to the society's area of interest are welcome to contact us by writing to the California Area Historical Society, P.O. Box 624, California, PA 15419-0624.

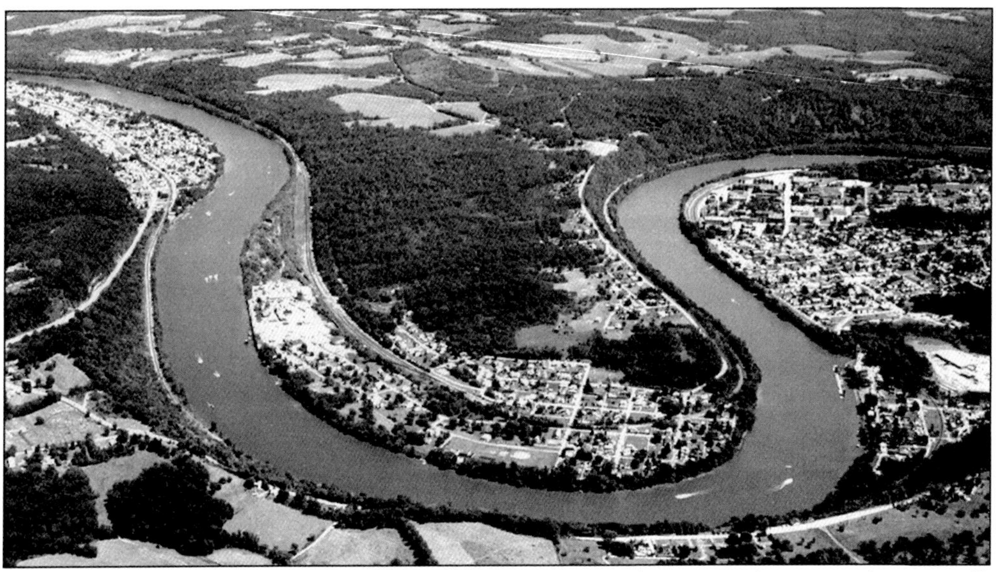

HORSESHOE BEND. This aerial view shows, from left to right, the towns of Roscoe, Elco, Newell, Coal Center, and California near the scenic horseshoe bend in the Monongahela River.

Contents

ACKNOWLEDGMENTS

Harry Harris set up his first photography studio in a tent in California, Pennsylvania, *c.* 1900. Later, he built a wooden studio where he continued to capture photographic images of the town, its people, and its activities until his death in 1951. Many of the images in this book are from the Harry Harris Collection, donated to the California Area Historical Society (CAHS) by his daughter Catherine Harris.

Appreciation is extended to all those who contributed photographs for the book and to the CAHS members who aided in researching the text. Special recognition is given to Patricia Cowen, Gerald Cowen, and Mary Beth Graf, who compiled and prepared the material for publication.

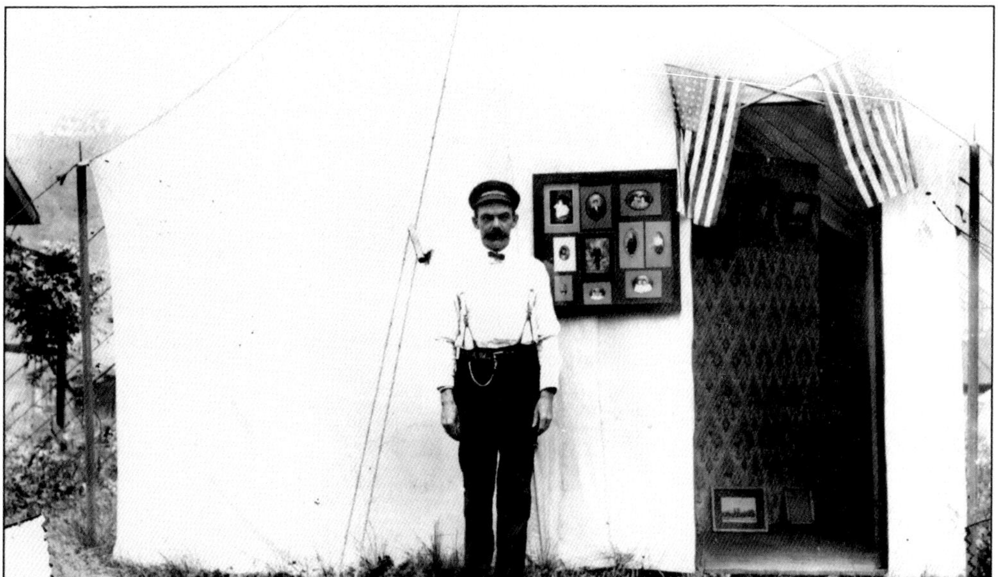

HARRY HARRIS. Pictured is the tent that Harry Harris used for his original photography studio.

INTRODUCTION

The village of California, originally a part of East Pike Run Township, was conceived by a group of industrious men. These entrepreneurs—Samuel Ashmead, Abraham Fry, George W. Hornbake, William Jackman, Job Johnson, and John Wood—laid out the village in May 1849 during the excitement of the California gold rush. The land once belonged to Indian Peter and had subsequently been passed down to Robert Jackman, who was the first to obtain a land patent for the area. Jackman's son William formed a company to charter the town.

The location of California near the graceful Greenfield bend on the Monongahela River became the site of riverboat construction. Skilled carpenters and artisans arriving to begin work in the boatyard often saw their first glimpse of California from a packet boat. The boatbuilding industry increased the population of the town and took advantage of the river as a major communication and transportation channel to the West. The river attracted other entrepreneurs, and the town slowly grew to include brickyards, a glass factory, a foundry, sawmills, and lumber companies.

By the 1880s, the coal industry was emerging. The ventures of local businessmen attracted immigrants to western Pennsylvania in search of work. A number of mines were soon operating in and around California. In the early 1900s, the Vesta No. 4 Mine was the largest and most productive mine in the country, and it remained so until it closed in 1957.

From the earliest years, providing education for all of the community members was an important priority. The California Academy was established in 1852. This institution became the Southwestern State Normal School and, in 1928, was transformed into a state teachers college. Now known as California University of Pennsylvania, the school has been a benefit to the entire Monongahela Valley area. While some industries have come and gone, education has implanted itself firmly in the community.

The citizens of California have met the challenges of their 150-year-old history. Whether mining coal or earning college degrees, the people of California have demonstrated their ability to adjust to the times and succeed. To the generations of families who have lived and worked in the area, there will always be a California, Pennsylvania.

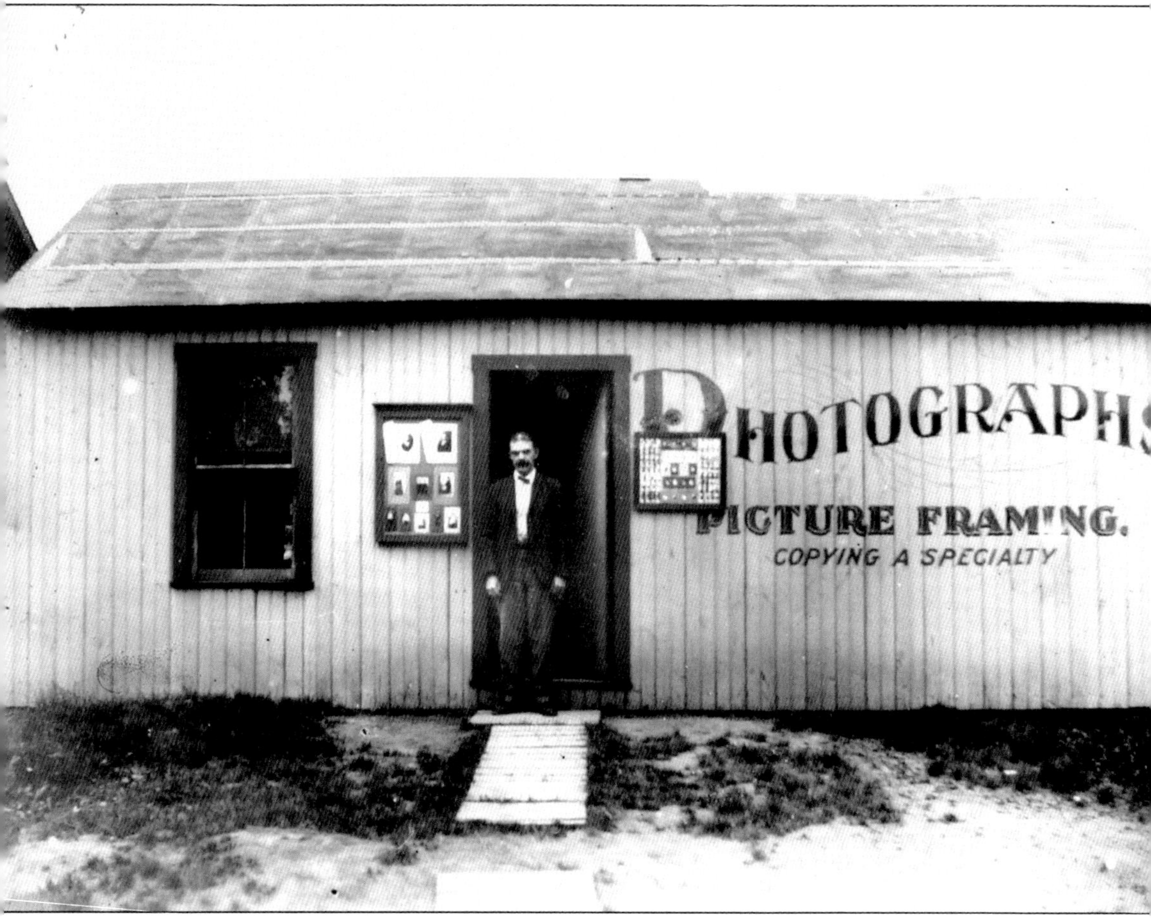

THE HARRY HARRIS PHOTOGRAPHY STUDIO. This wooden building was the second business establishment of Harry Harris. Through his camera lenses, Harris left a legacy of photographic images documenting the history of the California area. The collection donated to the California Area Historical Society numbers in excess of 1,000 photographs and negatives.

One

The Early Days

Gold was discovered in the western state of California c. 1849, and the discovery led to many Easterners abandoning their roots to follow the trail to the West, but the promise of prosperity could be found as well in western Pennsylvania along the Monongahela River. The fertile river valley and moderate climate attracted farmers and businessmen to the area known as East Pike Run Township. These early settlers realized the value of being near the river. Intelligent, ambitious, and resourceful, they remained and founded their own California. The community grew from a settlement of farms into a town. Mindful of the difficult routes they themselves had traveled over to get to the area, the early settlers planned wide streets to accommodate the businesses and homes, provided education and religious institutions, and valued the river and coal as natural resources. Within 30 years of settlement, the town of California had established itself on the Monongahela River as an active and productive community.

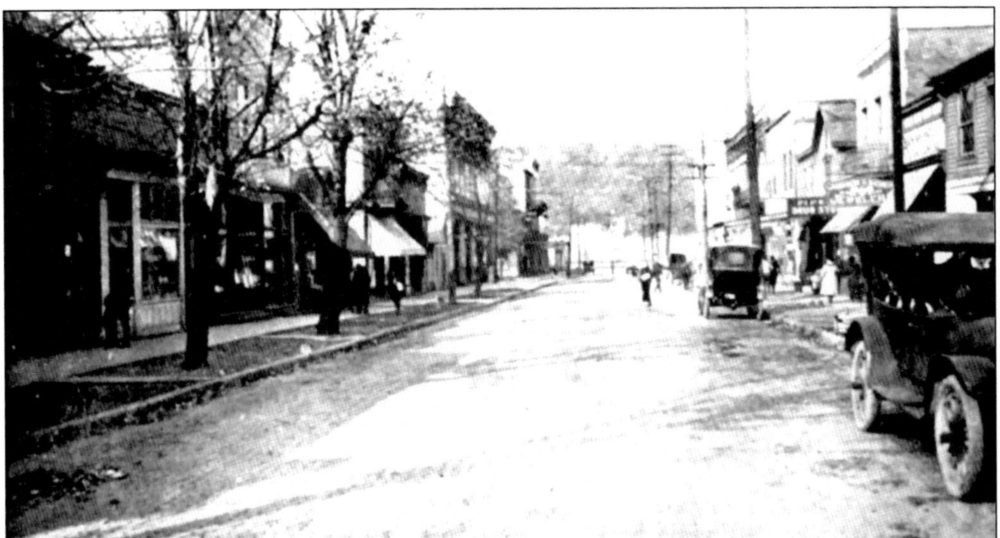

Wood Street, North. This early photograph of Wood Street shows buildings still in existence today. The buildings have housed many different enterprises over the years. Only the bank on Second Street remains in its original location.

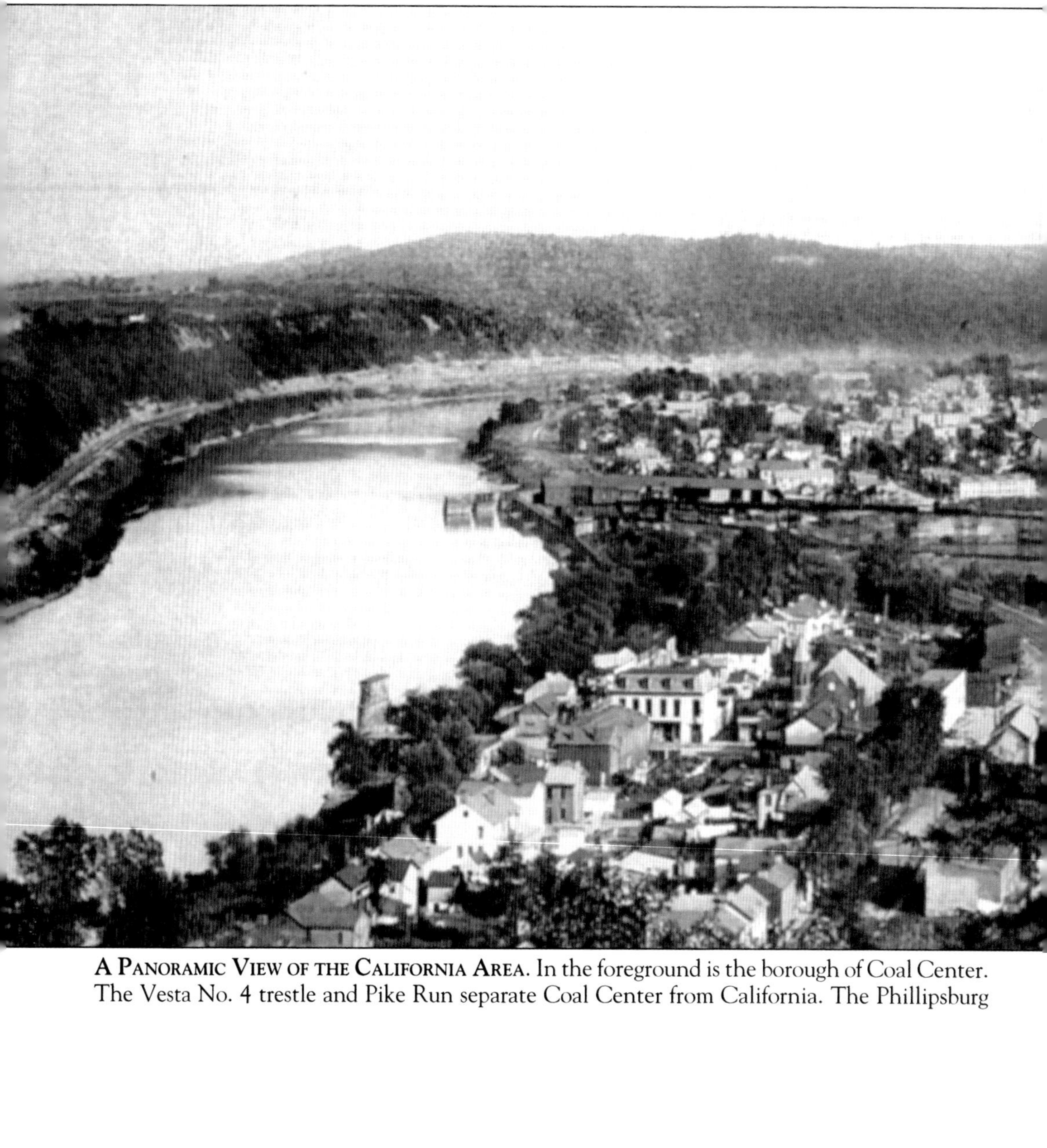

A Panoramic View of the California Area. In the foreground is the borough of Coal Center. The Vesta No. 4 trestle and Pike Run separate Coal Center from California. The Phillipsburg

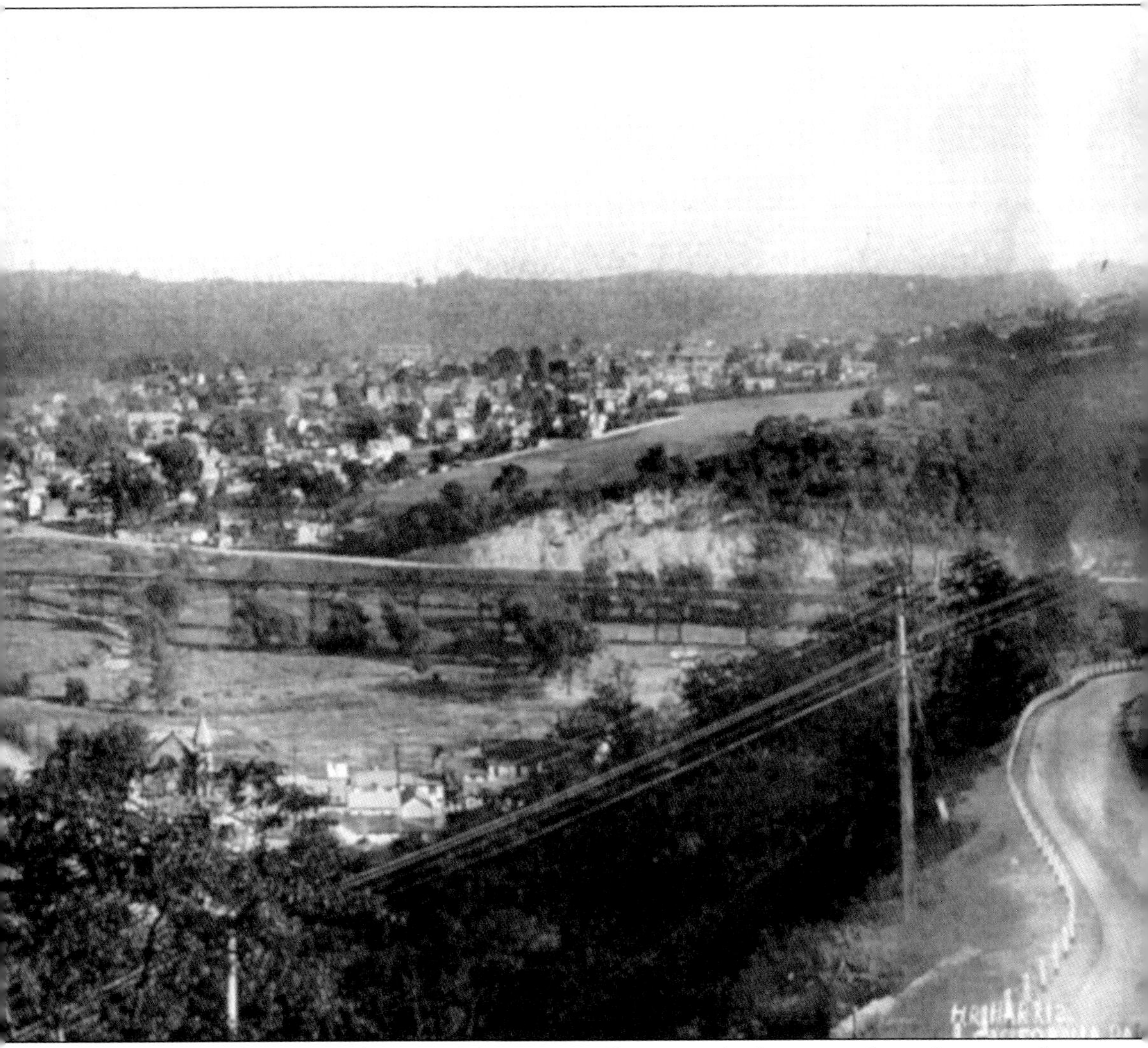

community can be seen at the top of the picture. Shown to the bottom right is the original Route 88, the access road from the north to the borough of California.

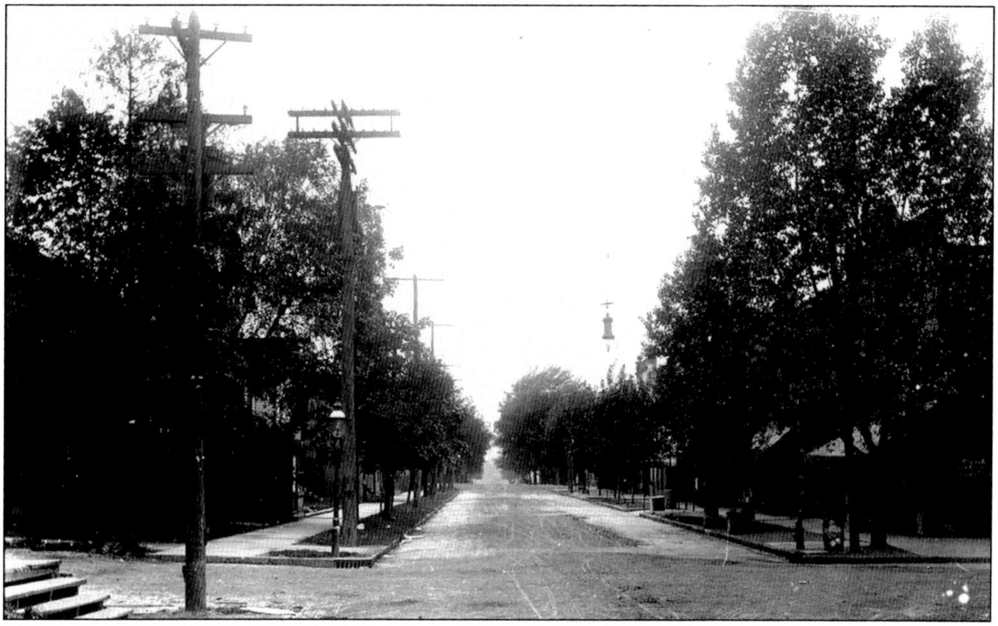

Third and Wood Streets. The busiest intersection in California is at Wood and Third Streets, but in 1900 there was no Quick Fill, Savage Hotel, or Rite Aid. The light from a single light bulb on a pole in the middle of the road aided travelers after dark. This view looks west from the middle of town.

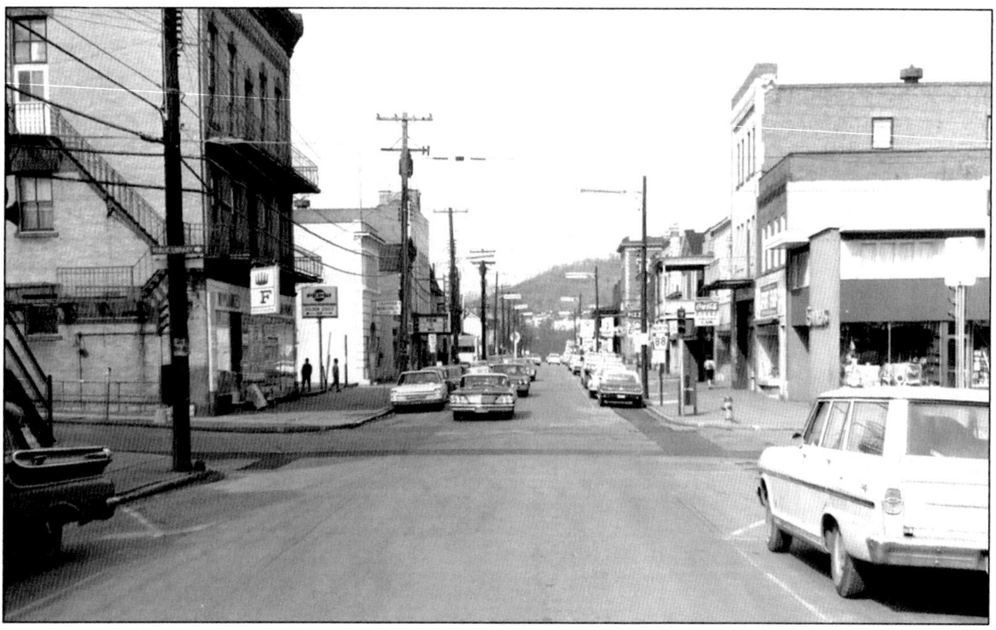

Third and Wood Streets. Fifty years after the previous photograph was taken, the busiest section of California shows growth. The types of stores have changed as the needs of the residents changed. (Courtesy Charles Keller.)

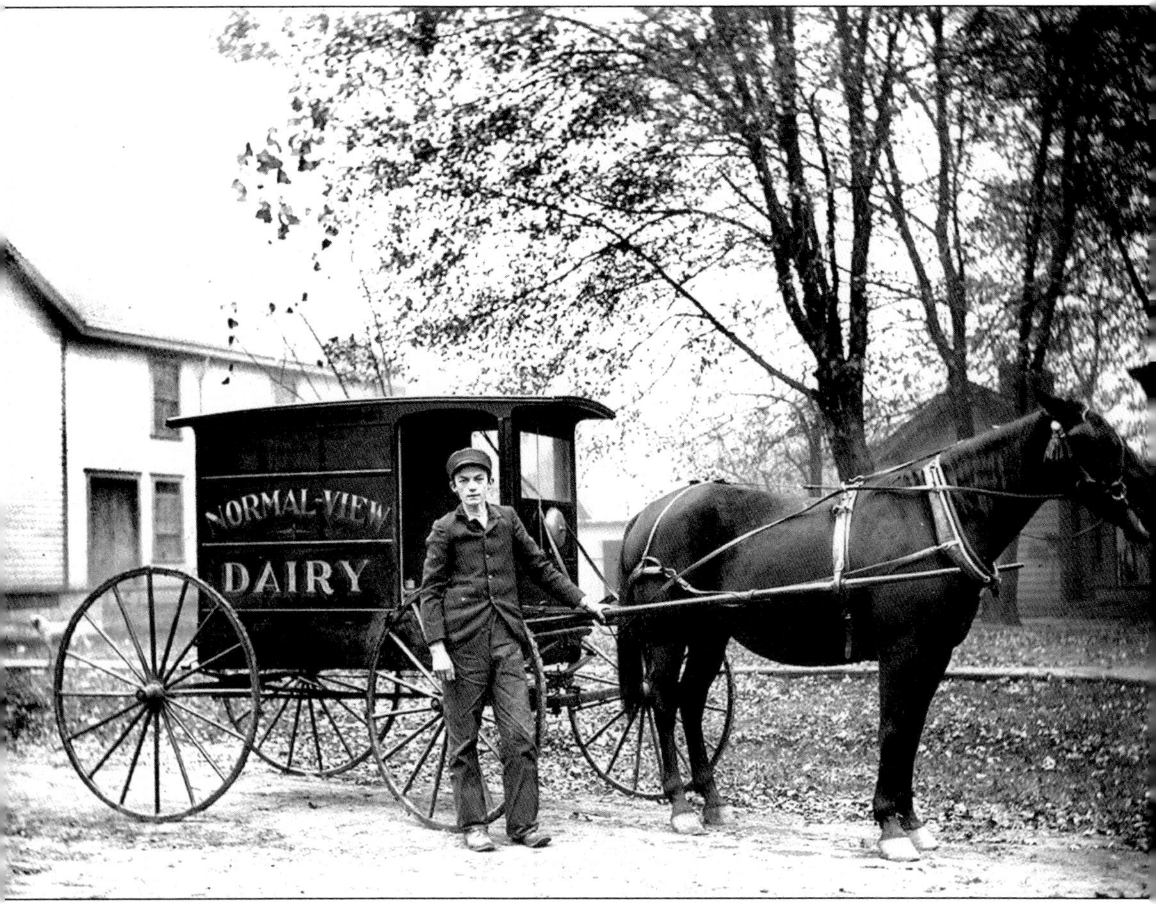

NORMAL VIEW DAIRY. Normal View was the part of East Pike Run Township overlooking the Southwestern State Normal School. This farmer delivered milk to his customers with horse and carriage. He came "off the hill" to sell his dairy products to Second Street and Southwestern State Normal School residents.

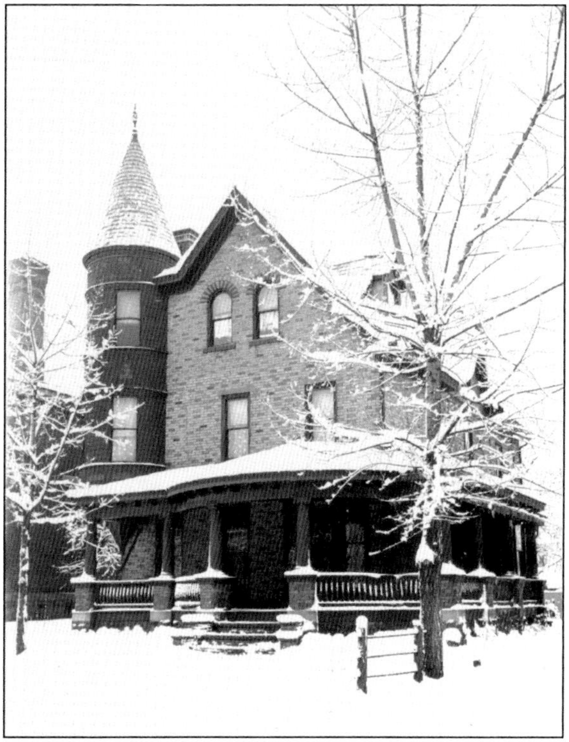

The Lewis Morgan House. Lewis and Anna Jane (Gregg) Morgan raised a family of eight children in this home. Morgan was superintendent of the Methodist Sunday school for 21 years and was an early town historian. He and Solomon Sibbitt opened the first general store in California in 1850.

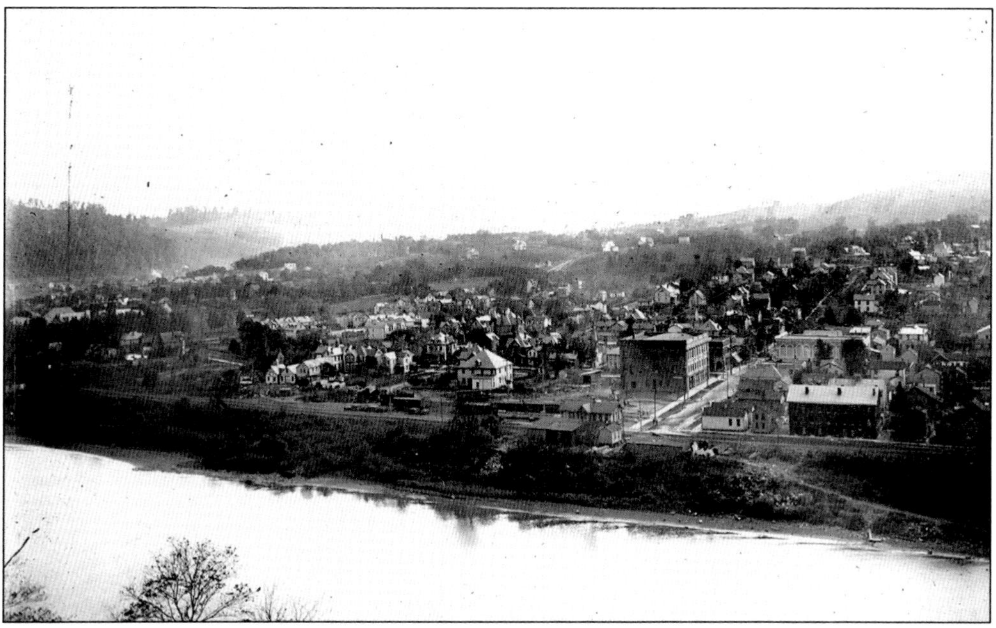

Downtown California. This undated picture gives clues about its age. Shown are the Job Johnson Hotel, the marble works, the driveway to the river, the wooden train depot, and the Phillipsburg community. What can you locate that is still here or long gone?

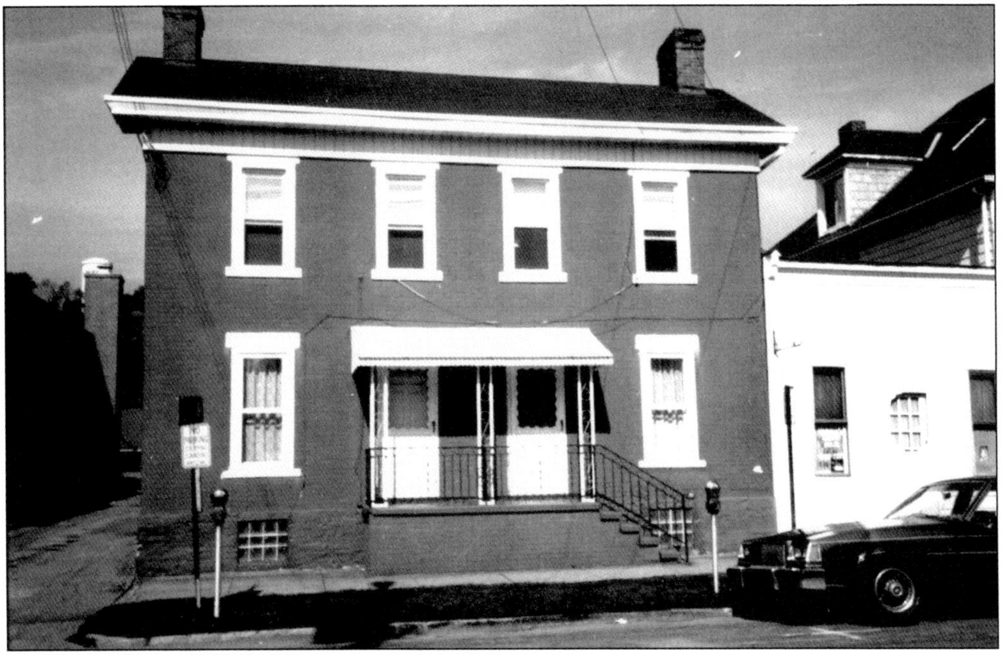

The First House. The Thomas Moore house, on Second Street and Temperance Alley, was the first home built in California. The bricks were made in town from clay dug on the banks of the Monongahela River. Long gone is the elaborate wooden trim designed to represent the trim on the paddle-wheel boats that were so prominent on the river.

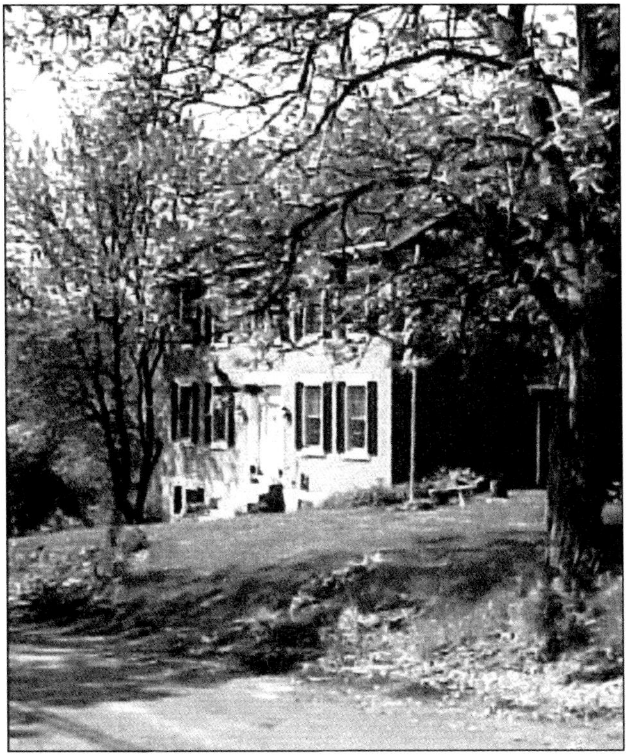

Bailey's Farm. Isaac Bailey and his sister Maria (Bailey) Kinder purchased two pieces of land in 1841 from David Duvall and Samuel Krepps. Isaac Bailey built this house between 1841 and 1860. Excluding the years from 1978 to 1998, the house has been in the Bailey-Worley-Harrison-Vitchoff family for 160 years. The beautiful brick home and barn have been restored and include five of the original fireplaces and original floors, closets, moldings, and stairways. (Courtesy Lorraine Vitchoff.)

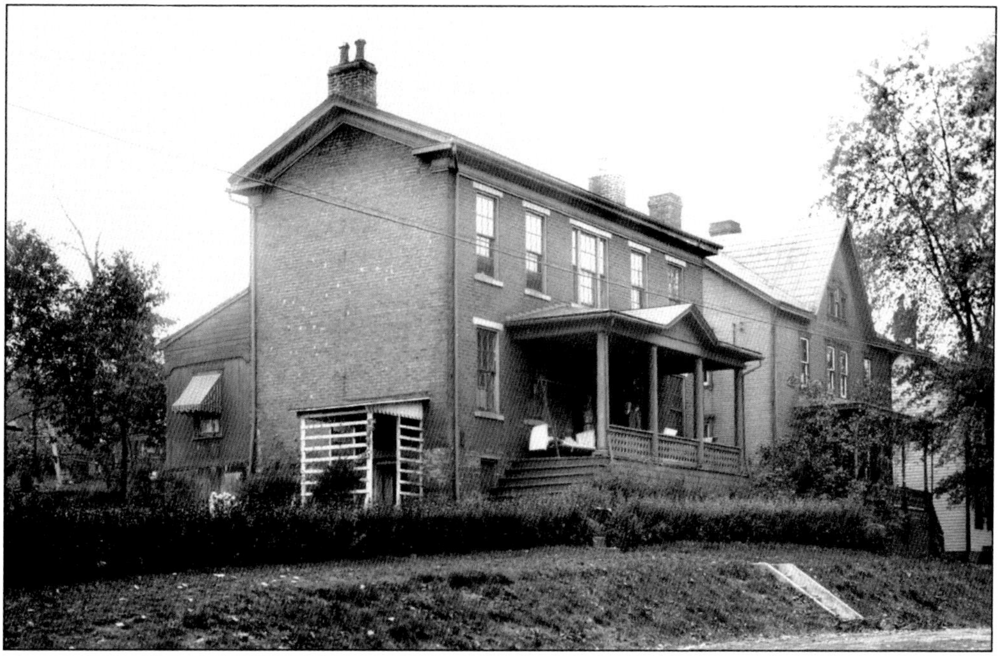

The Cairns Home. Still standing at Fifth and Liberty, the home built by Andrew Cairns was one of three new homes built in 1849 in the town. It is made of riverbank clay, a type especially suited for this kind of construction.

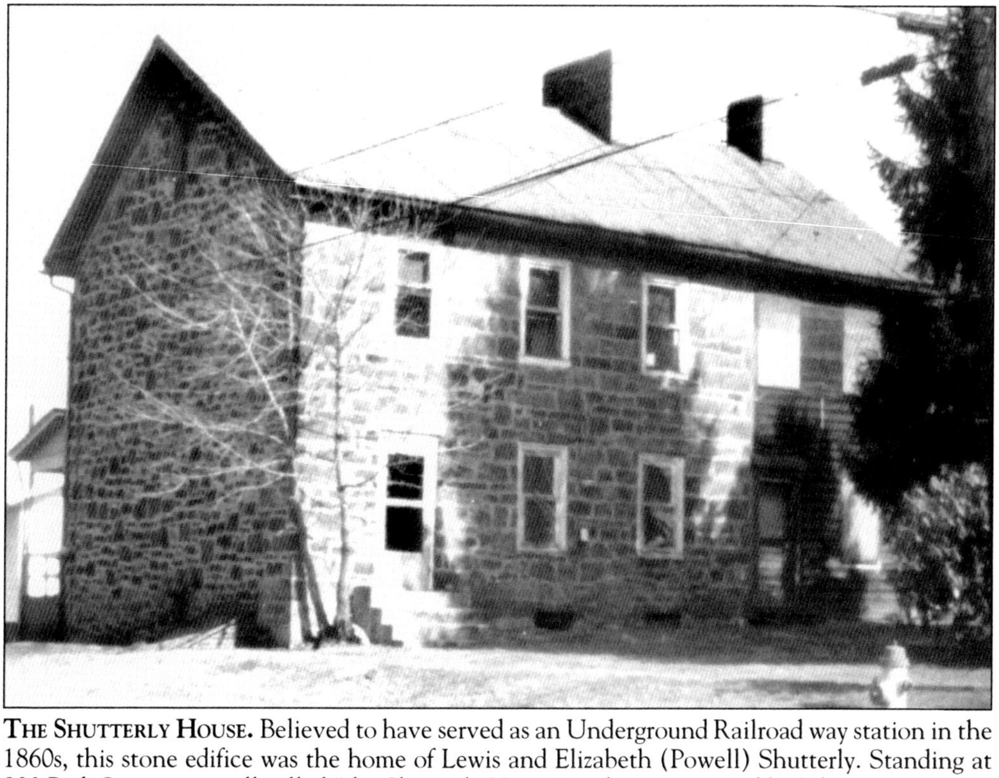

The Shutterly House. Believed to have served as an Underground Railroad way station in the 1860s, this stone edifice was the home of Lewis and Elizabeth (Powell) Shutterly. Standing at 800 Park Street, it is still called "the Shutterly House" and is now owned by John Mariscotti.

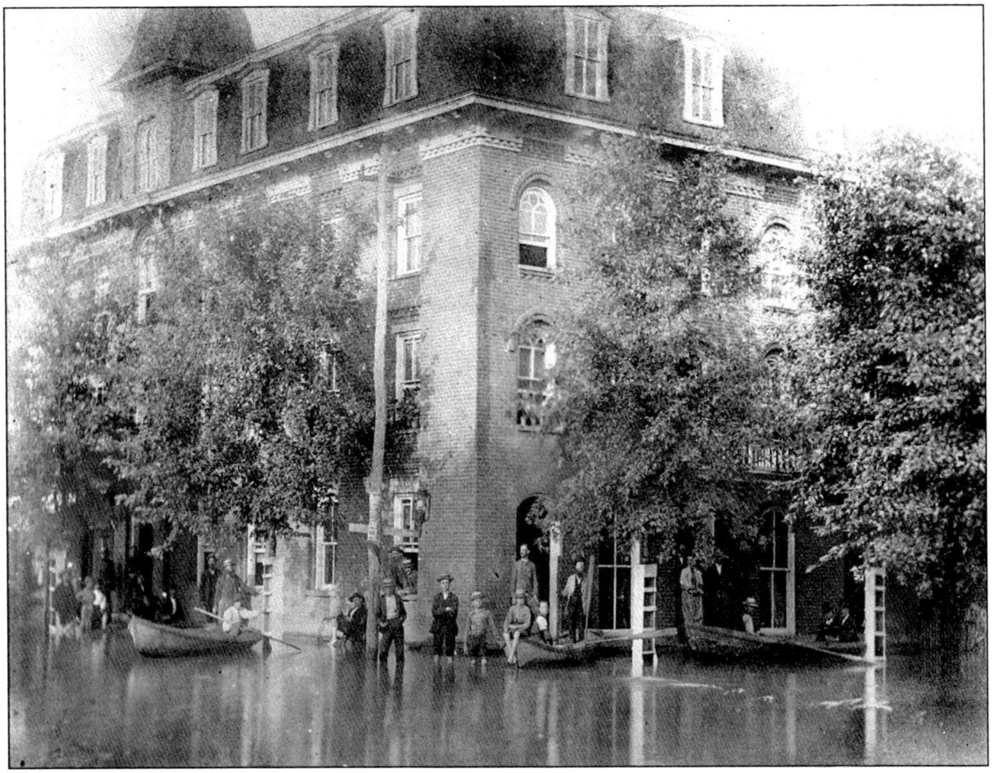

The Arlington Hotel. The Arlington Hotel is shown in 1888, when the Monongahela River rose to its highest level in history. Standing at the corner of Union and Second Streets, the hotel was originally built by Solomon Fry as a dwelling place. Purchased by A.J. Letherman in 1887, additions were built, and then it was converted into a hotel with a first-floor restaurant.

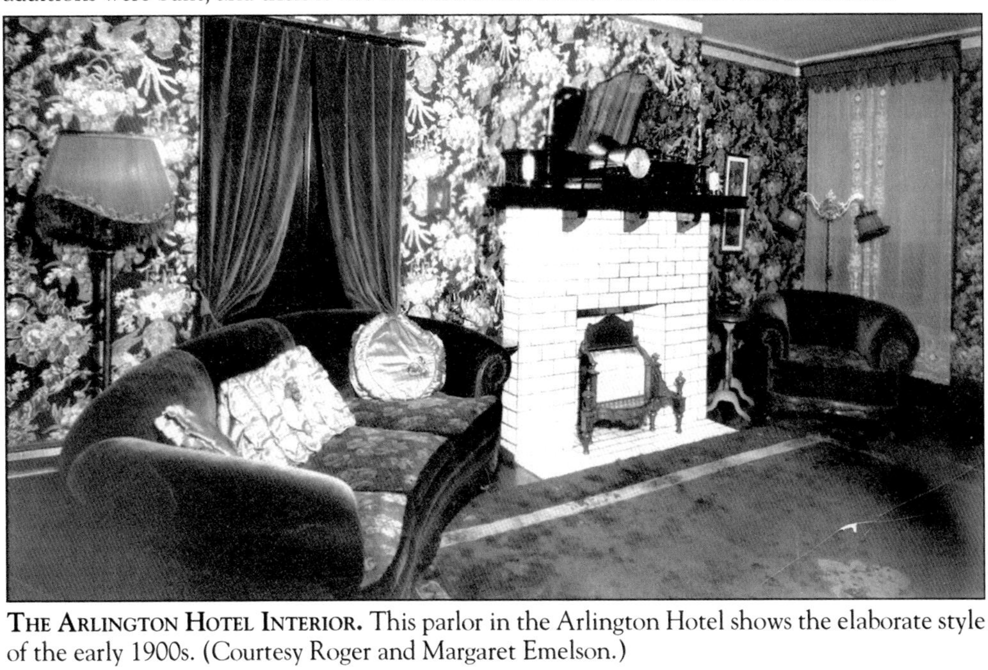

The Arlington Hotel Interior. This parlor in the Arlington Hotel shows the elaborate style of the early 1900s. (Courtesy Roger and Margaret Emelson.)

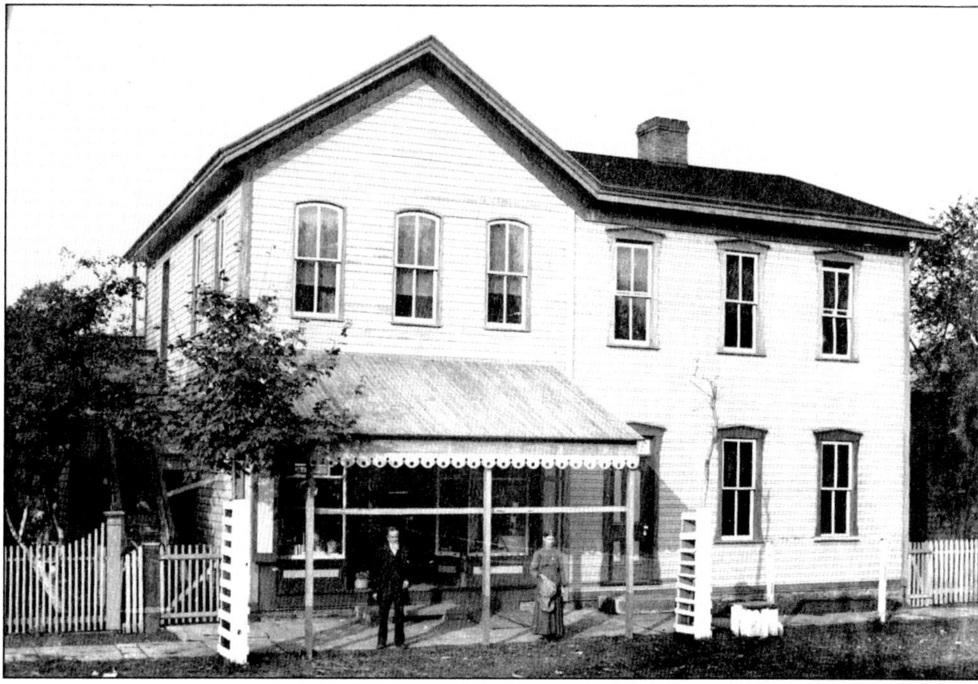

THE SOLOMON ZOOK STORE. This grocery store, at 450 Third Street, was owned by Solomon and Lydia (Binns) Zook *c.* 1880. (Courtesy W. Floyd Gillis.)

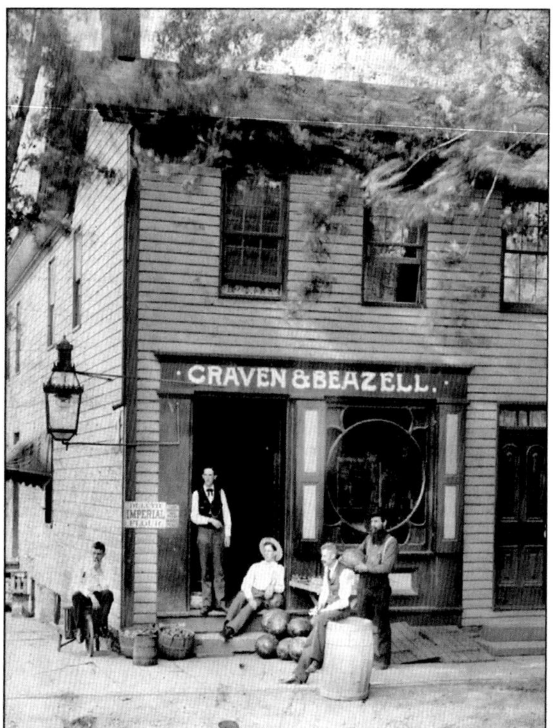

CRAVEN AND BEAZELL GROCERIES. In August 1894, at the corner of Third and Liberty Streets, employees and customers pose for a picture in front of Craven and Beazell store. They are Edgar Abel (on wheelbarrow), manager Fred T. Wilkins (standing in doorway), Frank H. Wilkins (seated in doorway), James Wilson (on barrel), and J.B. Shallenberger (purchasing watermelon). The store was purchased on July 9, 1894, by Fred H. Wilkins and was managed by his two sons.

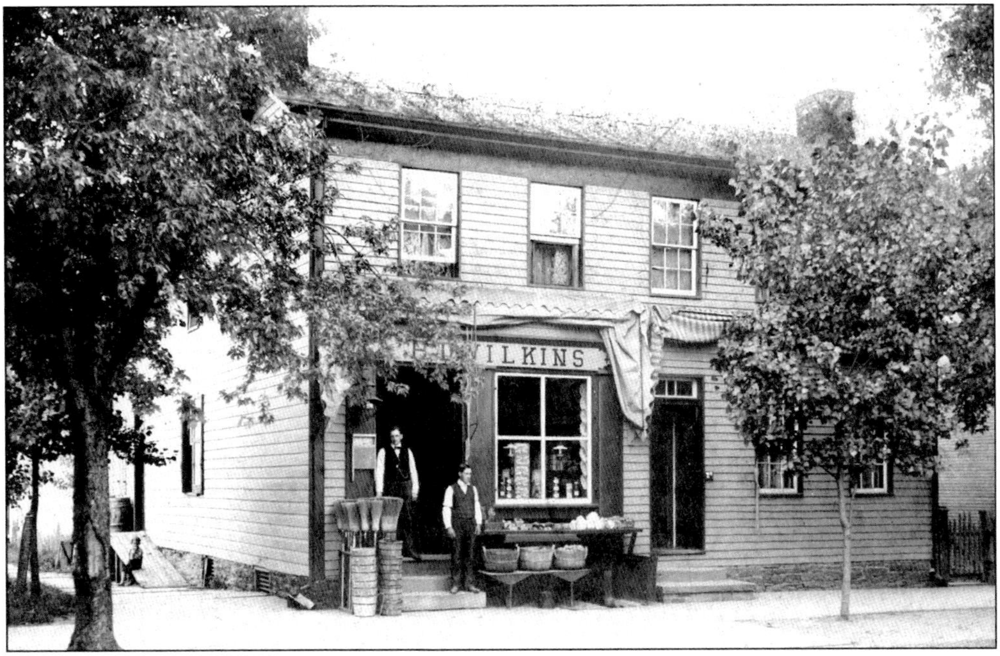

The Wilkins Grocery Store. Henry Wilkins opened this grocery store in 1894. Because he was master and pilot of the river steamer *Belle McGowan*, the management of the store became the responsibility of his sons, Fred and Khramer. Their aim was to transact business in a fair and honest manner, carrying only high-quality stocks of groceries, Queensware, and feed. The building is located on the corner of Third and Liberty Streets. (Courtesy Robert Grimes.)

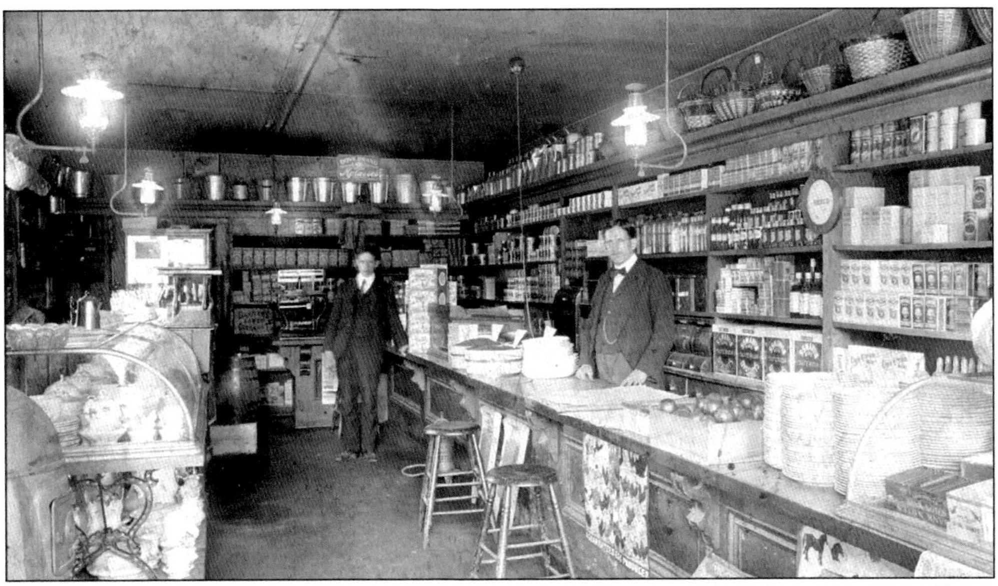

The Wilkins Grocery Interior. The Wilkins grocery was purchased in 1894 from Frank Craven. Frank H. and Fred T. Wilkins stand behind the counter in the store they managed. This interior photograph shows the variety of items they sold. (Courtesy Richard Wilkins.)

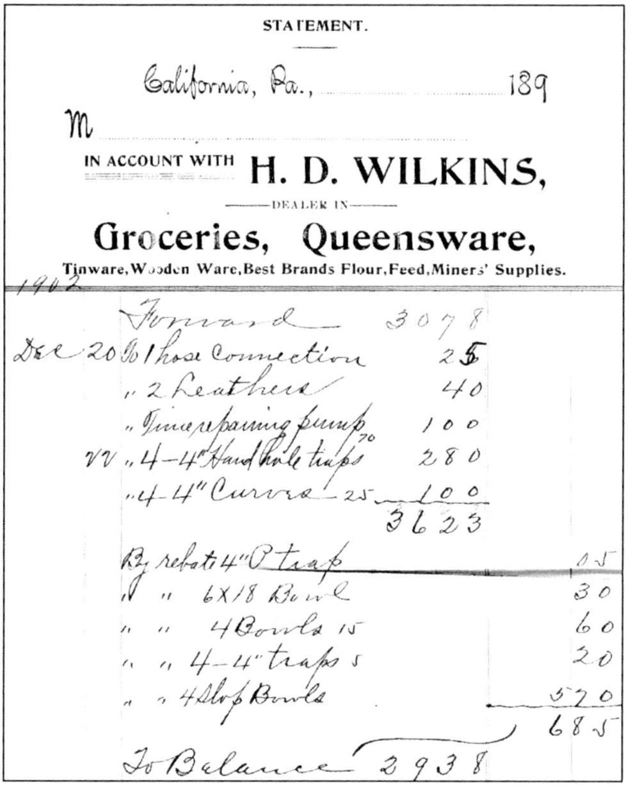

STATEMENT.

California, Pa., 189

M

IN ACCOUNT WITH H. D. WILKINS,

DEALER IN

Groceries, Queensware,

Tinware, Wooden Ware, Best Brands Flour, Feed, Miners' Supplies.

1902

Forward 30 78
Dec 20 To 1 hose connection 25
" 2 Leathers 40
" Time repairing pump 1 00
" 4-4" Hand hole traps 70 2 80
" 4-4" Curves 25 1 00
36 23
By rebate 4" P trap 05
" " 6X18 Bowl 30
" " 4 Bowls 15 60
" " 4-4" traps 5 20
" " 4 Slop Bowls 5 70
6 85
To Balance 29 38

A STORE STATEMENT. In 1902, you could buy on credit, as shown on this statement to C.N. Savage for purchases of plumbing supplies.

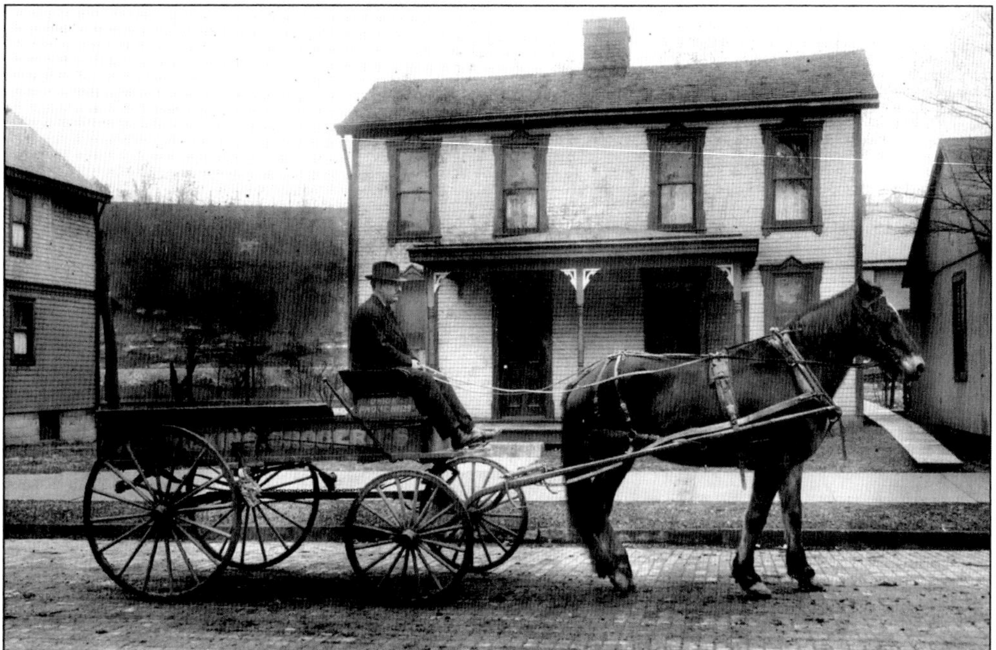

WILKINS DELIVERY SERVICE. In the 1900s, the H.D. Wilkins store offered the service of delivering purchases by horse-drawn carriage. The driver is on Second Street beside the photography studio of Harry Harris. (Courtesy W. Milton Sisson.)

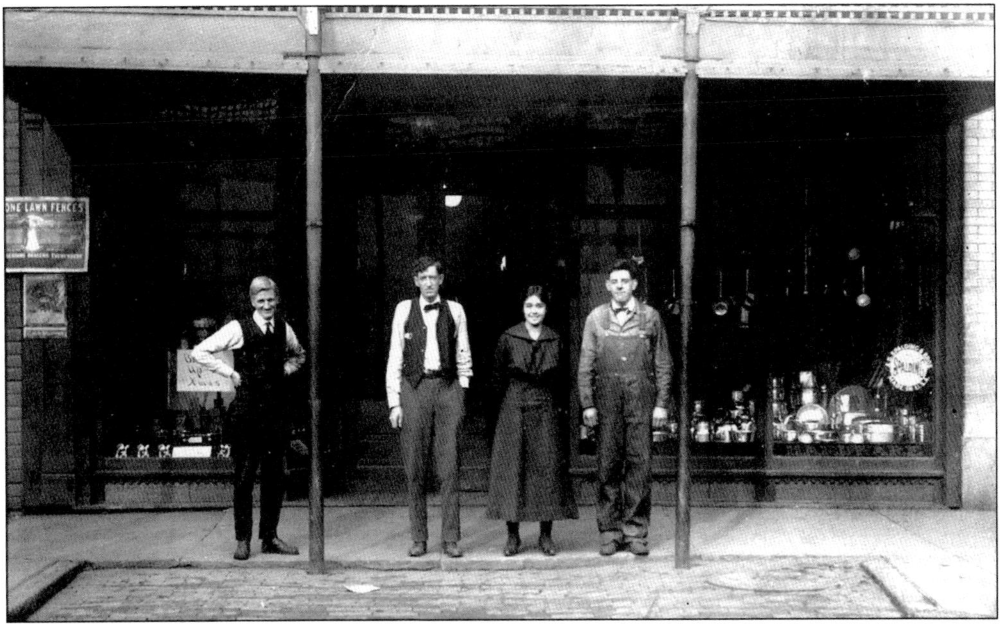

Sisson Hardware. Edwin Sisson had his hardware store at 334 Third Street c. 1926. Sisson is shown in the center in front of the store with Jessie Bunting and two employees. (Courtesy W. Milton Sisson.)

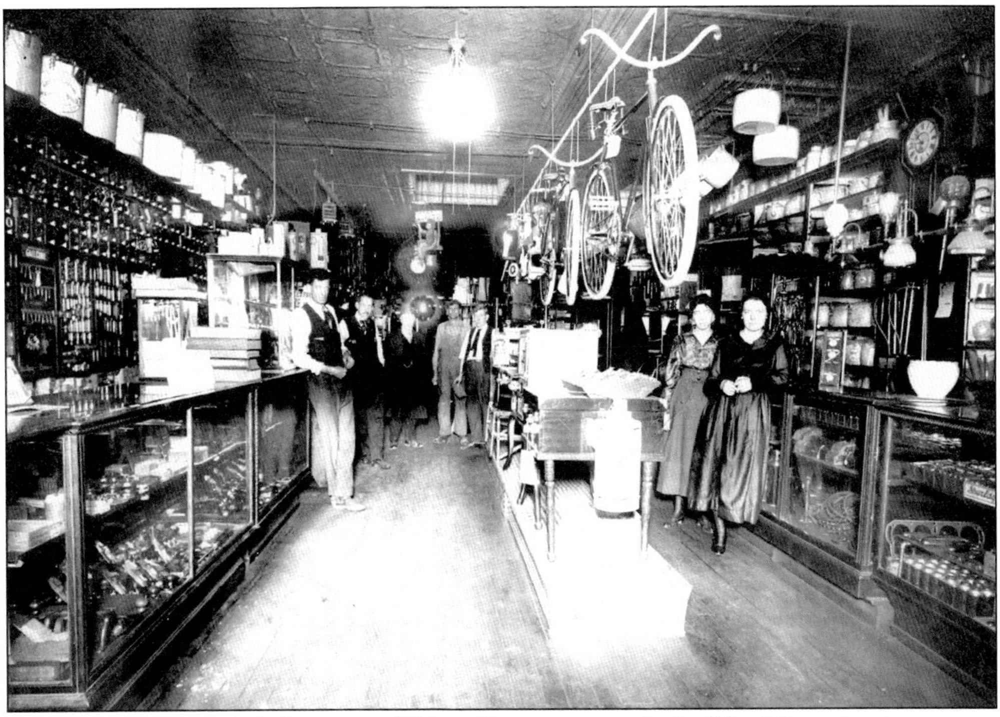

Savage Hardware. C.A. Savage and Edwin Sisson pose inside the Third Street hardware store. As of 1915, the store belonged to C.N. Savage. Since then, it has remained a hardware store but had a number of different owners. In 1926, it was owned by Sisson and a Mr. Keller; from 1930 to 1938, by Edwin Sisson alone; and in 1948, by Harry Lightcap. (Courtesy W. Milton Sisson.)

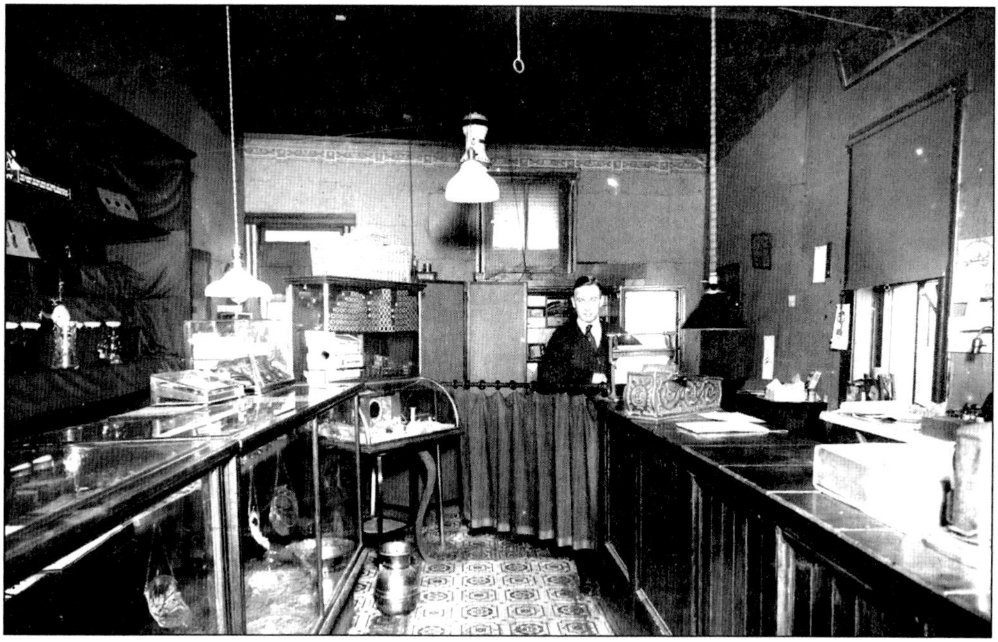

TAYLOR'S JEWELRY STORE. Earl Taylor had a jewelry store at 235 Wood Street from the 1920s to 1970. This photograph shows his store in 1927. Many changes took place over the years, but Taylor and his wife, Hallie, never stopped offering jewelry items during the time they owned the store. (Courtesy Roger and Margaret Emelson.)

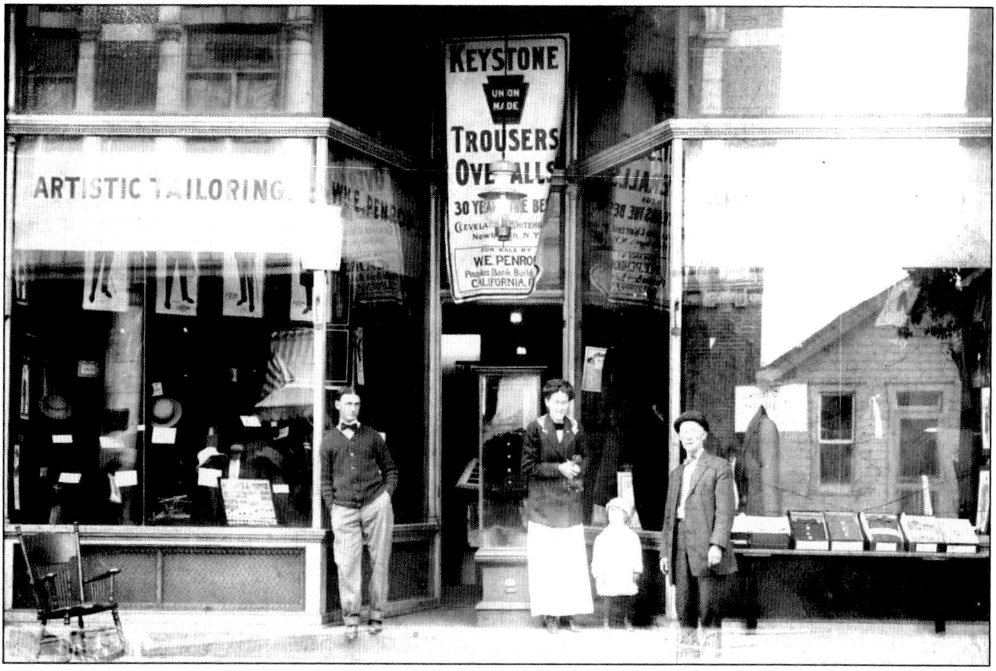

THE PENROD STORE. William Penrod operated his large department store at 200 Wood Street in the People's Bank Building from 1909 through the 1930s. The store advertised "gentlemen's furnishings." Penrod had a similar business in Coal Center, before moving to California. (Courtesy Barry Niccolai.)

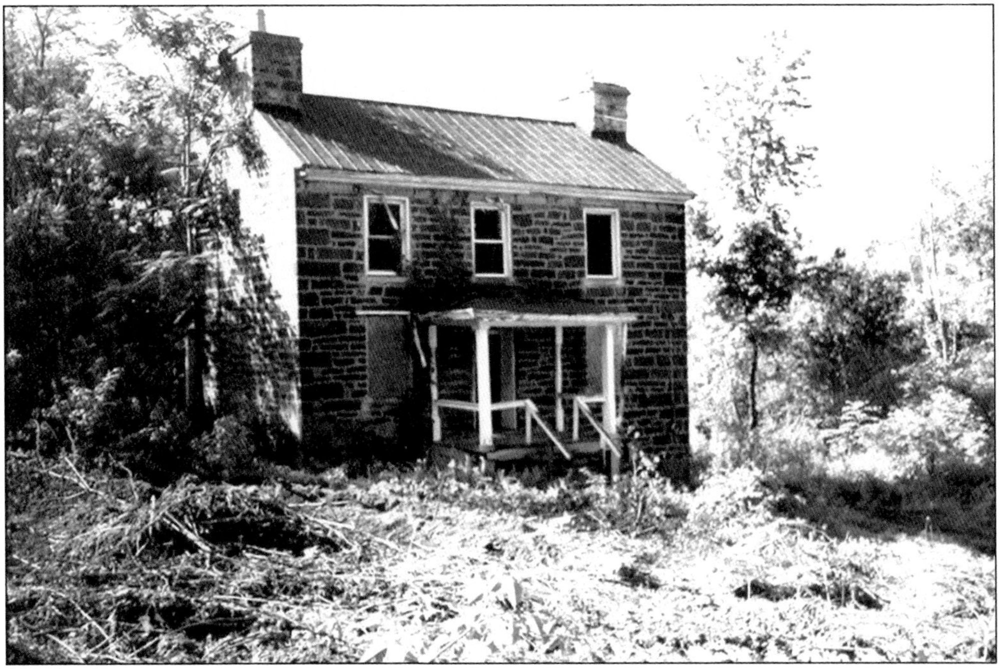

The Ellis Lilley Farm. The last occupant of this stone farmhouse built by Ellis Lilley on Highland Drive was Lieza Gettings. Some stone from the house is featured in the landscape gardens of the Center in the Woods, the California community senior citizen center on Route 88.

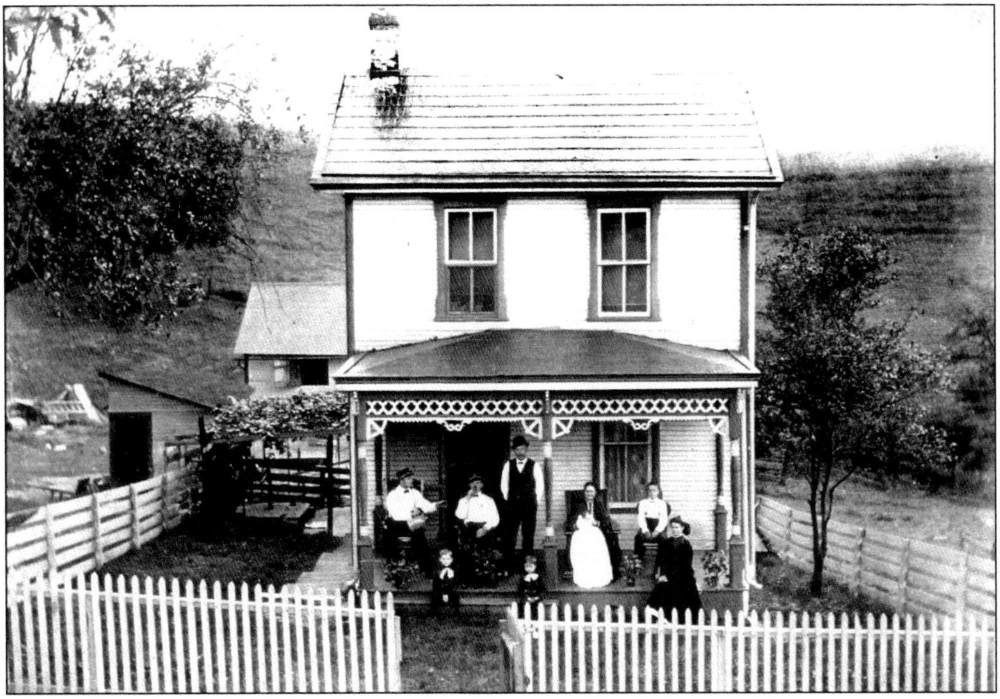

The Tentler House, the 1800s. The family of John and Maria Tentler pose for a picture on the porch of their home on the Old Pittsburgh Road (Edward Street). Today the rolling hills in the background have been given over to Route 88. (Courtesy Adelia Birkinsha.)

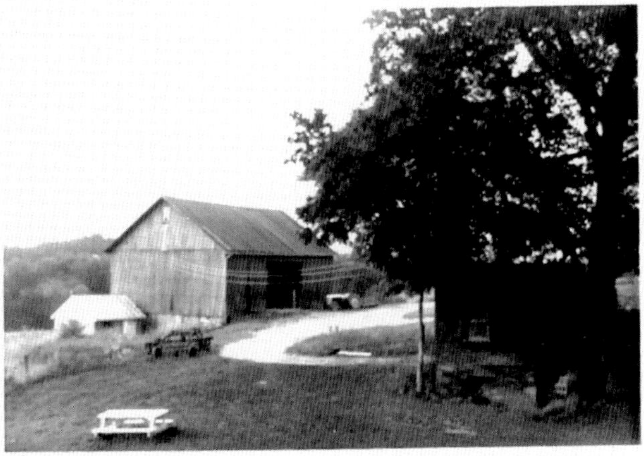

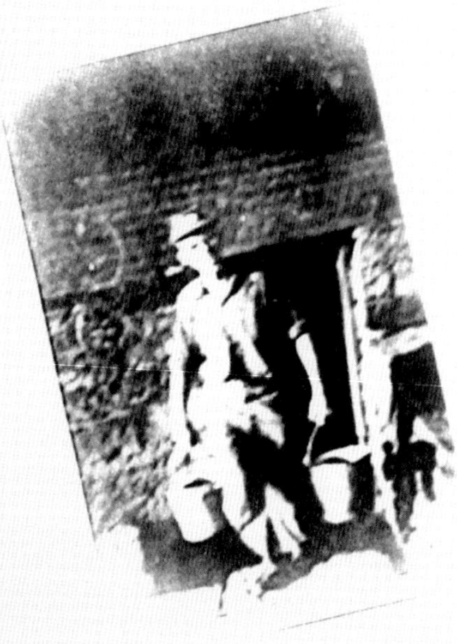

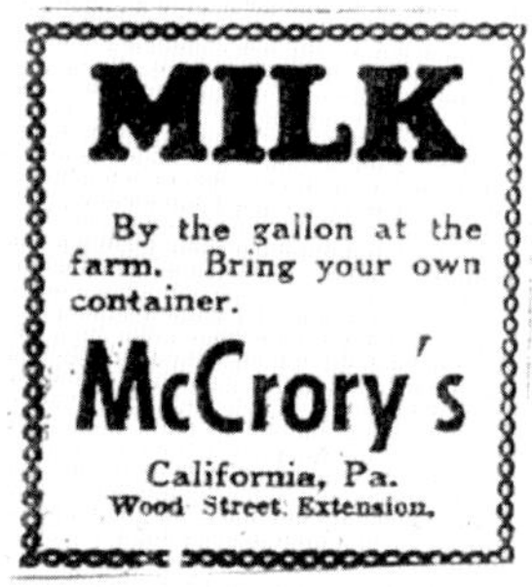

The McCrory Farm. In the 1930s, townspeople sent their children with empty gallon containers to the McCrory farm to buy milk for 25¢. At the lower left, Carl McCrory carries pails of milk from registered Guernsey cows from the springhouse. (Courtesy Pearle McCrory.)

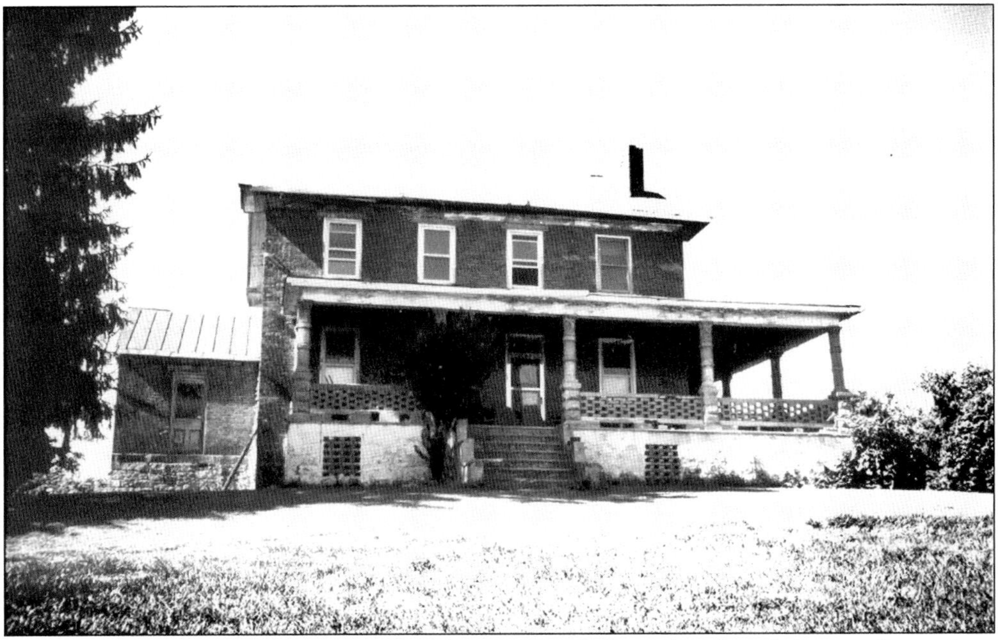

The Isaac Ailes Farmhouse. In 1790, this property belonged to Joseph Brown. It was later owned by his son-in-law Amos Ailes. For four generations, it was passed through the Ailes family. The older section is barely seen to the left in the photograph. The addition was built c. 1820, and the house is still a family home today. (Courtesy W. Floyd Gillis.)

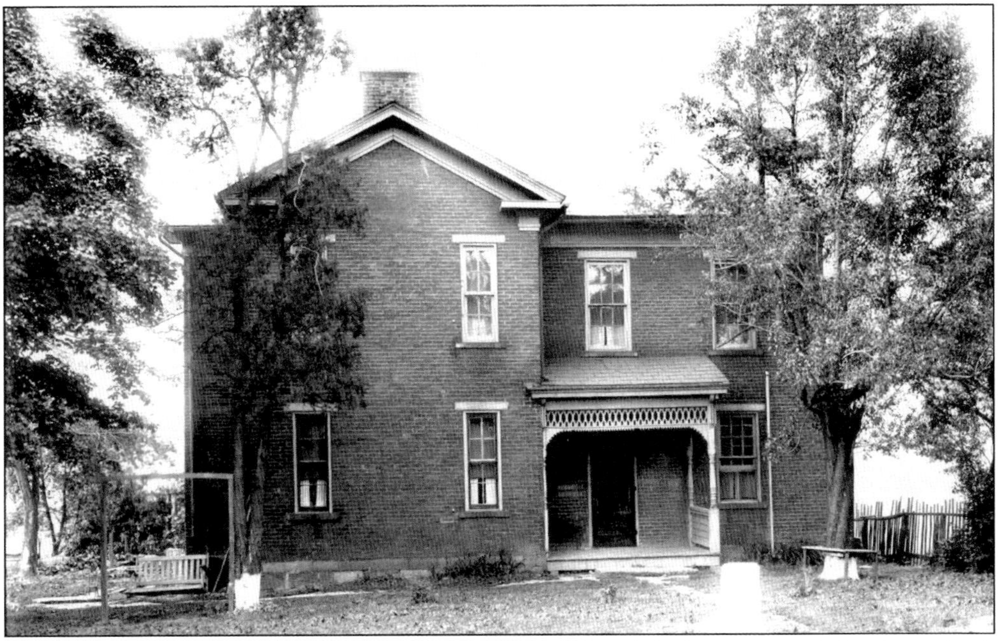

The Jackman Farmhouse. William W. and Eliza (Miller) Jackman owned this large brick home on a hill overlooking "the bottoms" of the Pike Run Creek. Jackman was one of the men responsible for laying out the town and was one of the founders of Southwestern State Normal School. Today, this house is used as the Italian Club of California in its original location at the west end of Pennsylvania Avenue.

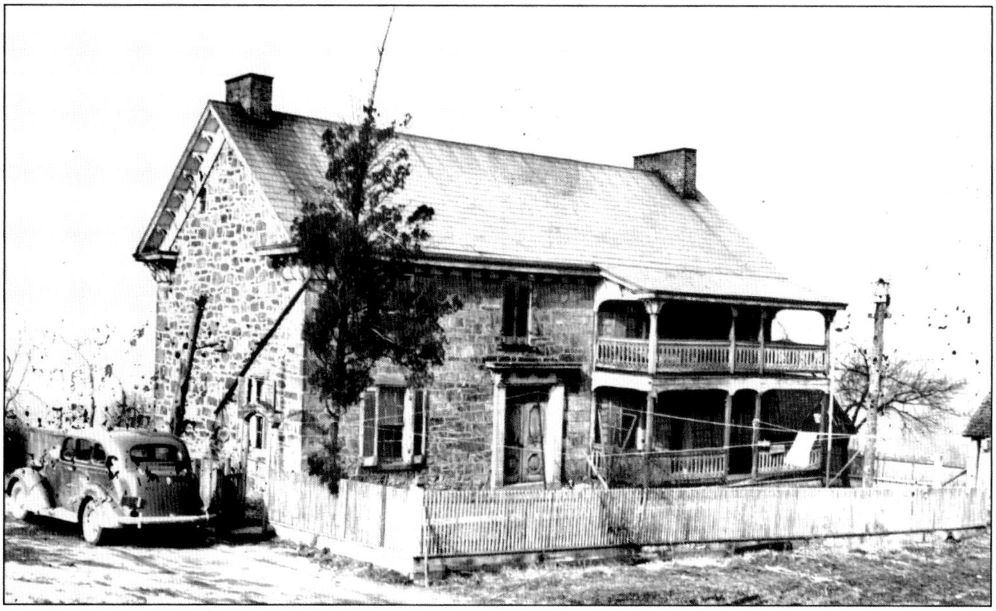

The Thomas Lilley House. This house belonged to Thomas Lilley and was built in 1810. It was constructed of hand-hewn chestnut beams and 18-inch sandstone walls. The floor joist in the house predates sawmill construction. In addition to being farmers, the Lilleys owned the Lilley Coal and Coke Company in West Brownsville. (Courtesy Archives, California University of Pennsylvania.)

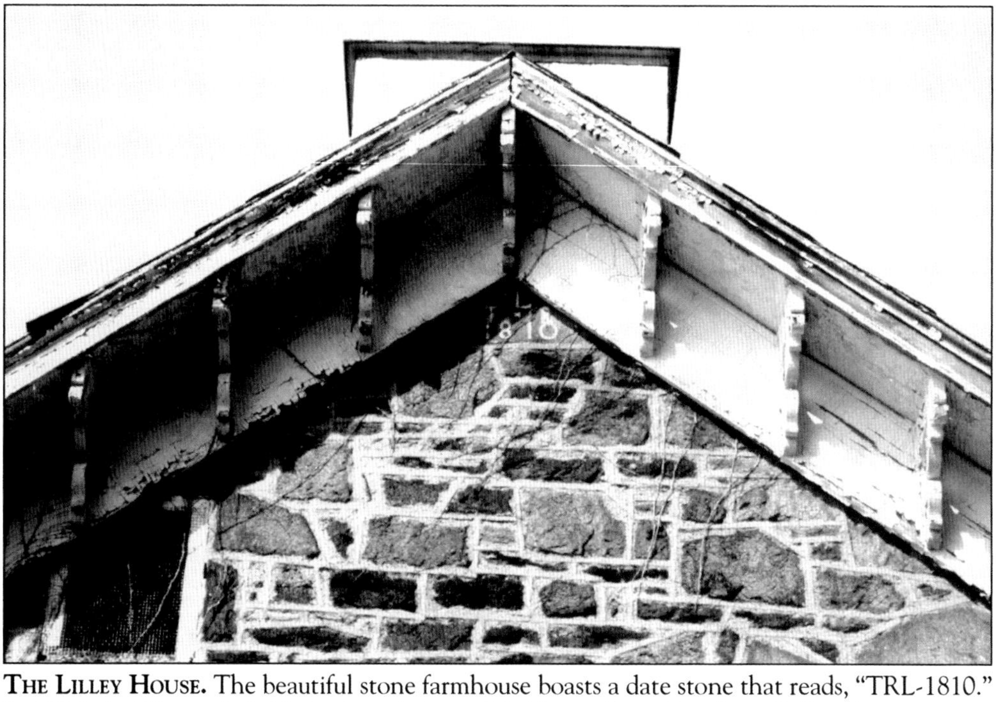

The Lilley House. The beautiful stone farmhouse boasts a date stone that reads, "TRL-1810." In 1930, the Women's Athletic Association of California State Teachers College began raising money to purchase the Lilley land. By 1937, enough funds had been raised to purchase the property, which became the College Farm.

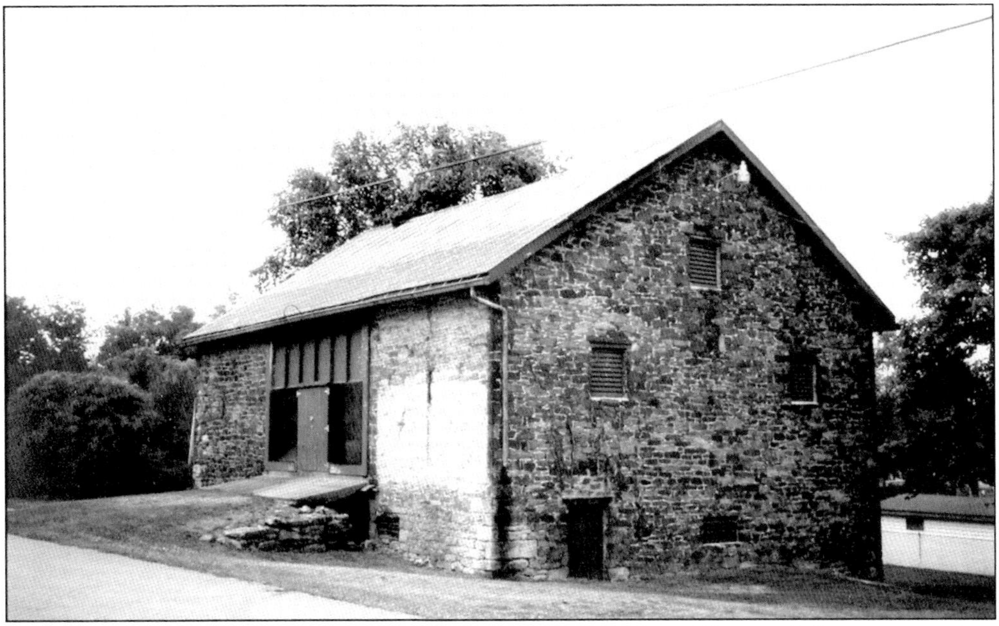

The Thomas Lilley Barn. The picturesque stone barn built by Thomas Lilley is depicted in the 1876 Caldwell atlas as being distinctive because of its sandstone construction. In 1999, fire destroyed most of the roof and wood trim, but the basic stone structure still stands.

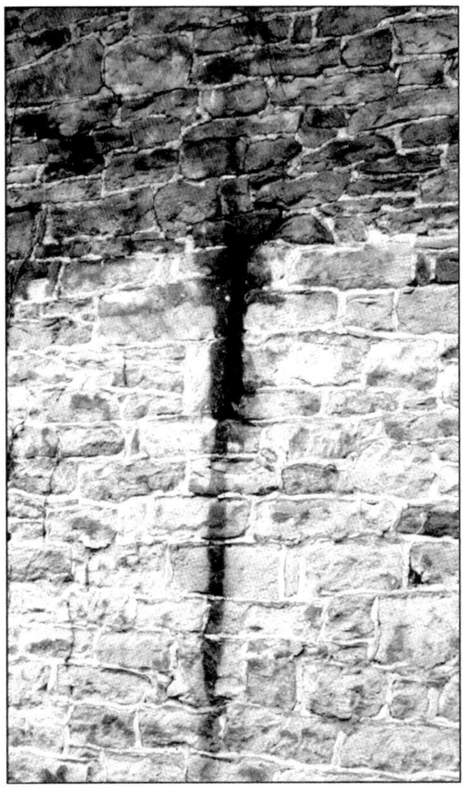

The Thomas Lilley Barn. Narrow slits in the thick stone walls of the Lilley barn are conveniently placed so that during a Native American raid or even an attack during the Civil War, the farmers on the inside could shoot through the slits without arrows or gunfire hitting them.

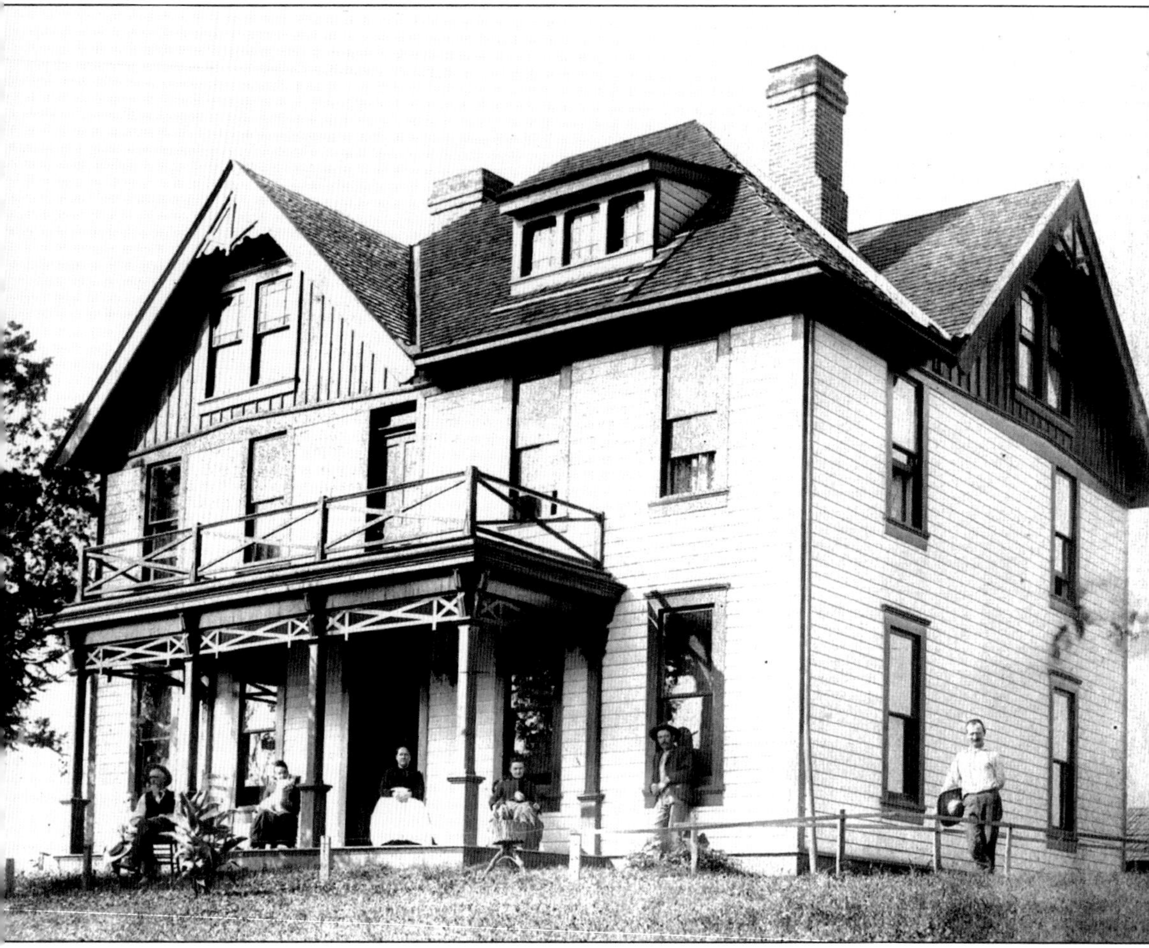

The Ailes Farm. This house was the farm home of William Jackson Ailes and later of his son James Burnett Ailes, who operated the Grandview Dairy Farm. The house is located on Route 88 near High Point and overlooks the Monongahela River.

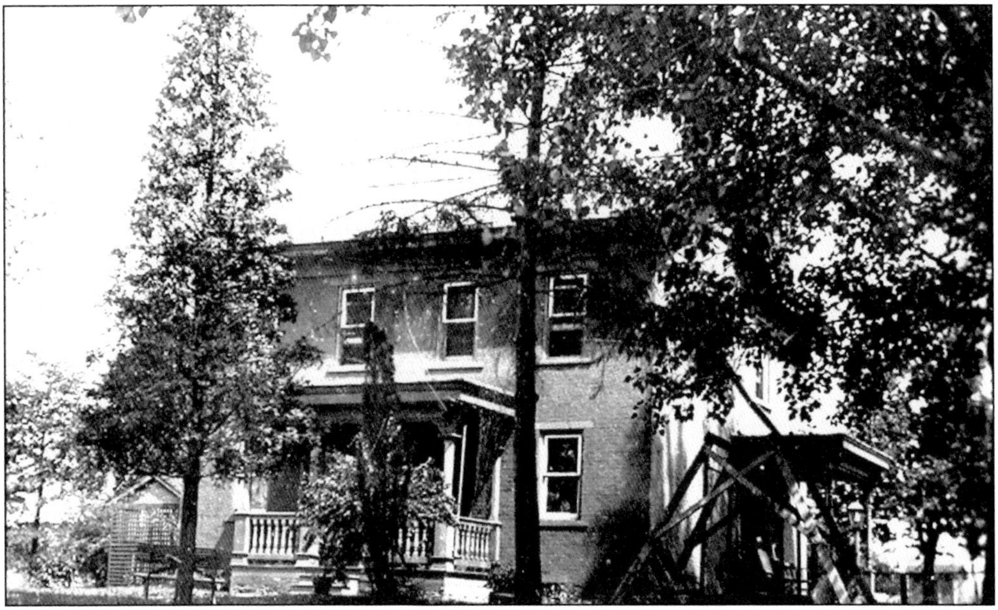

The Wilkins Family Home. Not long after the end of the Civil War, Capt. Henry Wilkins and his wife built and lived in this red-brick house on Wood Street in California. They owned much of the land behind their home, where many houses now stand, and it served as the Wilkins family homestead until the late 1960s. On its site now sit the offices and garage of a utility company. (Courtesy Richard Wilkins.)

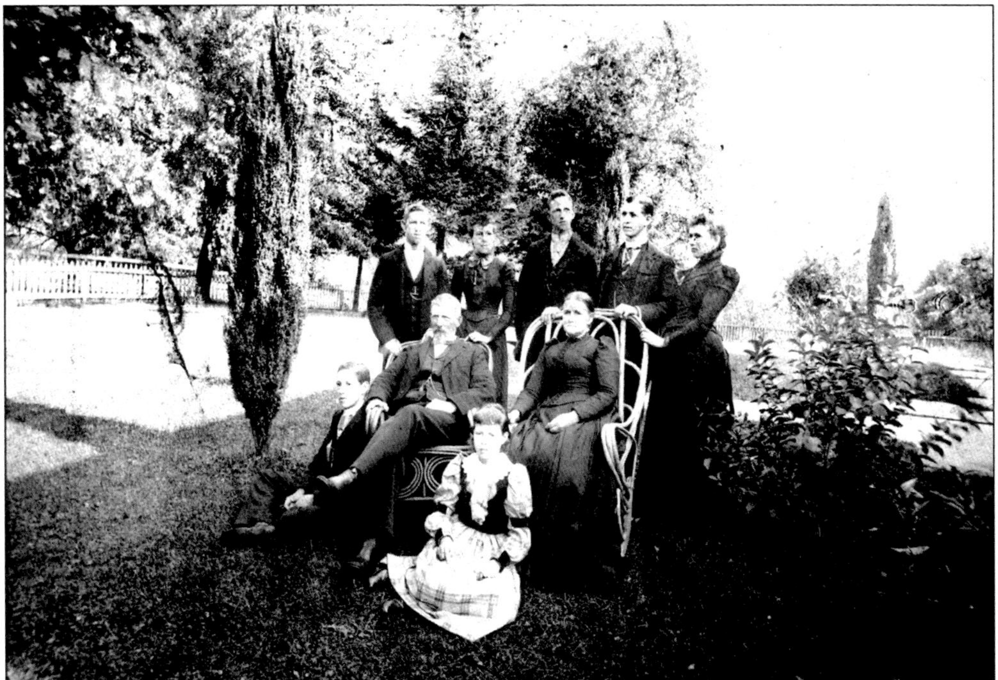

Captain Wilkins and Family. Riverboat captain Henry D. and Anna (Piper) Wilkins pose with their children c. 1900. Standing are, from left to right, Frank, Mary, Fred, Charles, and Eva. Wilkins and his wife are seated with Khramer and Annie at their feet. (Courtesy Richard Wilkins.)

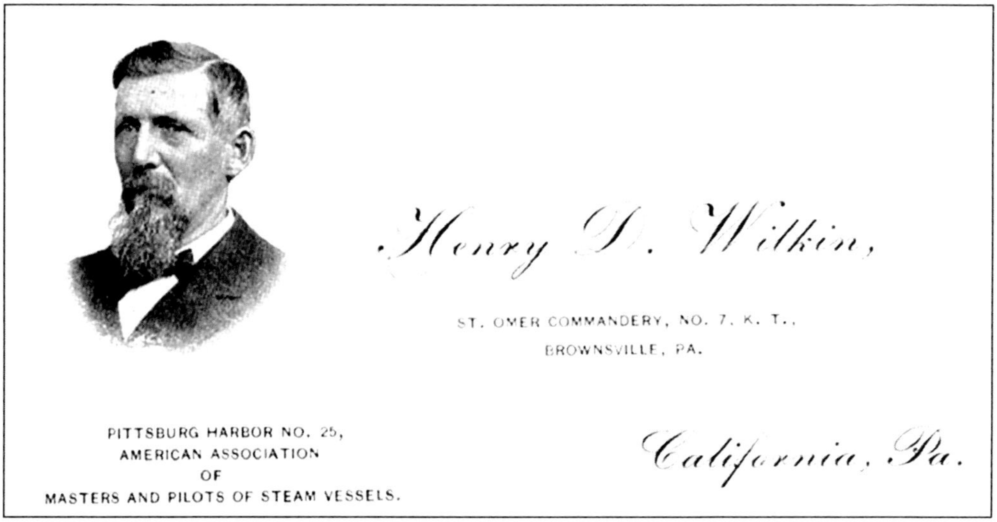

A WILKINS BUSINESS CARD. Well-known riverboat captain Henry D. Wilkins promoted his skills by introducing himself to those who could use his services with cards like this one.

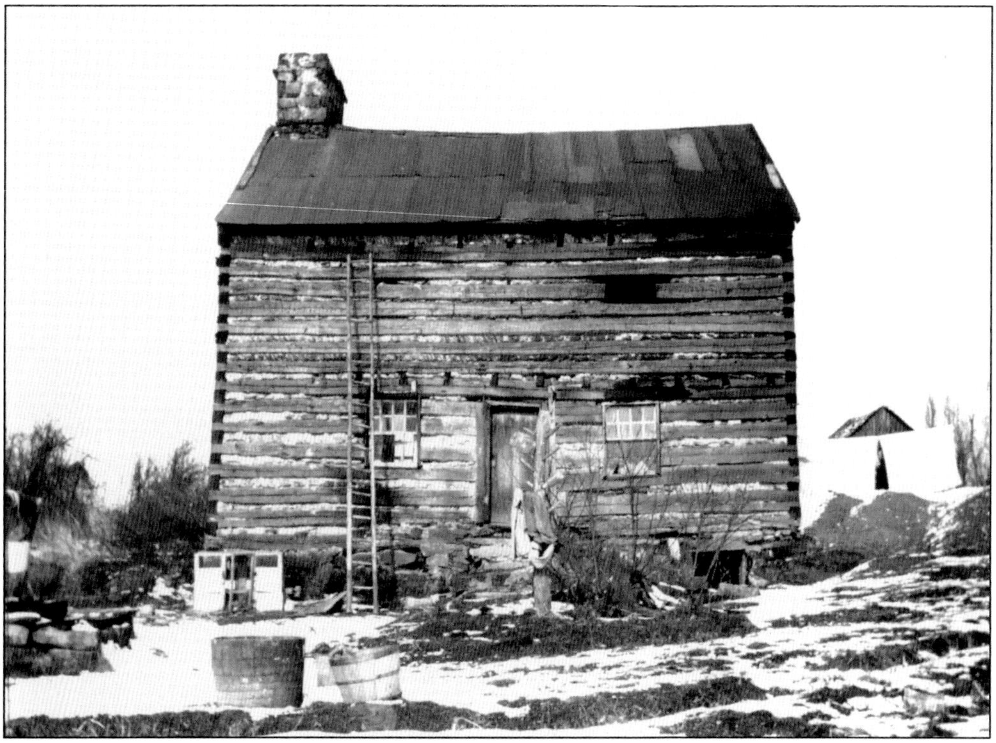

THE WILKINS LOG HOUSE. The first Wilkins settling in the area lived briefly in this old log house on Brenton Farm, Knob Road, West Brownsville. Shortly after, the family moved to Greenfield (Coal Center).

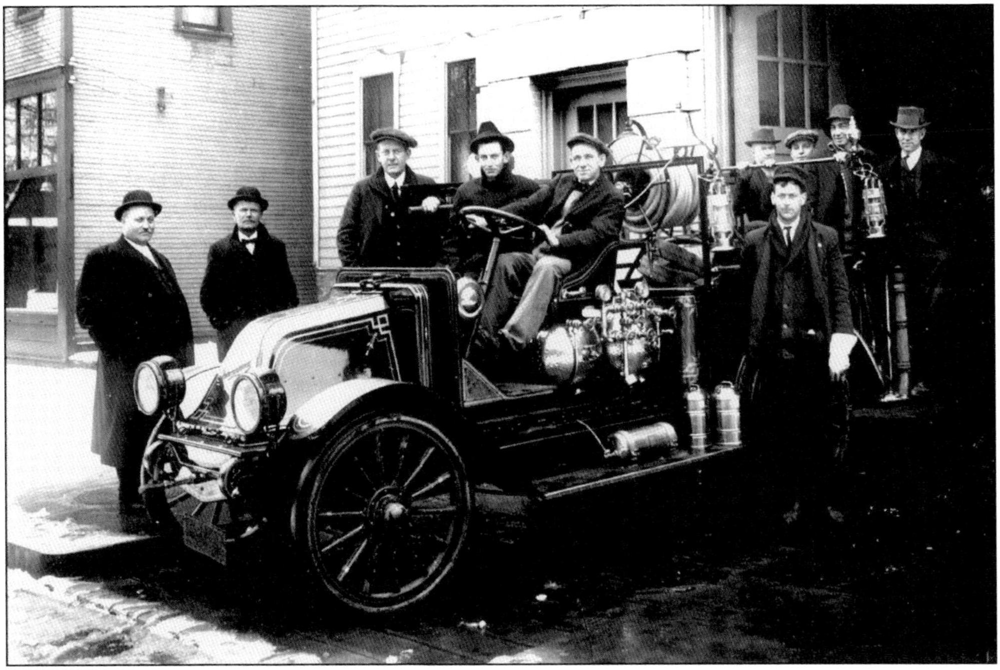

CALIFORNIA FIREMEN. Chief Barney Latta and a group of unidentified men pose with the new California fire truck in front of the fire station. This was the town's first motor-powered fire engine, a two-cylinder chemical truck that cost $1,300. The truck was affectionately dubbed "the Peanut Roaster."

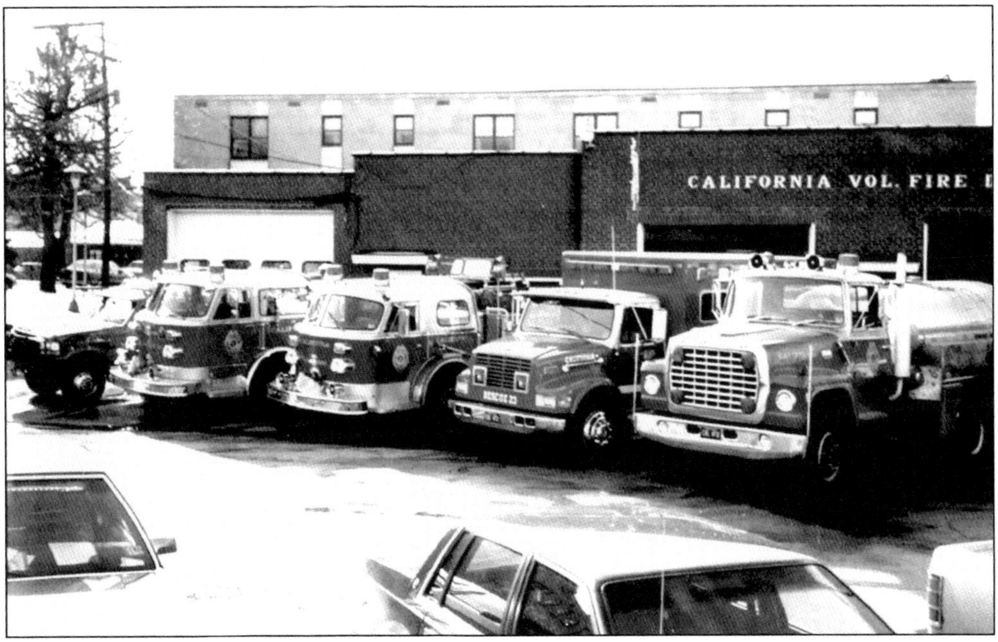

THE FIRE DEPARTMENT. By 1953, the fire company had outgrown its quarters on Third Street. This brick station at Wood and Water Streets was built on the site of the original 1909 fire station. Today, the department runs six trucks: two heavy pumpers, a 100-foot aerial, a rescue truck, a tanker, and a brush truck. (Courtesy Bruce McCrory.)

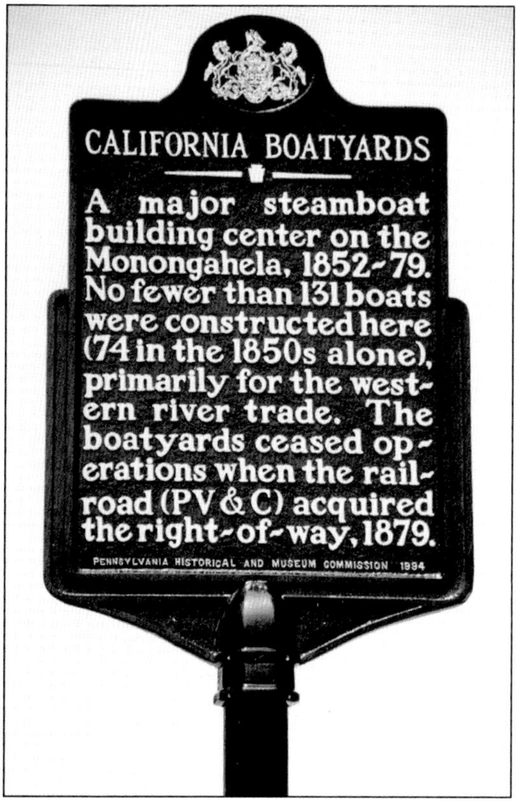

REMEMBERING THE PAST. This historical marker, sponsored by the Monongahela River Buffs Association, commemorates the town of California's significance as an early steamboat-building center.

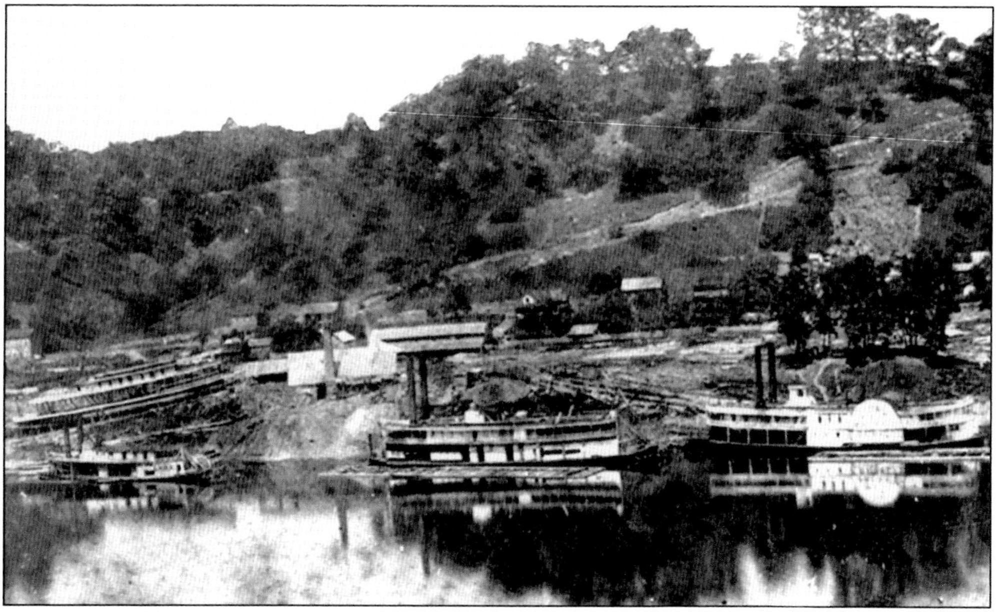

BOATYARDS, WEST BROWNSVILLE. This rare photograph of the Dawson and Bowman boatyards on the west side of the Monongahela River was taken *c.* 1870. It shows three steamboats in the water and a fourth under construction. Many famous riverboats were built here. Axton and Sons later owned a boatyard in the same location. (Courtesy Alva Harris.)

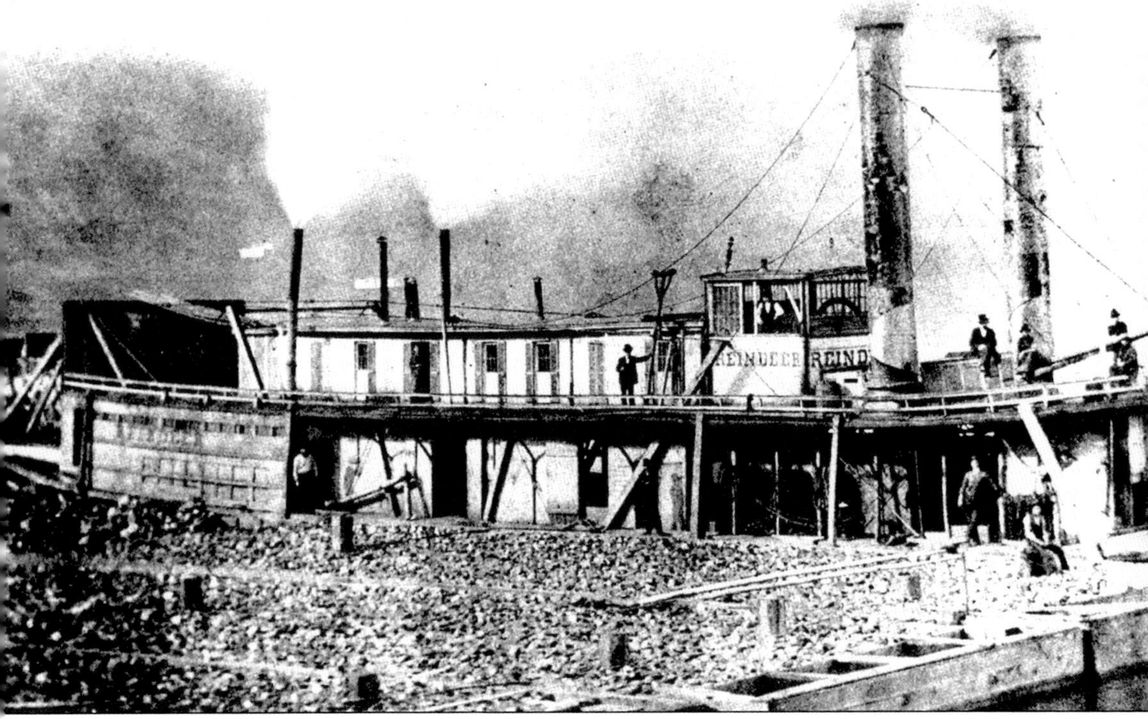

The Steamer *Reindeer*. The riverboat steamer *Reindeer* was launched on Christmas Day in 1825, just above Dunlap's Creek from the John Cock Boatyard (later known as the Pringle Boat Yard). The following year, *Reindeer* became the first steamboat to navigate up the Monongahela River to Morgantown, West Virginia. In 1836, the *Reindeer*, owned by the Dippold Coal Company, was piloted by Capt. Henry Wilkins. (Courtesy Archives, California University of Pennsylvania.)

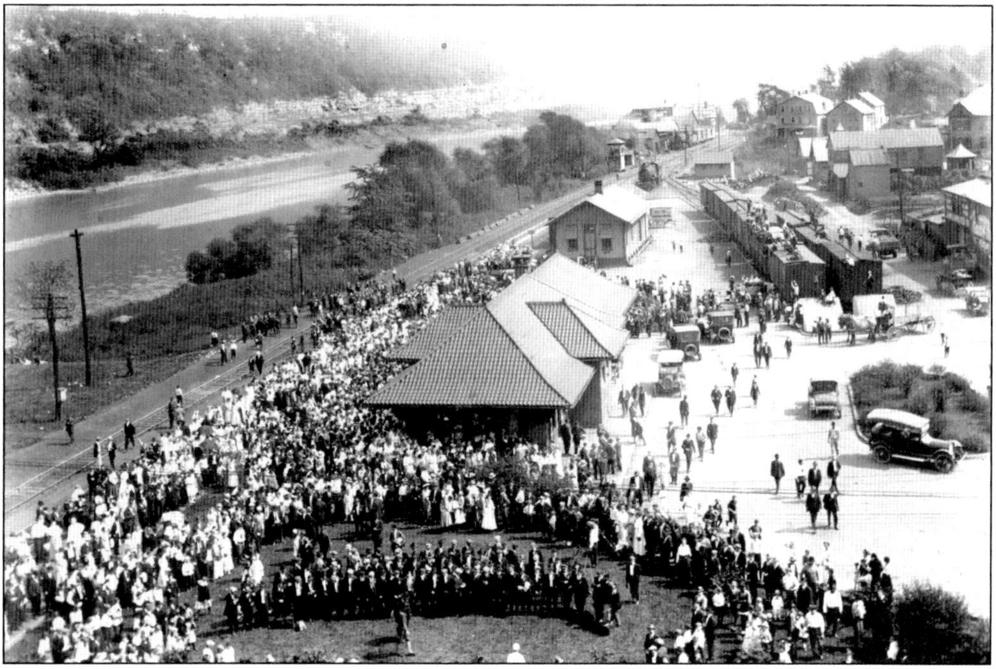

WORLD WAR I HOMECOMING. In 1917, hundreds of people gathered at the California train depot for a World War I homecoming celebration. In the foreground, grateful family and friends surround the returning soldiers. The center of the photograph shows the wooden baggage station and bunkers. (Courtesy Tom and Debbie Moore.)

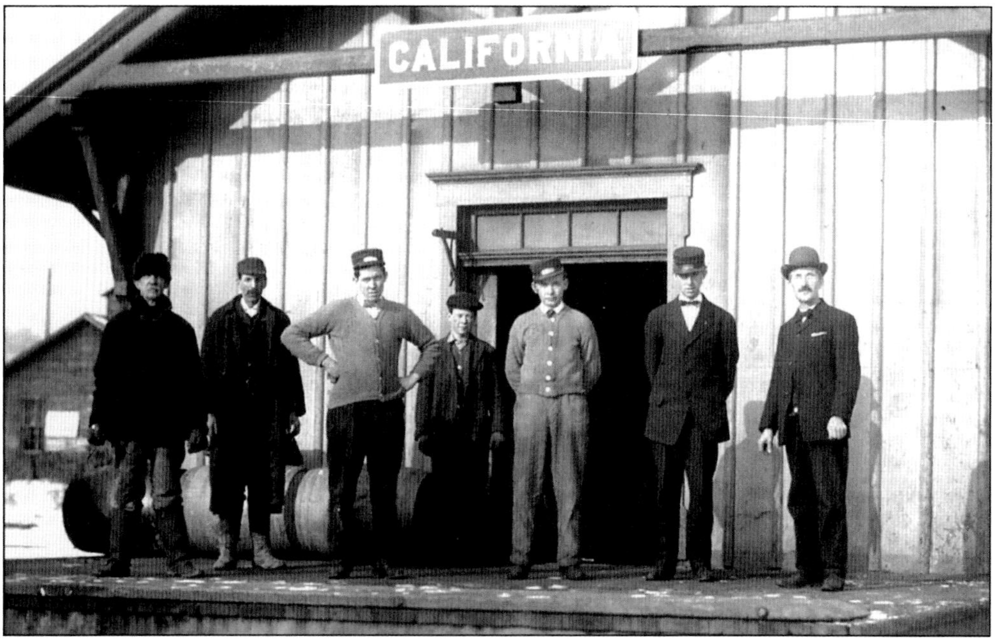

THE BAGGAGE STATION. The wooden depot built in 1885 was used only for baggage pickup after the new brick building was constructed in 1910. It was still in use during the World War II years.

Two

Around the Area

California, Pennsylvania, could not have survived without the cooperation that the communities surrounding it gave to each other. These neighboring communities include East Pike Run Township, Coal Center (Greenfield), West Brownsville (Blainesburg), Phillipsburg, West Pike Run Township, Roscoe, and Elco. All eventually became part of the California area school system, and their citizens laid the foundation for area growth. Each of these towns has its own interesting story. Some were anchored from their beginnings in agricultural pursuits, and others were dependent on the river, steel mills, or coal mines. While some of these communities are still in existence and others are only a memory, all combined to form a prosperous area when coal mines and steel mills were at peak production.

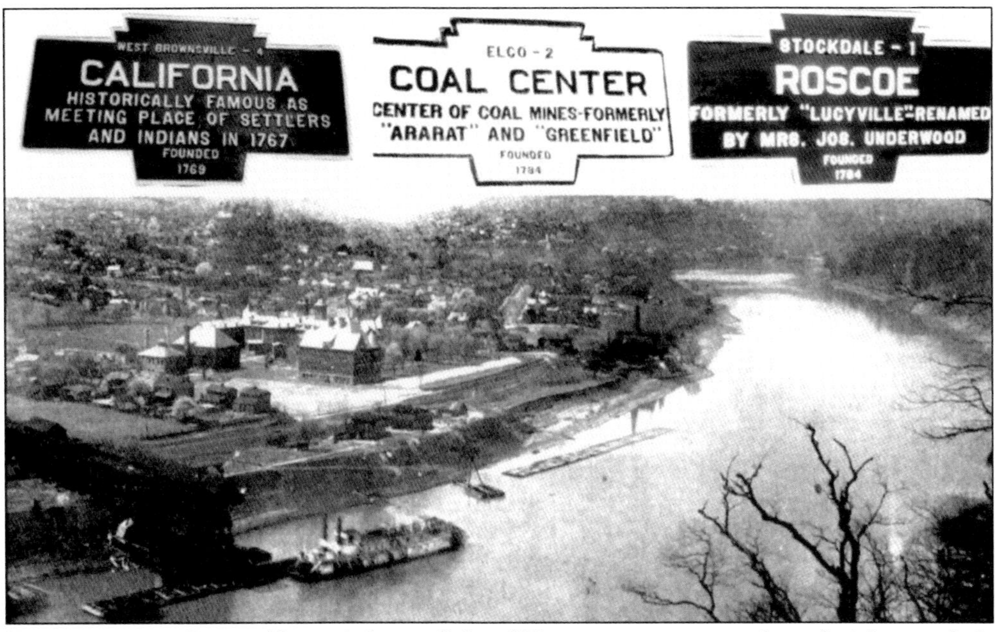

Town Markers. Roscoe (formerly Lucyville) and Elco are communities along the Monongahela River. The towns in this area are separated only by the surveyor's line. The markers tell much about the history of the three communities.

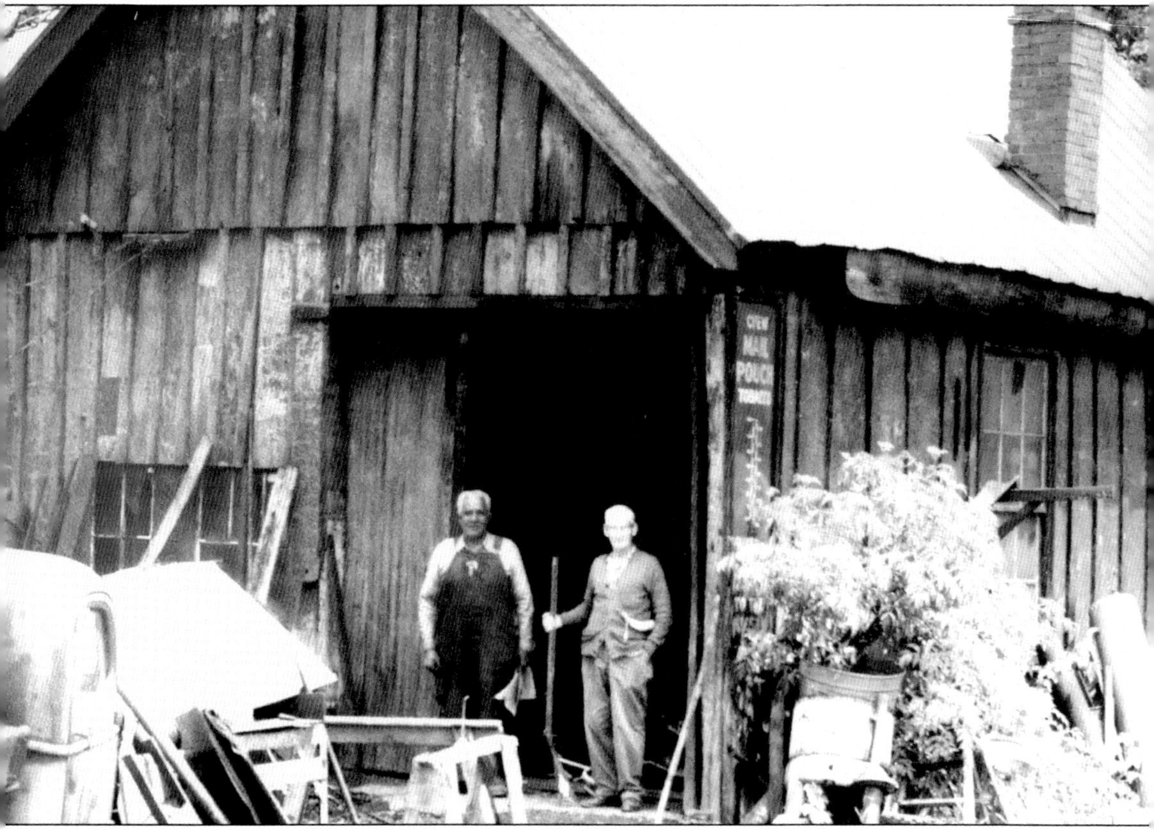

THE ANKRUM BLACKSMITH SHOP. James T. Ankrum owned a blacksmith shop on Water Street in Coal Center. He operated the shop until the early 1970s, when he gave it up due to ill health. He was well known in the area for practicing a craft that had almost become extinct after the need for horseshoeing waned. He served in the armed forces as a private in World War II. This photograph was taken in 1964 and shows Ankrum to the left. (Courtesy Walter Otto.)

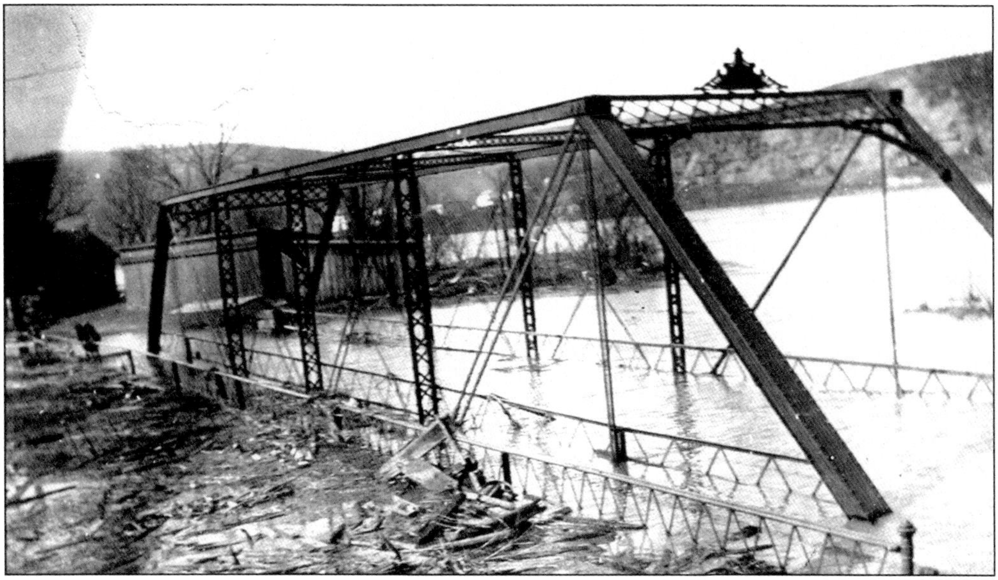

THE FLOOD OF 1936. Pike Run overflowed its banks during the flood of 1936. Transportation between California and Coal Center was halted until the Monongahela River receded to its normal height.

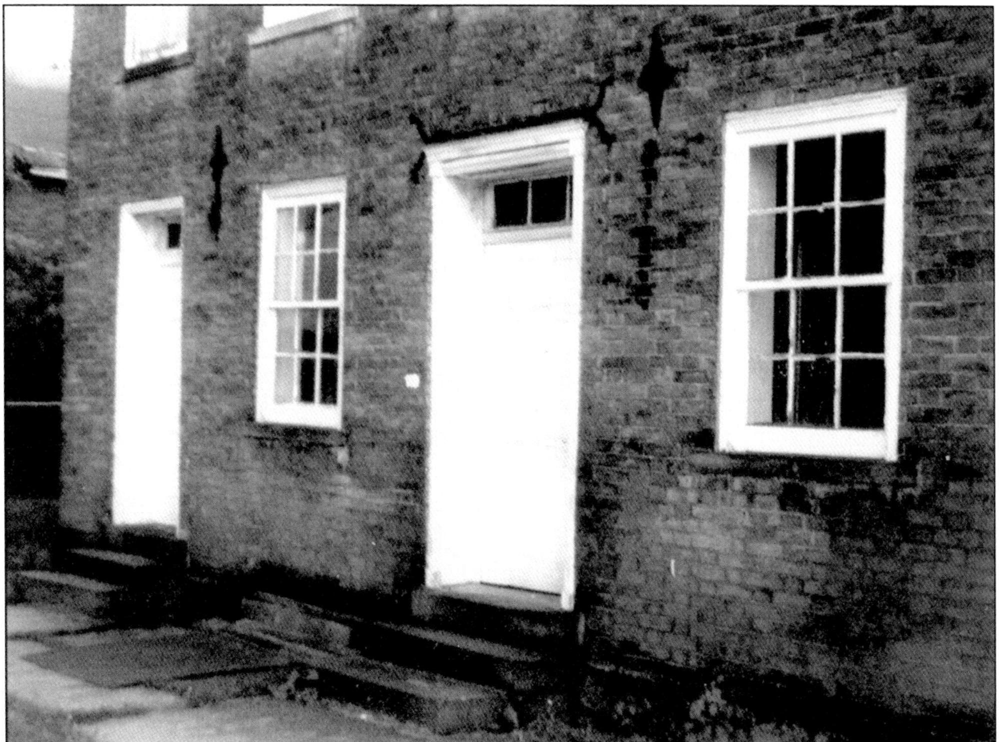

BOAT BARS IN COAL CENTER. The black iron hooks by the doorway of the Wilkins House in Coal Center were used to tie a boat when the Monongahela River rose over its banks. The water often reached the second floor of this house on Water Street.

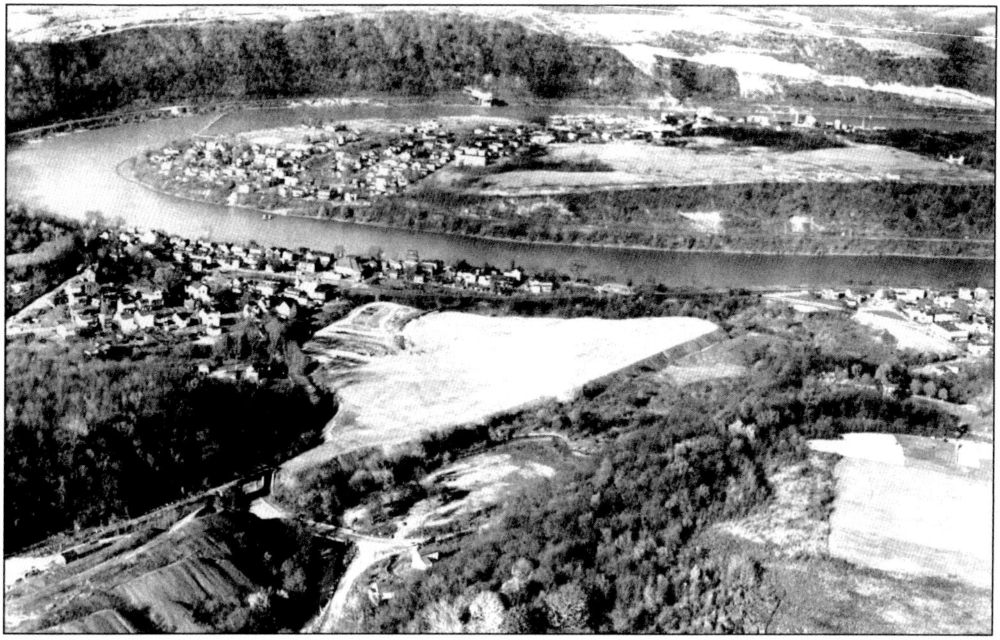

A Panoramic View. To the left is the borough of Coal Center. One mile to the right is California. Pike Run and the Vesta Coal Mine tipple separate the two boroughs. The large field once used by the coal company is now home to 84 Lumber Company. Across the river is Newell. Note the mine on this side of the river in Elco. (Courtesy Charles and Marguerite Cox.)

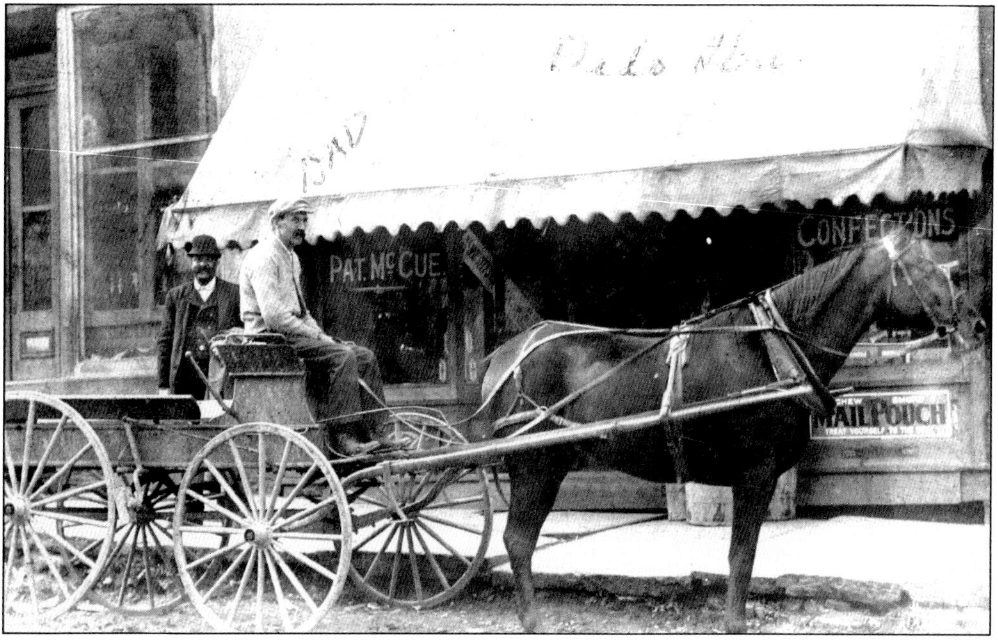

McCue Confectionery and Ice Cream. The genial Irishman Pat McCue had a store on Spring Street in Coal Center *c.* 1900. The store was famous throughout the valley for homemade ice cream and fresh roasted peanuts. In the front were a soda fountain and a display of candy, fruit, nuts, and tobacco. In the back was a parlor where patrons could sit and eat their fill. (Courtesy Cecil McCue.)

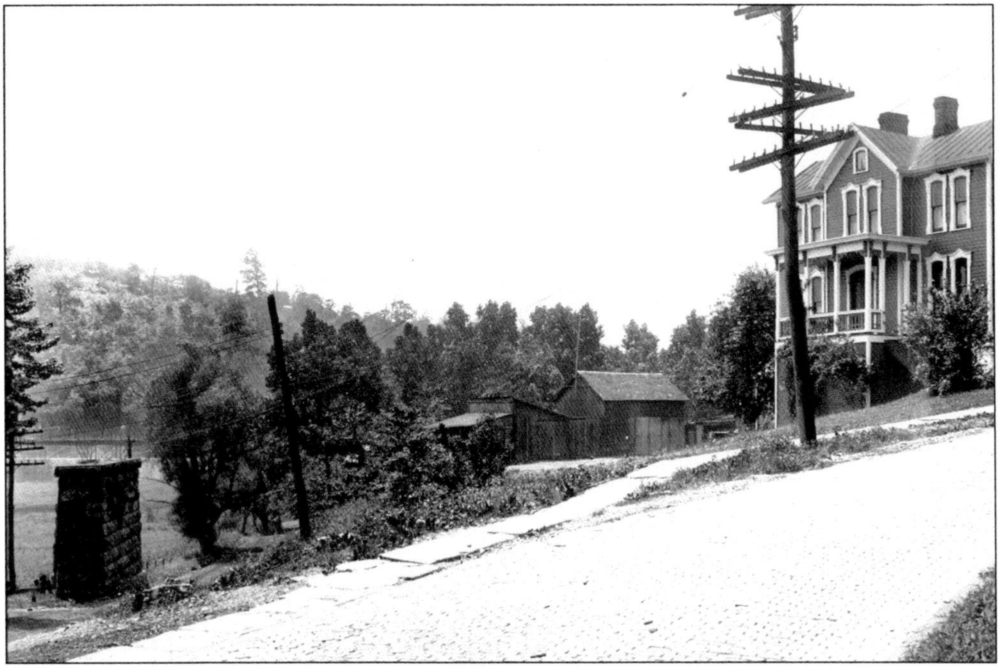

SPRING STREET (ROUTE 88). Route 88 on the outskirts of Coal Center was once known as Spring Street. On the left in this photograph is the dirt road connecting to Route 88, the "bottoms," and the Jones and Laughlin tipple.

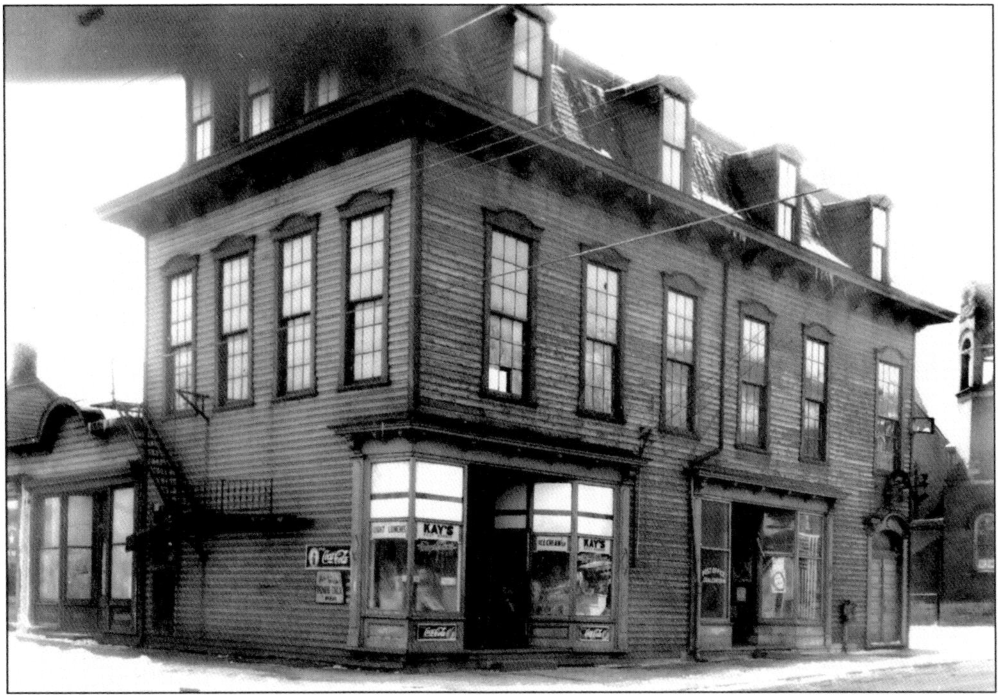

COAL CENTER. Seen *c.* 1931 at the corner of Water and Spring Streets are Kay's Light Lunches, the Coal Center post office, and the Cumberland Presbyterian Church.

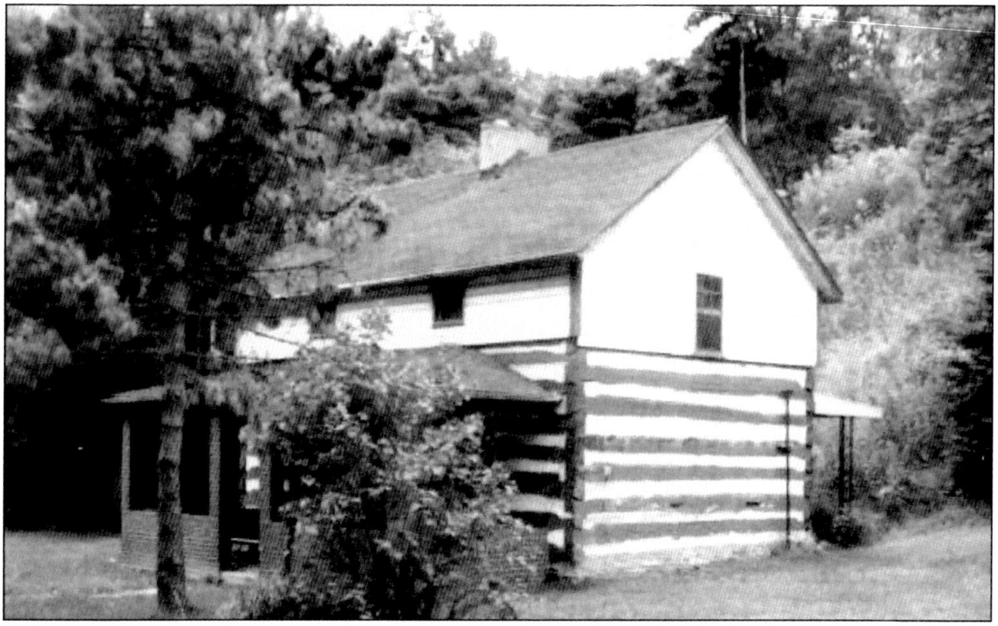

The Walter Grimes Home. When Walter and Isadora (Shibbler) Grimes married in 1895, they received this log cabin as a wedding gift from their relatives. They raised 11 children in this Granville Hollow location. (Courtesy George F. Harris.)

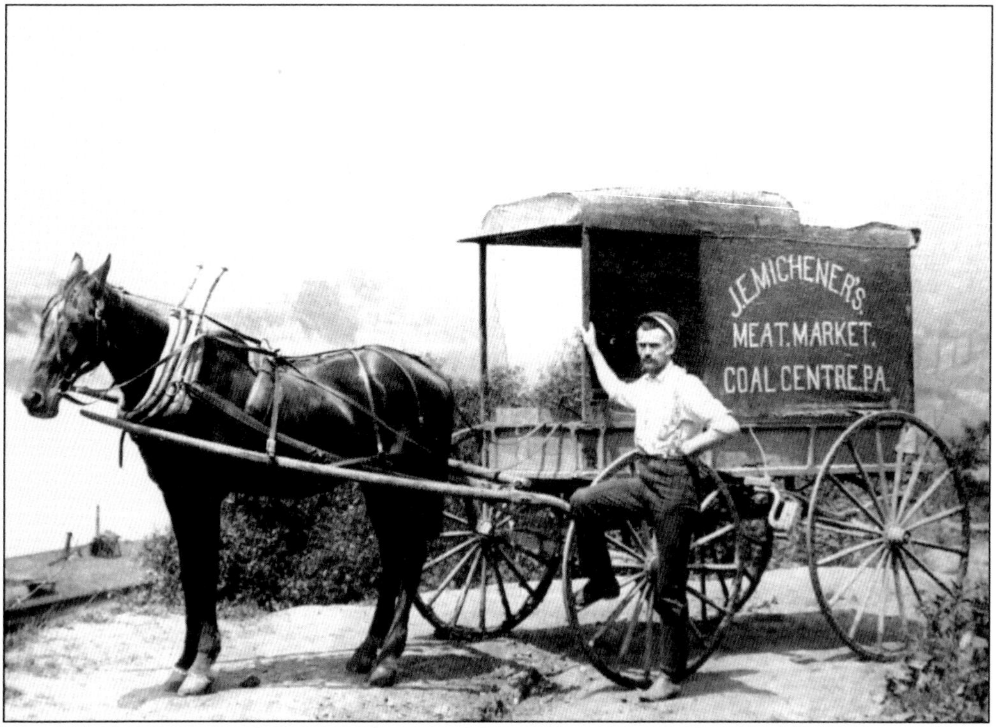

Michener's Market. The J.E. Michener's delivery wagon in Coal Center stops to rest before resuming its round of meat and groceries delivery. (Courtesy Belle Brutout.)

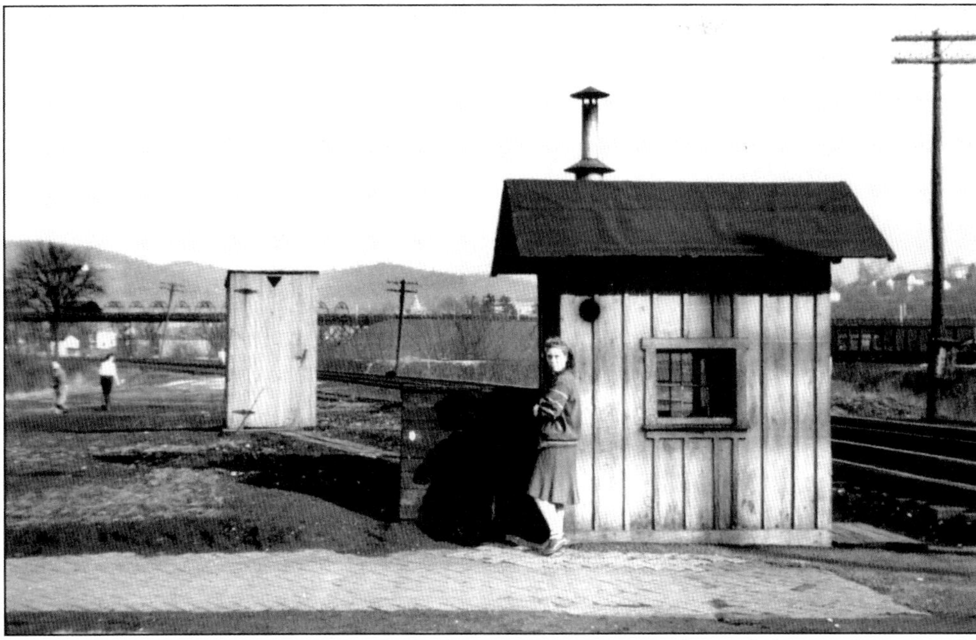

A Crossing Guard Shanty. This little shanty in Coal Center housed the watchman at the grade crossing. The guard came out with a stop sign when a train approached. The shanty was a borough storage shed for several years until an enterprising neighbor dragged it to his yard. (Courtesy John Staskavitch.)

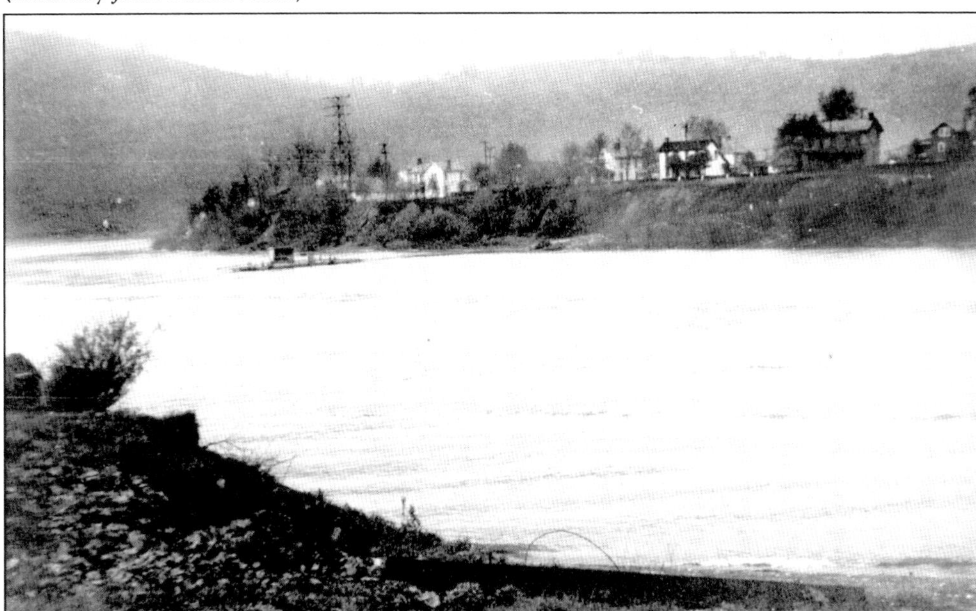

The Ferry Crossing. As early as 1879, there was a ferry at the Coal Center wharf with service between Coal Center and Newell. In 1910, it was moved to the site of the Greenfield bridge. The ferry was the quickest way for employees of the Newell Chemical Plant to cross from either side of the river. The ferry ceased operation in 1967. Travelers to Newell then crossed the river at Brownsville. (Courtesy John Staskavitch.)

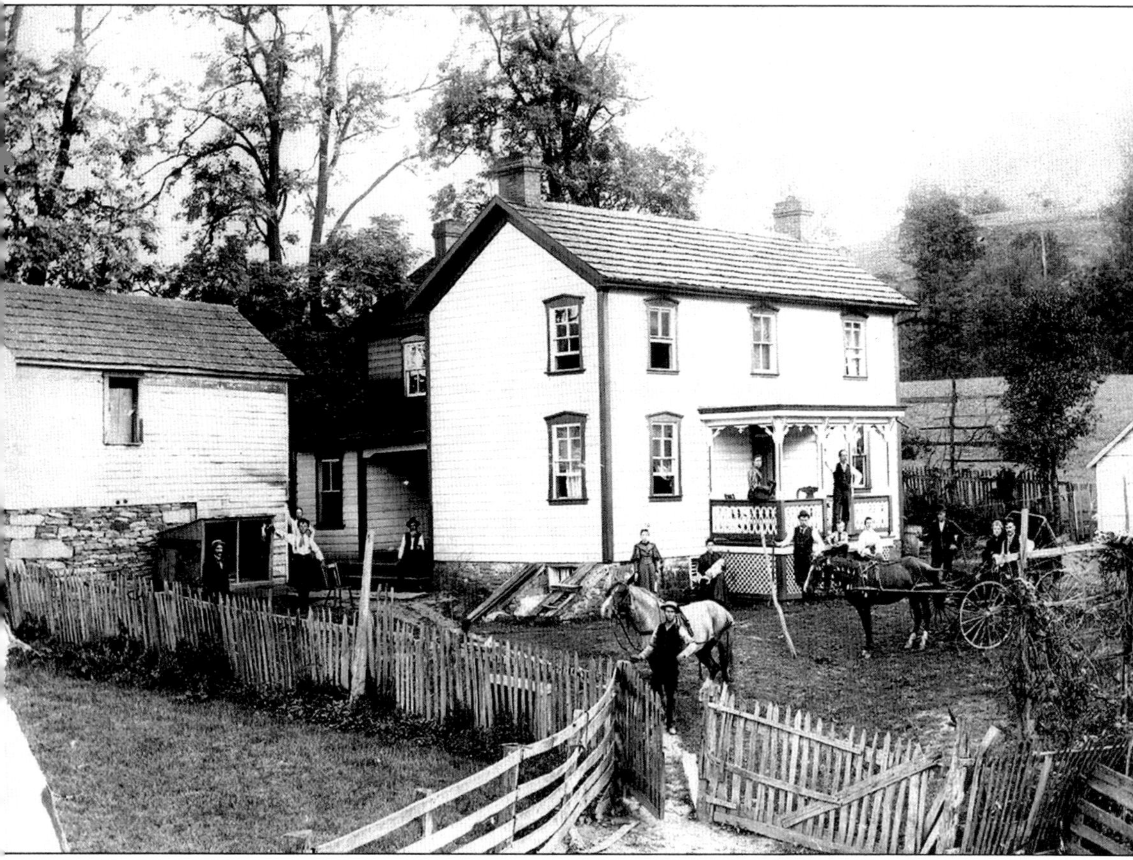

THE LUKE WRIGHT FARM AND HOMESTEAD. Taken in 1890, this photograph shows the home of Isaac and Mary Jane (Long) Wright. Born here were Luke, who fought in the Civil War, along with his brothers William Henry, Joseph, and Samuel. All were in Company B, 22nd Ringgold Calvary. All are buried in Taylor Cemetery, located in West Pike Run Township. Luke Wright owned coal mines on this land. His sons Lewis Isaac and Henry Ott died in mining accidents. Shown here are Luke Wright, on the front porch; Amanda Adeline Newman, holding an accordion; Frank Wright (son of Luke Wright), holding the reins of his horse; Cliff Wright (son of Luke Wright), leaning against the chicken coop; Charlie (son of Luke Wright), holding his rifle butt-end-down; and Ed Wright (son of Luke Wright), standing on the right side of the porch and holding a walking stick. The others are unidentified. (Courtesy Marcella Boyer Price.)

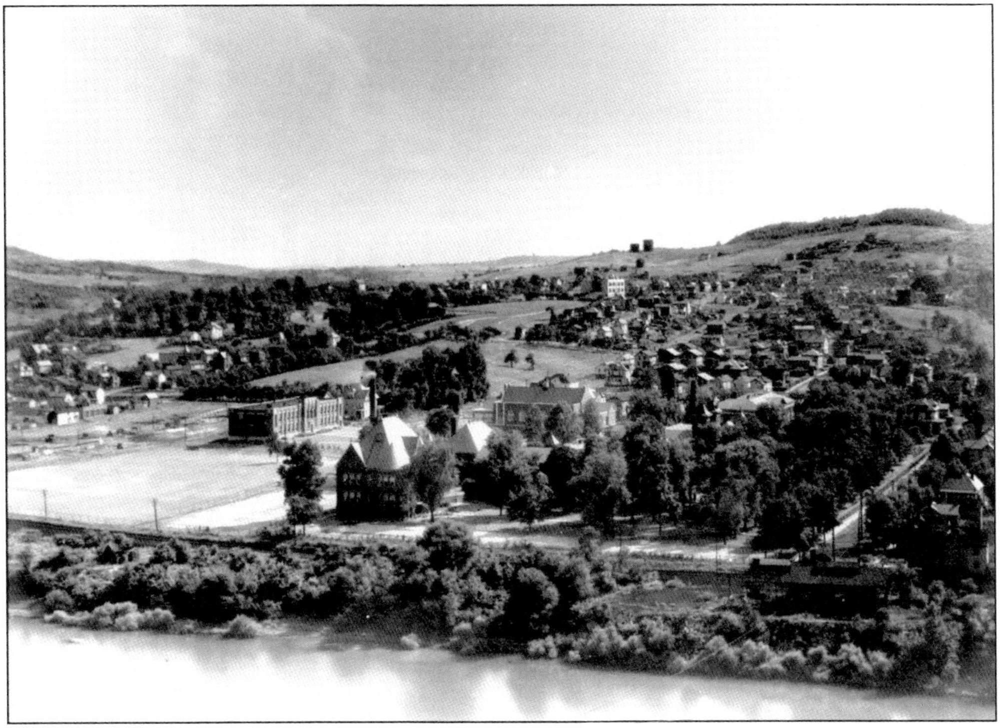

A View of California and Phillipsburg. To the left in this picture is the community of Phillipsburg, adjacent to the California State College campus.

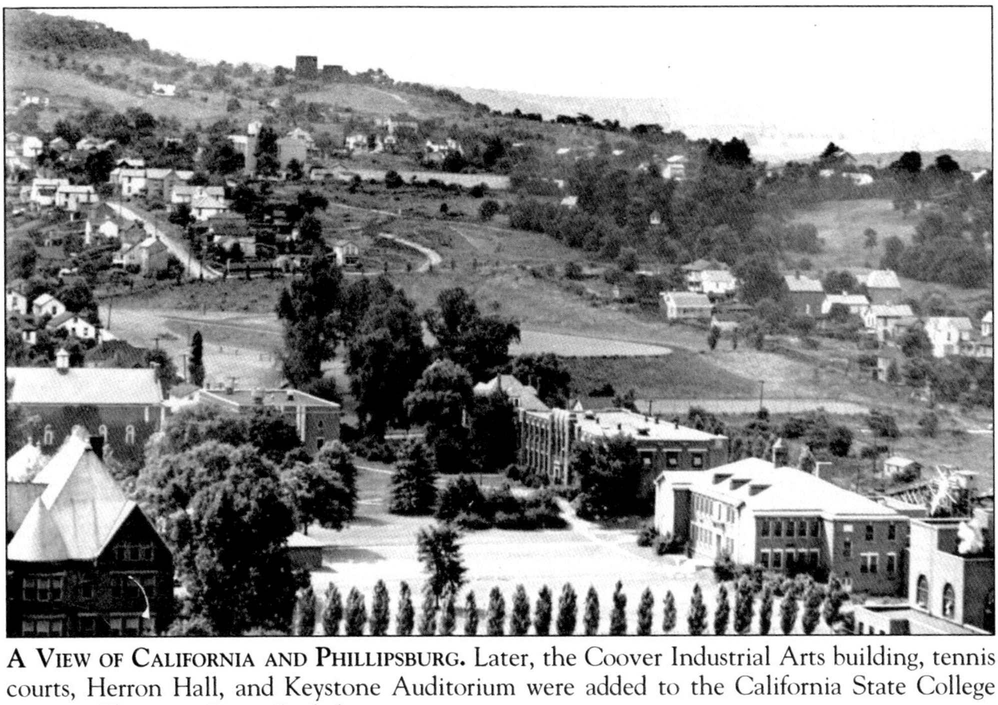

A View of California and Phillipsburg. Later, the Coover Industrial Arts building, tennis courts, Herron Hall, and Keystone Auditorium were added to the California State College campus. (Courtesy Roger Sealy.)

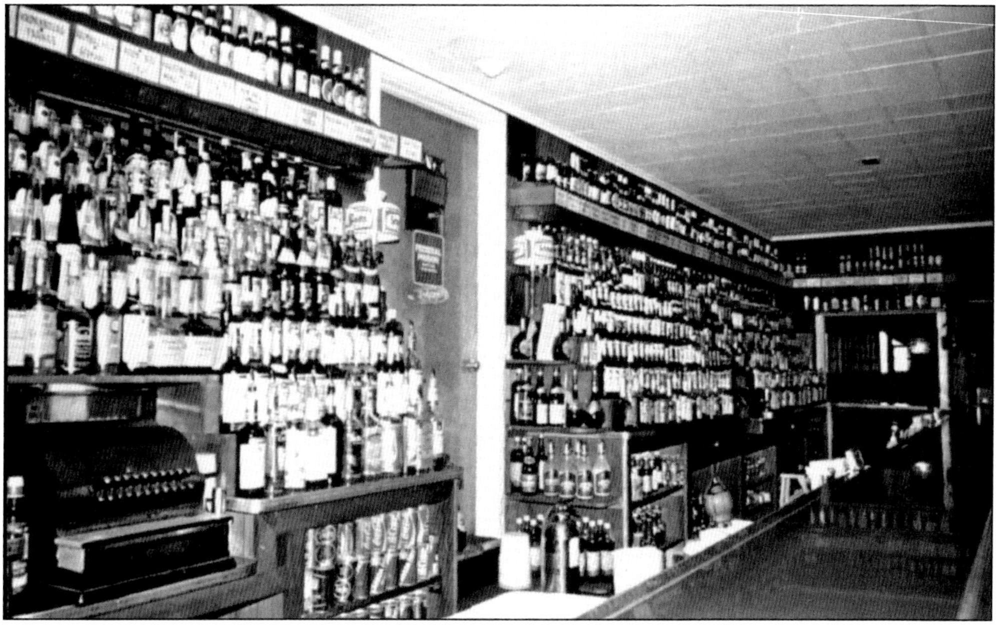

FRIENDSHIP LOUNGE. This gathering place features more than 450 varieties of beer from all over the world and a large stock of domestic and imported liquors. Located in Richeyville, it is where locals dance to polka bands on weekend nights. (Courtesy Barry Niccolai.)

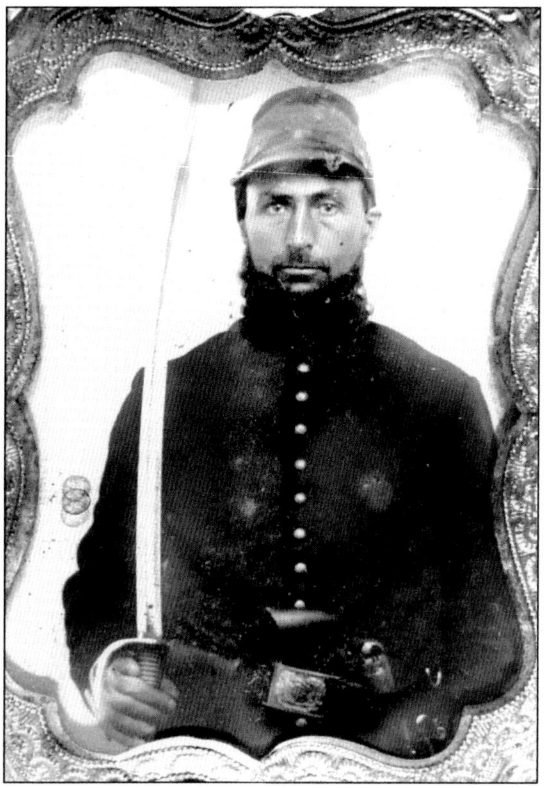

WILLIAM HENRY HORNBAKE. William Henry Hornbake is shown in his Civil War uniform in this copy of an 1863 tintype photograph. With several other volunteers from California and Coal Center, Hornbake enlisted in the 5th West Virginia Cavalry because the Pennsylvania regiments were full. William was the son of George W. Hornbake, who owned the Coal Center sawmills and lumberyards. (Courtesy Annamary Robin.)

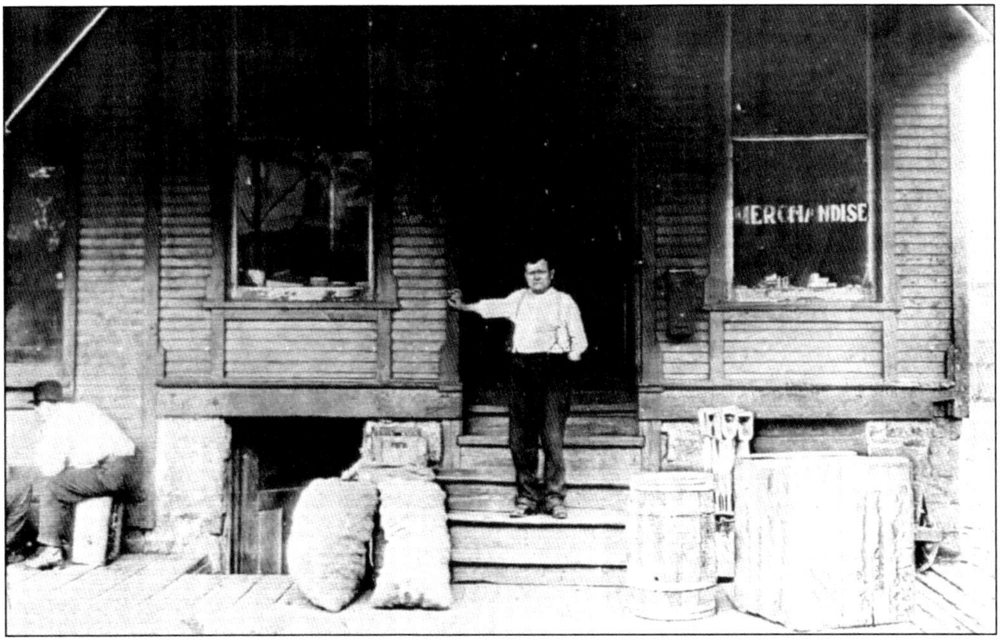

LETRICK'S GROCERY. Mike Letrick's was listed as one of five grocery stores in Phillipsburg in 1906. It was located on the corner of Boaz and Second Street. Mike Letrick was the father of John Letrick, who became superintendent of the East Pike Run Township schools. (Courtesy Peter Horvath.)

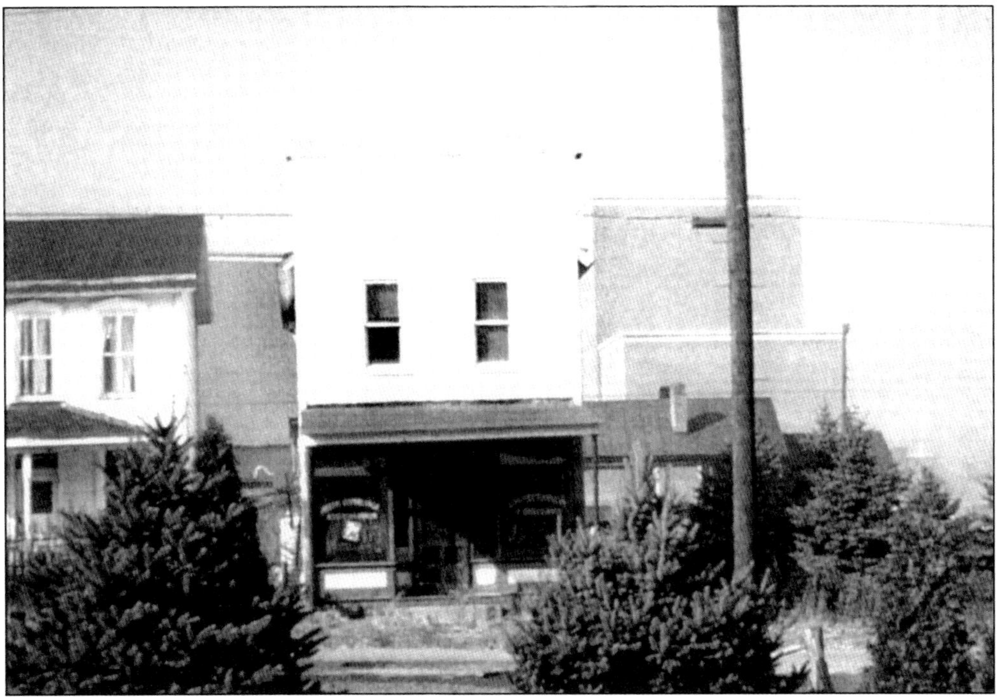

CAPPALONGA'S STORE. This store in the middle of Phillipsburg was known for its baked goods and bread. Customers of the former store best remember the ice cream it sold. (Courtesy Ted and Juanita Frederick Barney.)

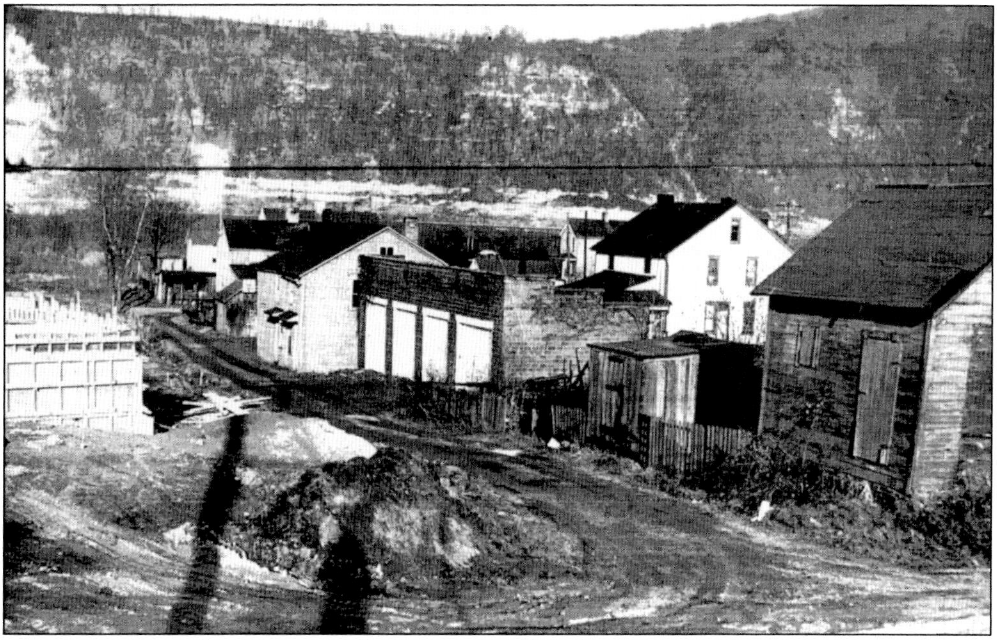

Phillipsburg. In the 1960s, California State College began expansion of its campus, and by 1964, the Hammer Hall gymnasium was under construction. What was once the Phillipsburg community is now part of the college campus. (Courtesy Special Collections, California University of Pennsylvania.)

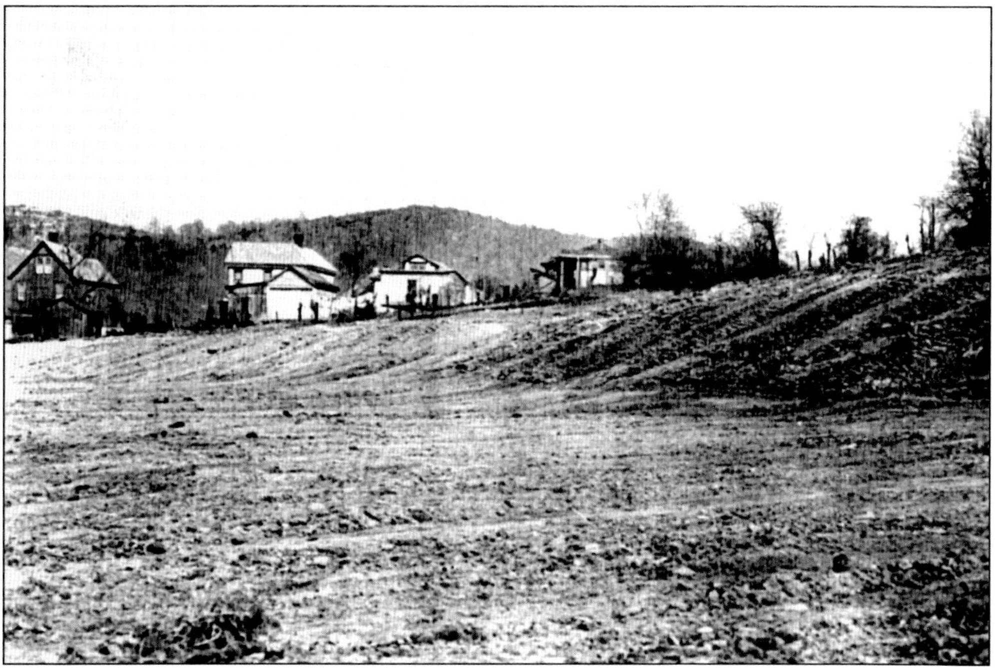

Phillipsburg in Transition. Here the land of Phillipsburg is being prepared for the expansion of the college. Dr. William H. Phillips founded and named the town in honor of his father, James, who originally farmed the area. (Courtesy Special Collections, California University of Pennsylvania.)

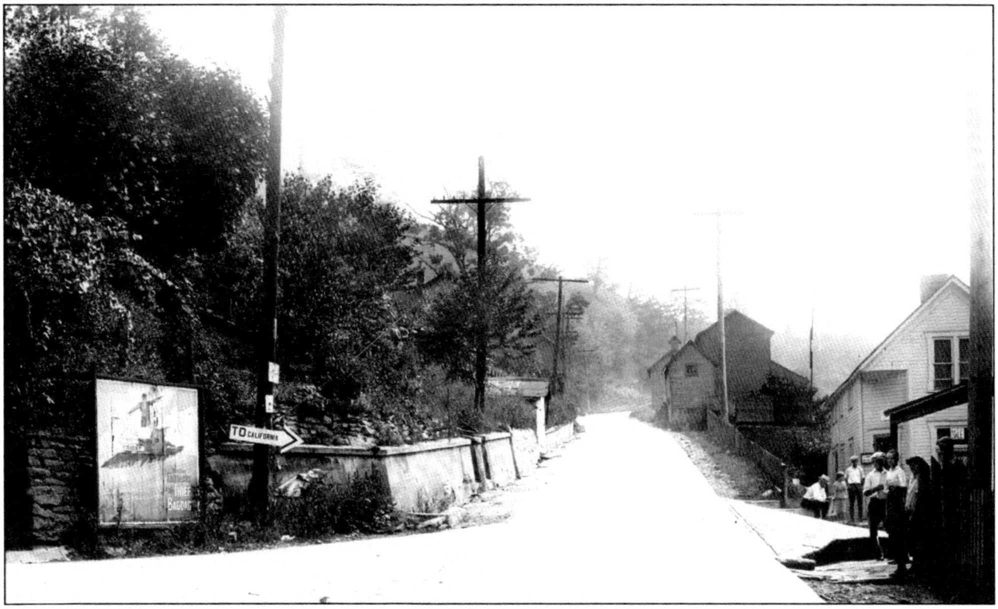

Granville to California. The road to California winds through Granville, originally called Wilna. Most of the inhabitants were miners. The town is situated on both sides of Pike Run and Gorby's Fork.

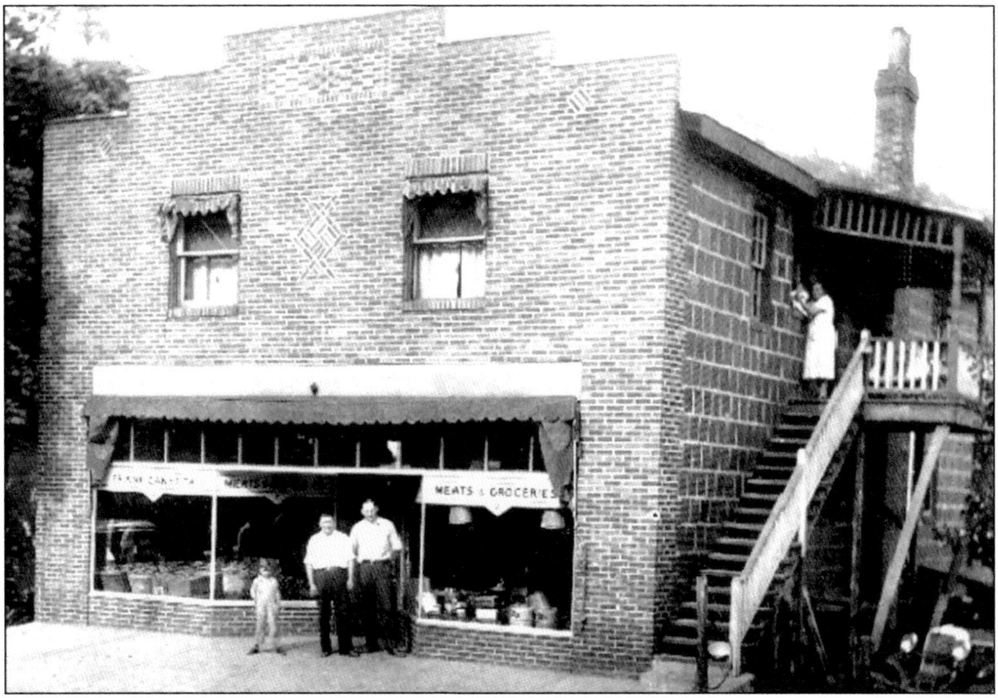

Frank Zanetta's Grocery Store. The residents of Granville purchased their groceries and meats at Frank Zanetta's store. The Zanetta family lived in an apartment over the store. (Courtesy Glen Dixon.)

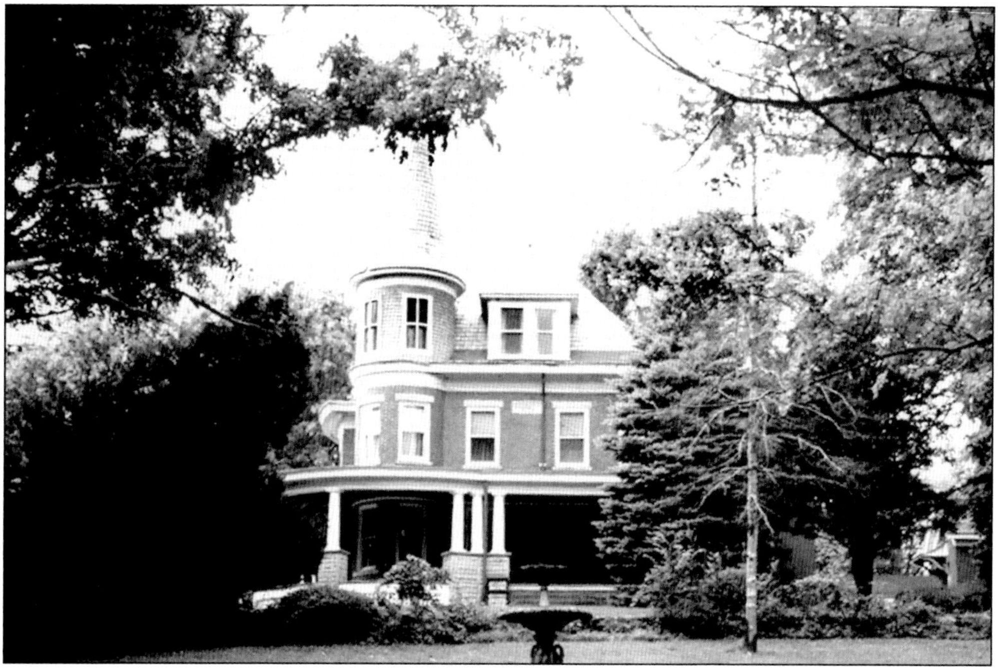

THE WALKER MANSION. Samuel G. Walker built this family home in 1903 in a small mining community. Because of its size compared to the patch houses, it was called a mansion. The area was called Walkertown. (Courtesy Rene Kraus.)

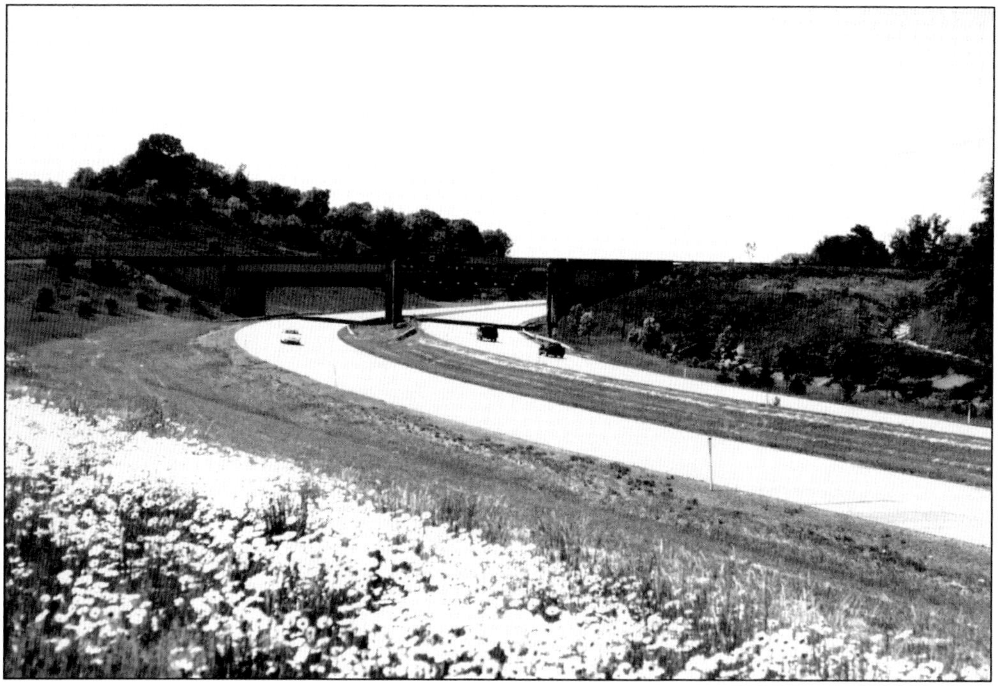

ROUTE 43. A new expressway, Route 43, promises future industrial expansion to the California area. This photograph shows the turnoff to town and the Malden overpass. (Courtesy Betty Carson.)

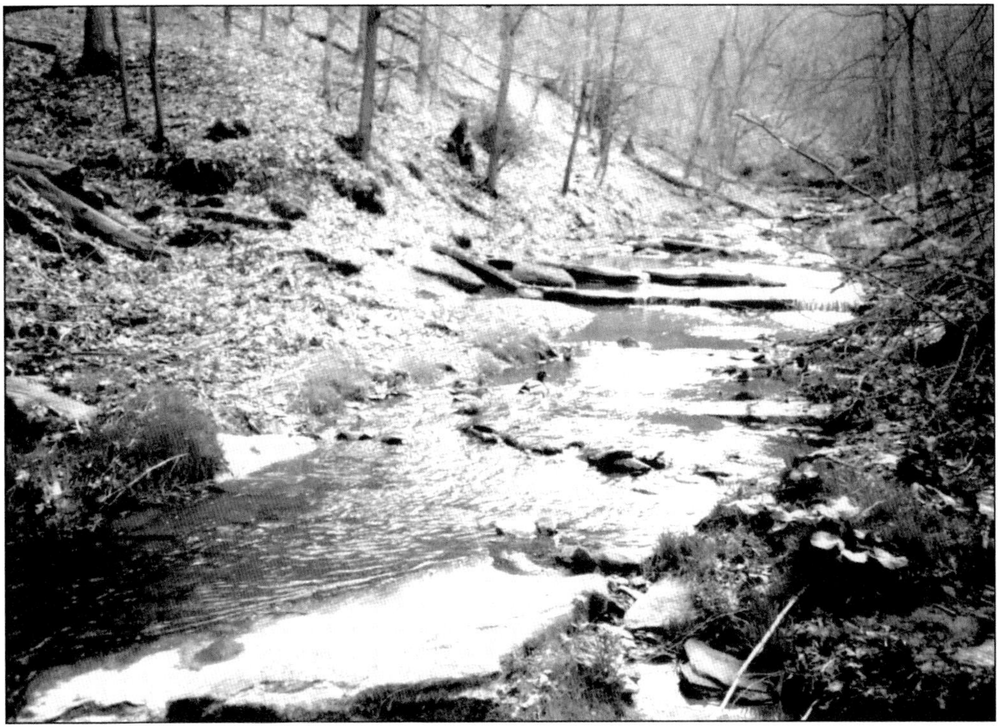

BABY HOLLOW. Along the banks of this stream, numerous species of western Pennsylvania wildflowers flourished.

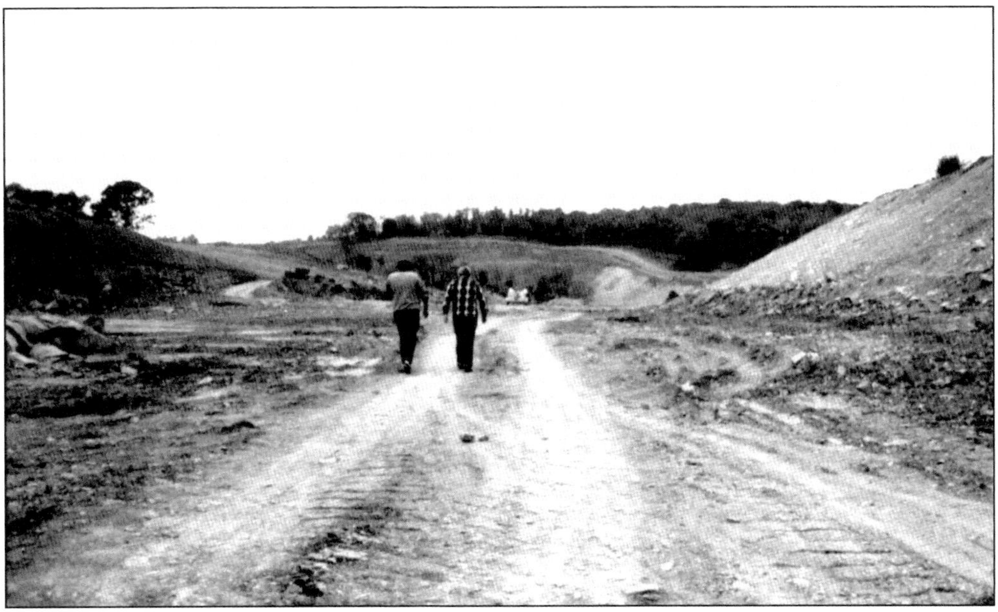

ROUTE 43 CONSTRUCTION. When the expressway was built, Baby Hollow was filled in to prepare the way for highway construction. Until completion of the new expressway in October 1990, Baby Hollow was still a favorite walking area. Fond memories remain of its many flowers and bubbling stream.

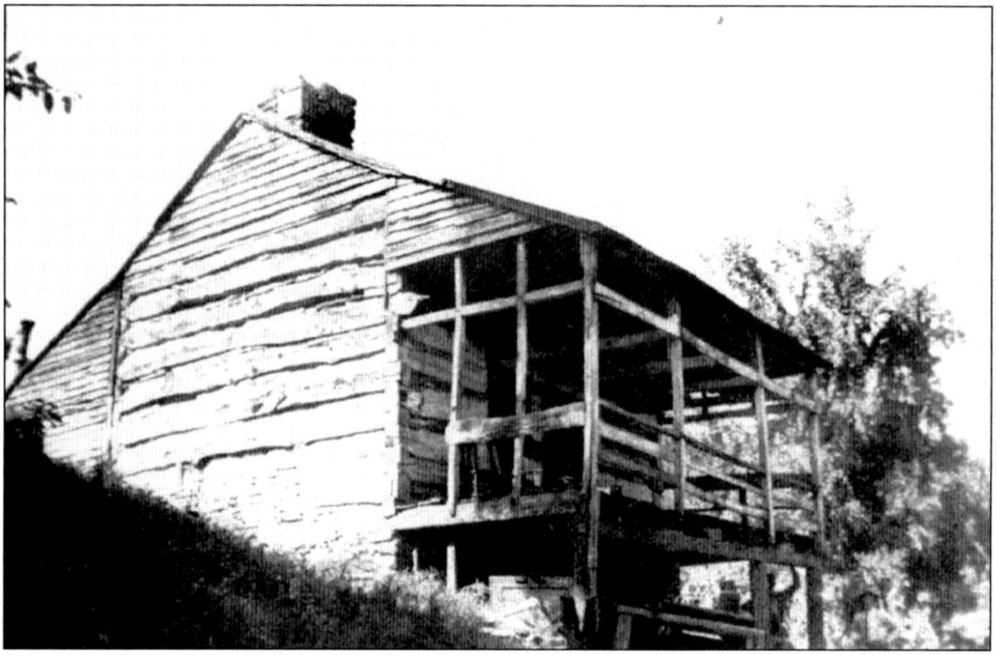

The David Hartman Home. In Granville Hollow on the west side of the road is the David Hartman house. The family moved into the house in 1844. David Hartman is listed in the 1850 census as a shingle maker. (Courtesy Midge Tomlinson and Glen Dixon.)

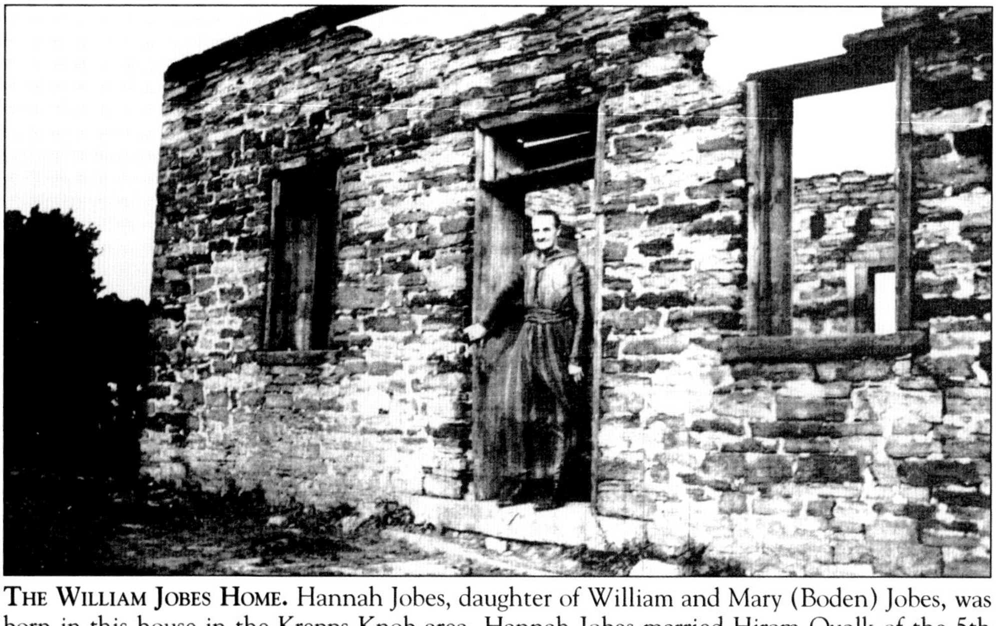

The William Jobes Home. Hannah Jobes, daughter of William and Mary (Boden) Jobes, was born in this house in the Krepps Knob area. Hannah Jobes married Hiram Qualk of the 5th West Virginia Cavalry, which served in the Civil War. Qualk was wounded in a skirmish at Dublin Depot, Virginia, in 1864. The couple raised seven children in the Coal Center area. (Courtesy Glen Dixon.)

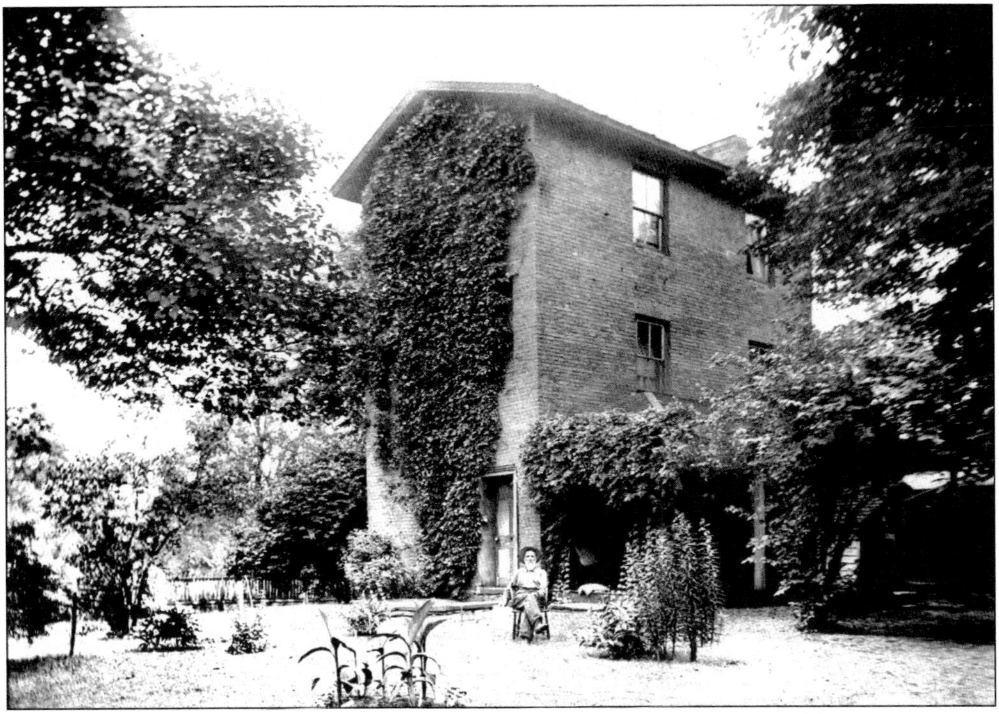

The Lucius Marchand Homestead. Lucius Marchand owned a homestead farm of 130 acres, located five miles below Brownsville. In 1873, he laid out the village of Marchand on his land. It is now called Newell. Noted as a successful farmer, Marchand is shown here sitting in his yard by his spacious three-story home. (Courtesy W. Floyd Gillis.)

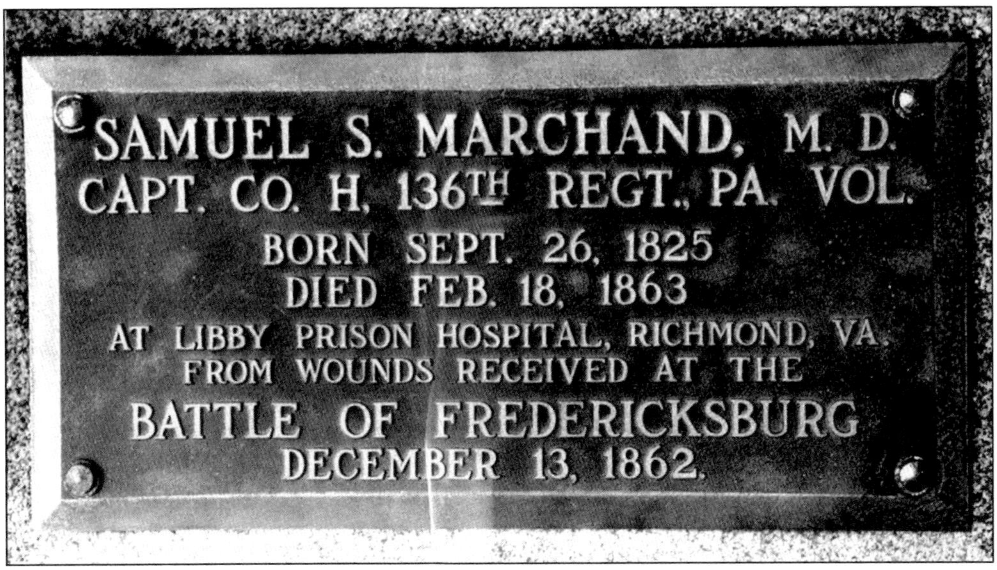

Samuel Marchand. Samuel Marchand was the son of Louis and Sarah (Sackett) Marchand. He practiced medicine before enlisting in Company H, 136th Pennsylvania Regiment, during the Civil War. He is buried in Highland Cemetery, California, and his military service marker is shown here.

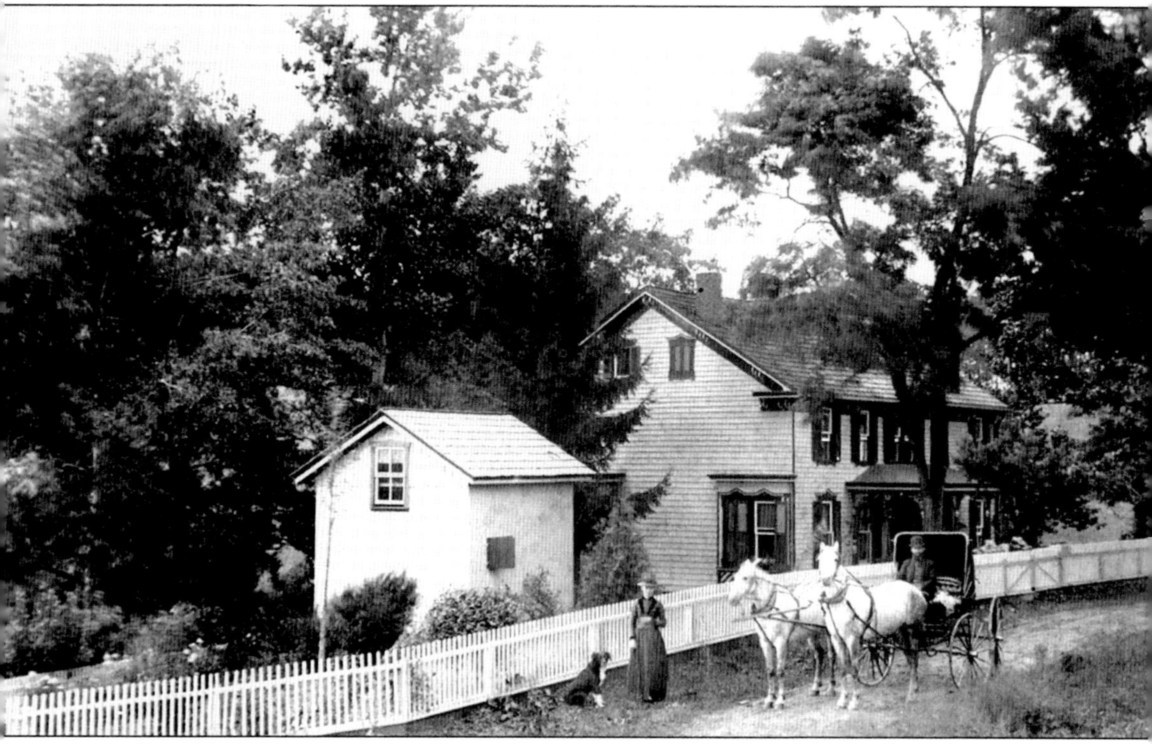

THE CLEAVER FARM. The Mitchell house, on the Cleaver Farm, is believed to have been the home of Nathan Cleaver. Renols Parker, a fugitive slave, escaped from a farm near Bentleyville and was captured while employed by Nathan Cleaver. Shown in the photograph are Martha "Mattie" (Cleaver) Mitchell and her husband, Hopkins Mitchell. (Courtesy W. Floyd Gillis.)

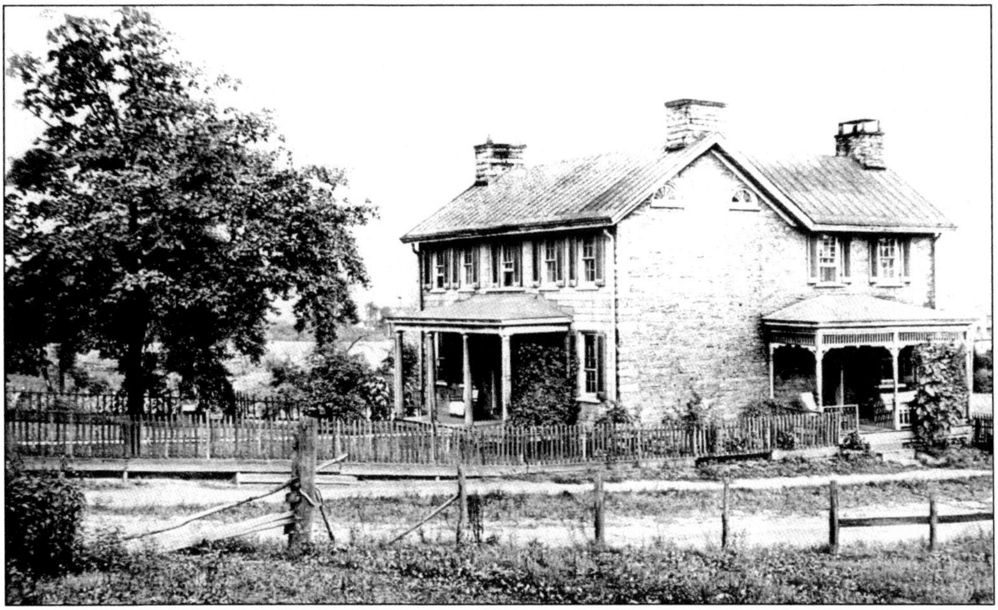

The Latta House. This stone house is listed by the Western Pennsylvania Architectural Survey as being the best representation of the Virginia plantation style found in Washington County. Built in 1805, the house was owned by the Stockdale, Allen, and Latta families. It is noted for two-inch-thick paneled doors, the walnut staircase, cupboards with hand-carved moldings, and a five-foot stone kitchen fireplace. (Courtesy Charles and Marguerite Cox.)

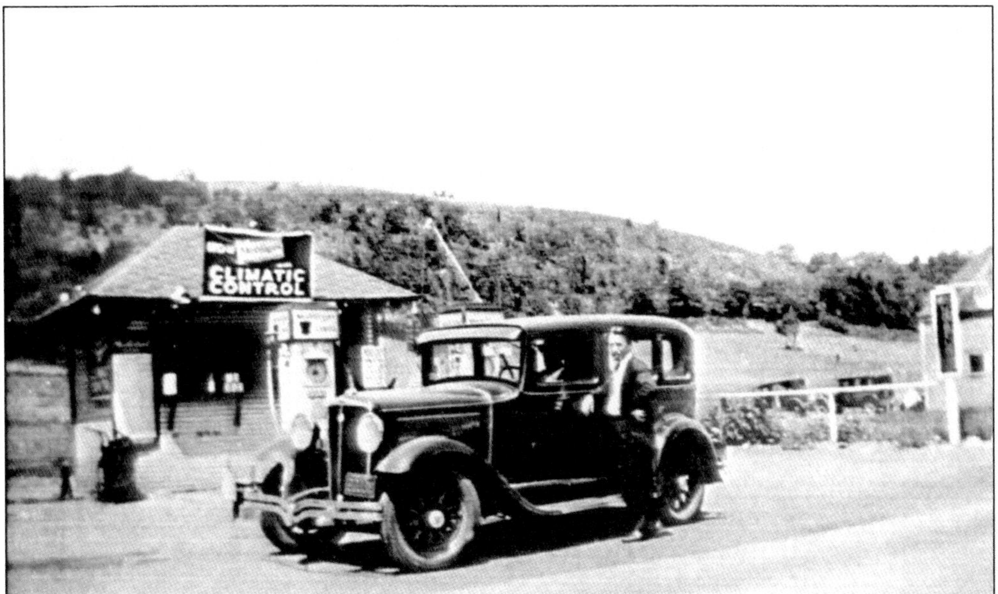

Roscoe Taxi. In the 1930s, people who missed the trolley or had no car could take the taxi in Roscoe for a reasonable fee. (Courtesy Charles and Marguerite Cox.)

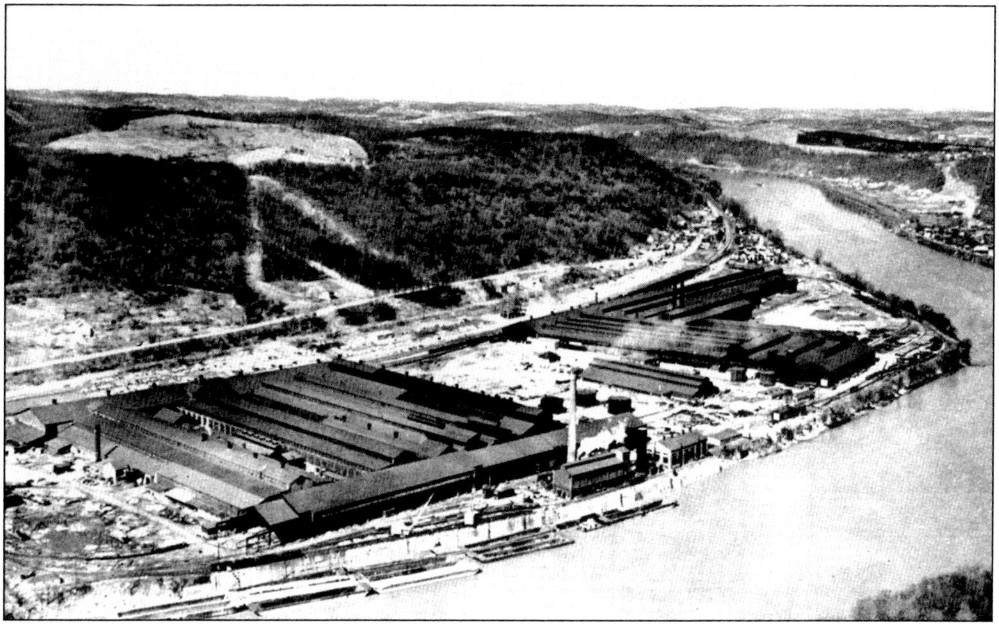

The Allenport Mill. In January 1918, the new Allenport plant of the Pittsburgh Steel Products Company began production. Some 400 tons of fabricated structural steel was used for construction of the Fort Pitt Bridge in Pittsburgh. The tube mill was noted for making the best seamless oil well tubing available. The plant is now in production as part of Wheeling-Pittsburgh Steel. (Courtesy Charles and Marguerite Cox.)

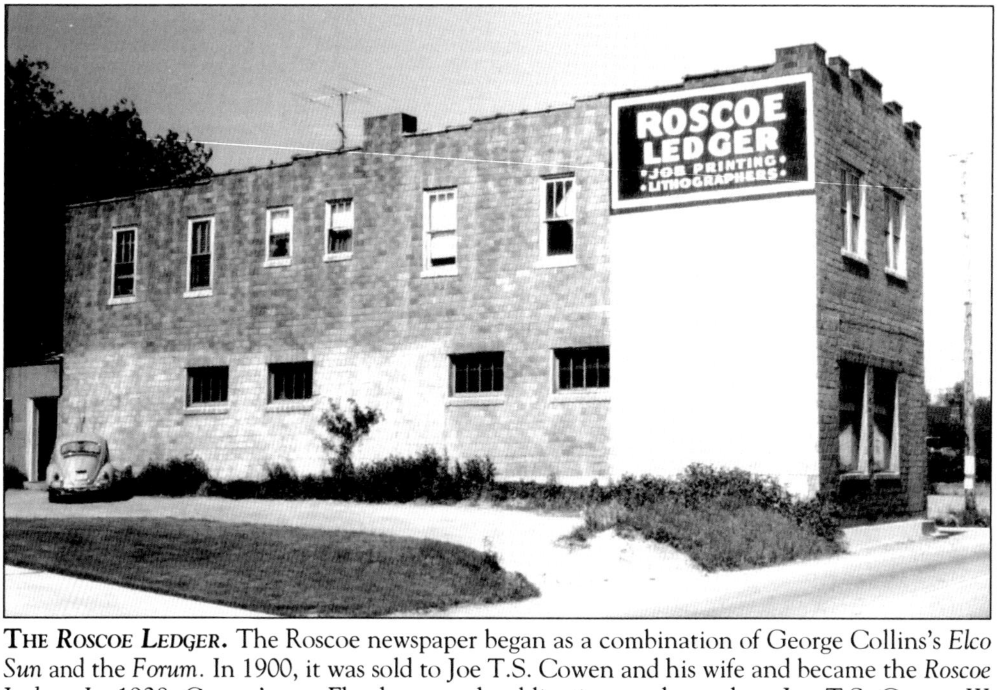

The *Roscoe Ledger*. The Roscoe newspaper began as a combination of George Collins's *Elco Sun* and the *Forum*. In 1900, it was sold to Joe T.S. Cowen and his wife and became the *Roscoe Ledger*. In 1938, Cowen's son Floyd assumed publication, and grandson Joe T.S. Cowen III continued to publish the paper until its final issue of February 29, 1952. (Courtesy Charles and Marguerite Cox.)

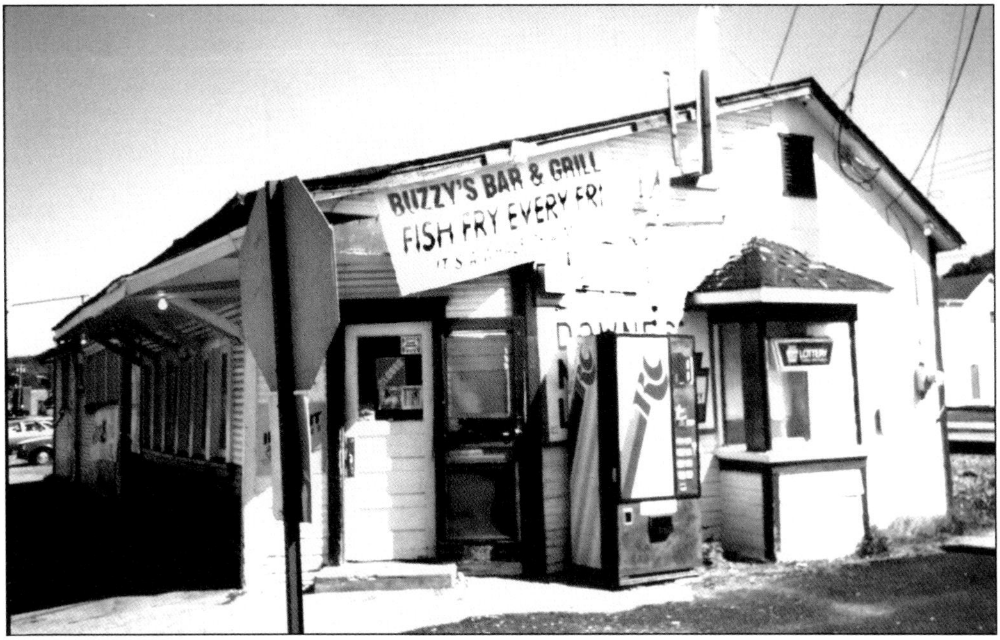

Downes Luncheonette and Newsstand. Owned by Sam Downes, this popular little business was the stop for the trolley. Many customers dropped in for coffee and a newspaper on their way to work. Crossing the railroad tracks for a 15¢ hamburger was worth the effort for the locals. Sam operated the luncheonette until it was destroyed by fire in 1994. (Courtesy Charles and Marguerite Cox.)

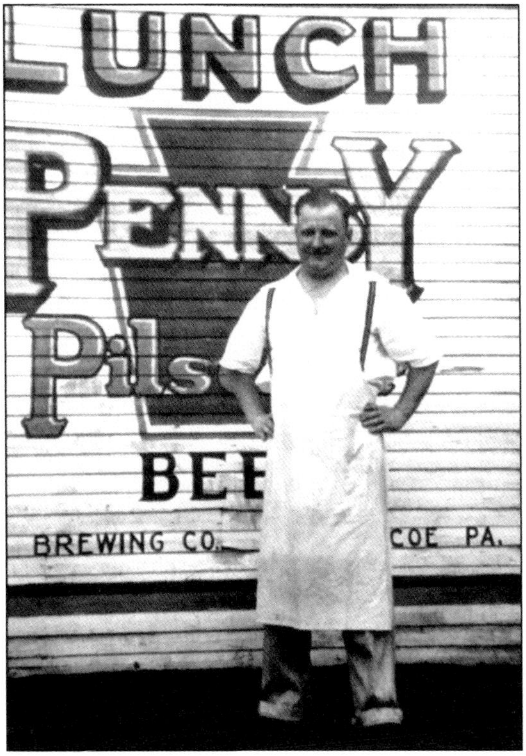

The Sam Downes Lunch Room. Raymond Pichard takes a break from work at the Sam Downes Lunch Room. Pennsy Pilsner, made by Roscoe's own Moose Brewery, is advertised in the background. (Courtesy Charles and Marguerite Cox.)

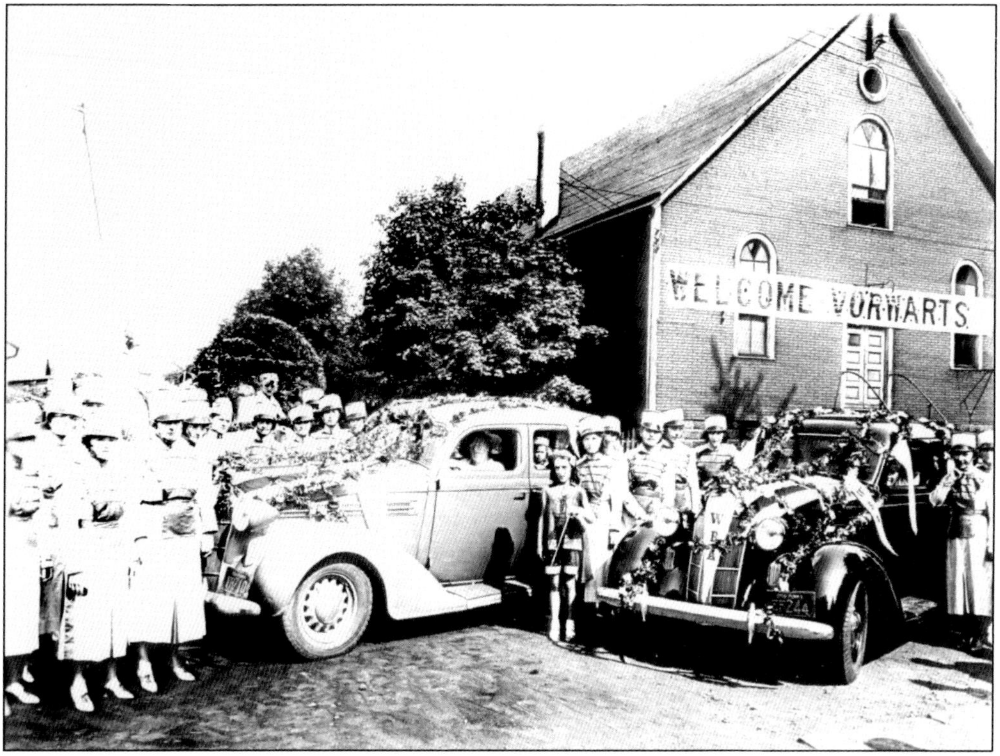

VORWARTS. The Vorwarts German Club was the starting place for a parade honoring Rear Adm. W. Rea Furlong, a Roscoe resident and U.S. Navy officer during World War I. The Vorwarts, popular with the German community in Roscoe, was especially noted for both the male and female singing groups organized there in the 1890s. (Courtesy Charles and Marguerite Cox.)

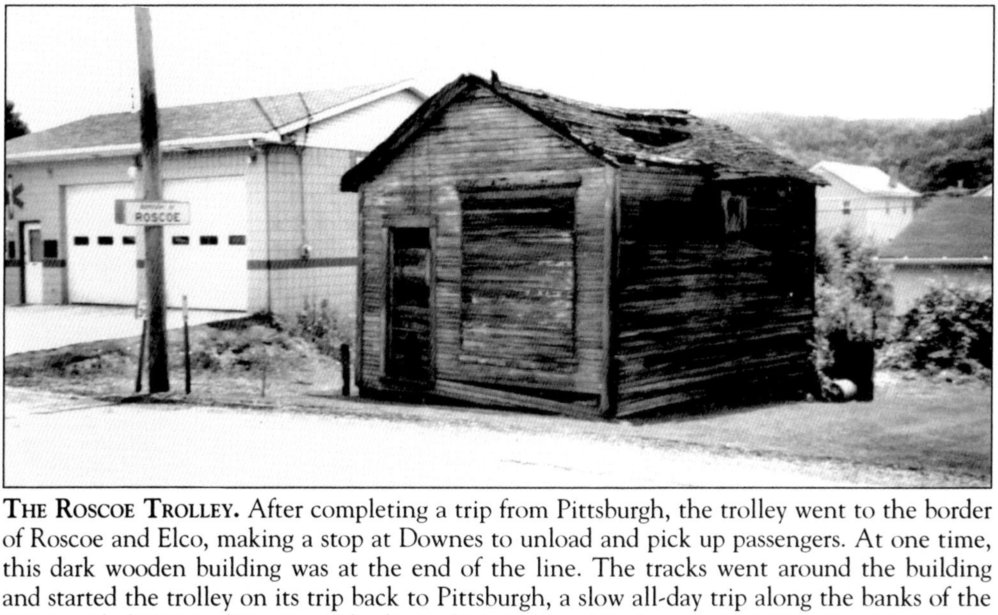

THE ROSCOE TROLLEY. After completing a trip from Pittsburgh, the trolley went to the border of Roscoe and Elco, making a stop at Downes to unload and pick up passengers. At one time, this dark wooden building was at the end of the line. The tracks went around the building and started the trolley on its trip back to Pittsburgh, a slow all-day trip along the banks of the Monongahela River. (Courtesy Charles and Marguerite Cox.)

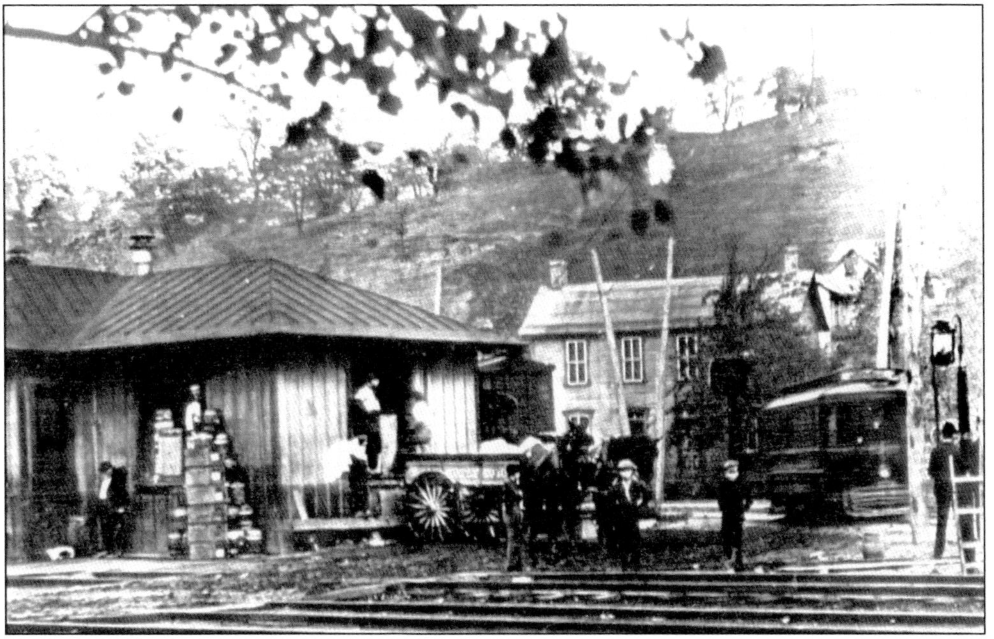

The Roscoe Railroad Station. The railroad was always a popular means of transportation. Roscoe had its own station. Here baggage employees wait for the train, carting the luggage that was entrusted to their care. (Courtesy Charles and Marguerite Cox.)

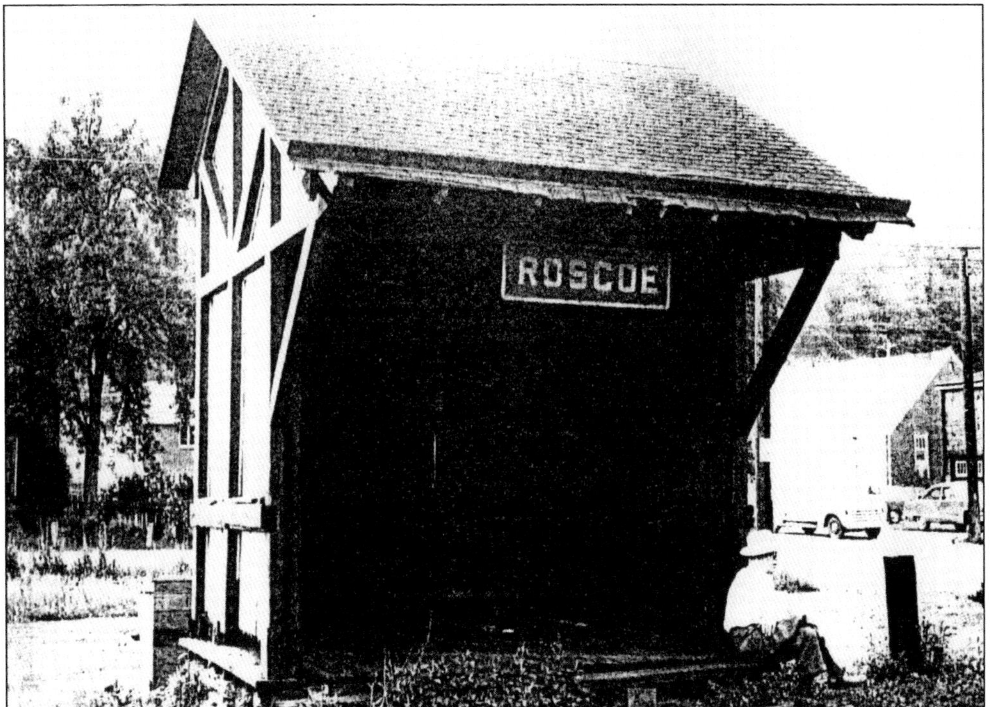

The Roscoe Shelter. As rail travel declined, this small shelter replaced the railroad station and baggage room. The shelter protected rail customers and was a reminder to the engineer that the train was approaching Roscoe. (Courtesy Charles and Marguerite Cox.)

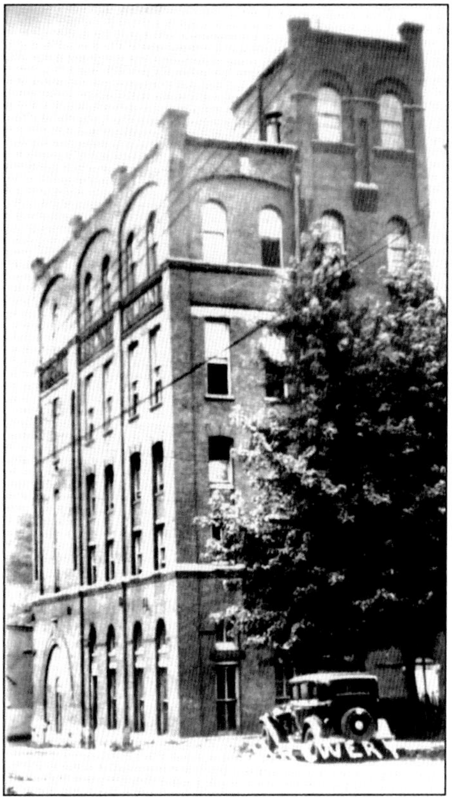

The Moose Brewery. The Moose Brewery of Lucyville was incorporated in 1874. The tallest building around, it became a landmark and supplied the area with thousands of barrels of beer each year. The brewery declared bankruptcy after World War II. (Courtesy Helen and Karen Webb.)

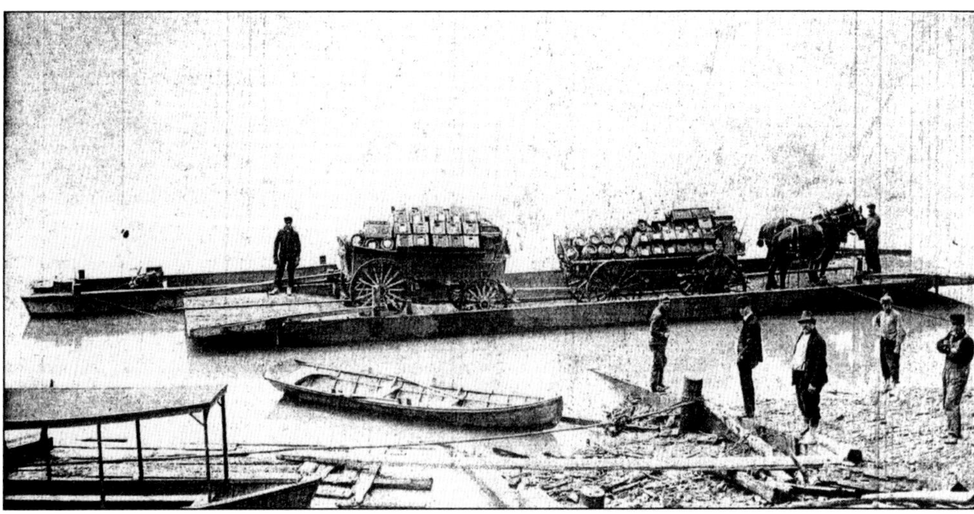

The Roscoe Ferry. Men load kegs and cases of beer from the Moose Brewery onto the ferry in 1915. Route 88 had not yet been built between Roscoe and California, so the horse-drawn wagons were taken to the next town for delivery. (Courtesy Helen and Karen Webb.)

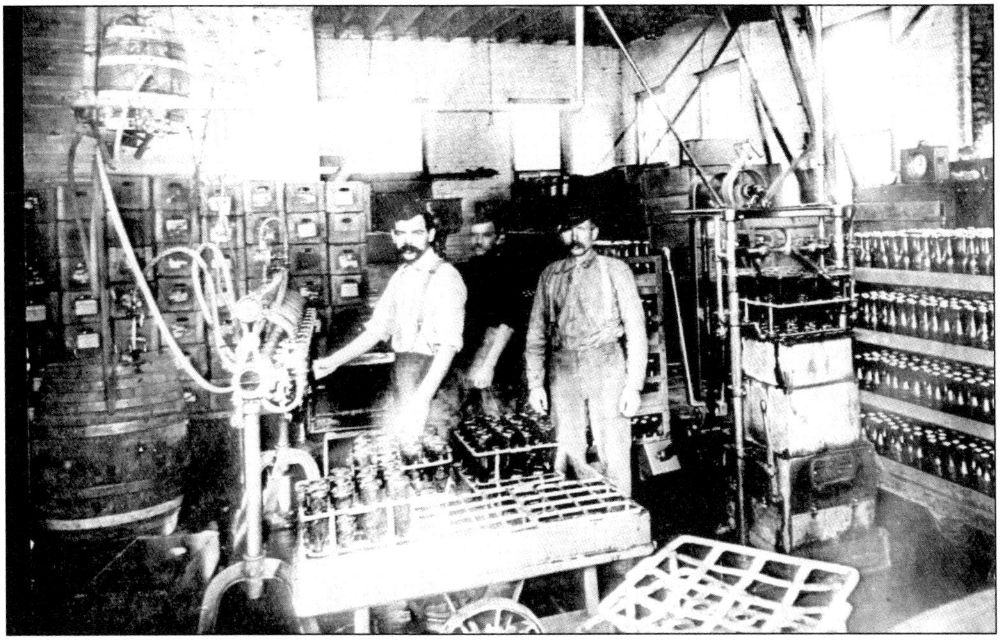

THE INTERIOR OF THE MOOSE BREWERY. Bottling beer at the brewery in Roscoe was done by machinery. The plant was self sufficient, with its own electric plant that generated light and power. It was also capable of making its own ice. John "Cowboy" Petrick (left) is operating the bottling machine. (Courtesy Helen and Karen Webb.)

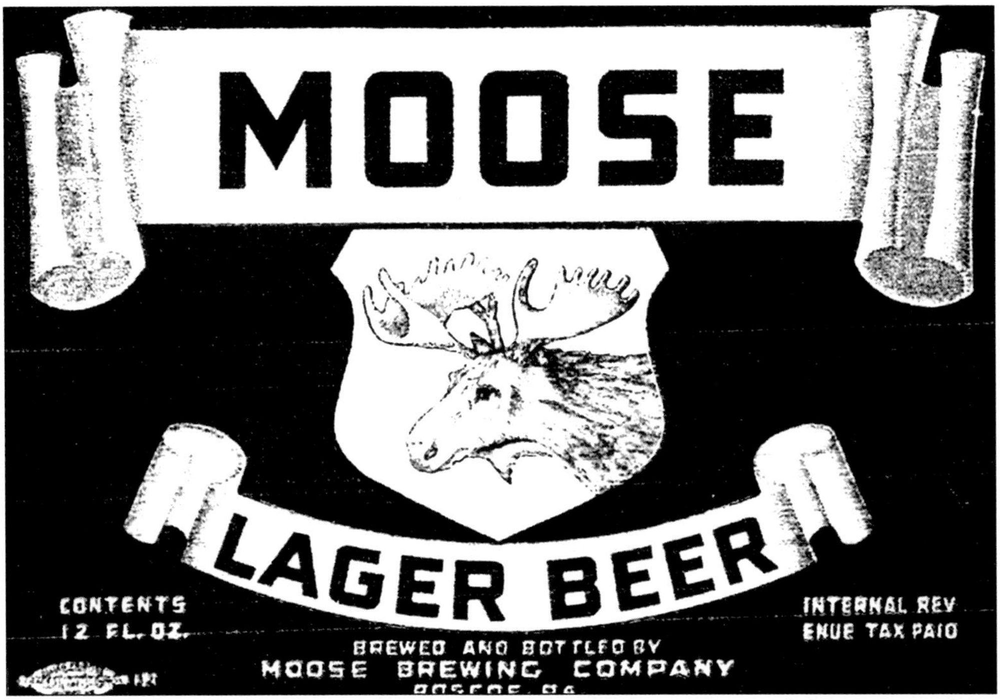

A MOOSE BREWERY LABEL. This label for a bottle of beer was one of several that showcased the kinds of beer made at the Moose Brewery. The brewery offered Bohemian Club, Pilsner, Bock, Lager, and Antler German. (Courtesy Charles and Marguerite Cox.)

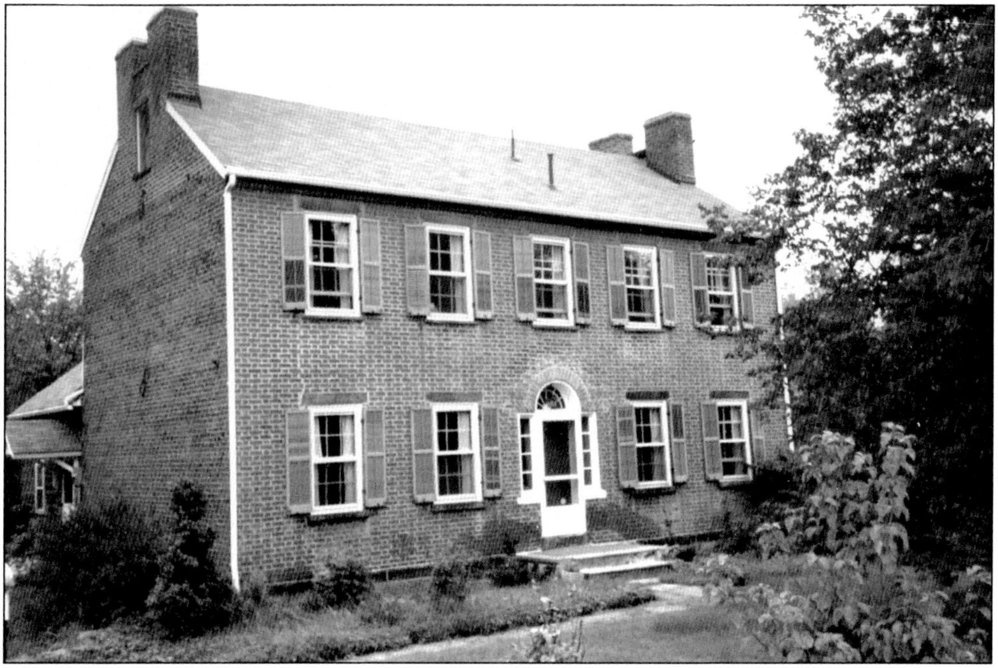

The Solomon Phillips Farm. In 1786, Solomon Phillips built a stone house and barn that are still in existence in East Pike Run Township, overlooking the Monongahela River. He and his wife, Martha, lived in this home, built in 1790. They were the parents of seven children.

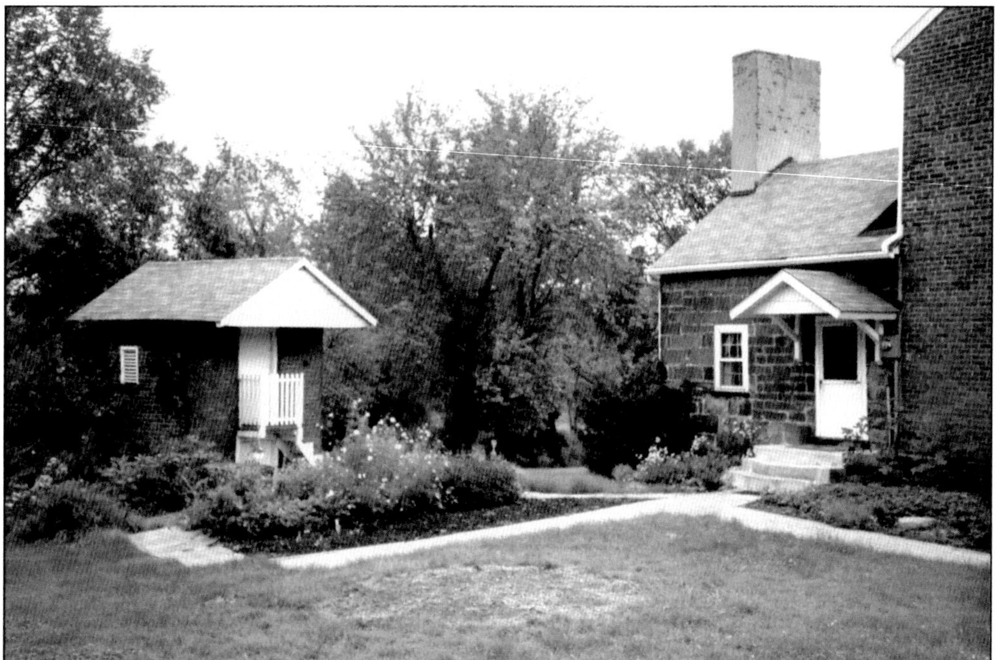

The Phillips House and Oven. This photograph shows the original single-room house built by Solomon Phillips. The outside oven house is to the left.

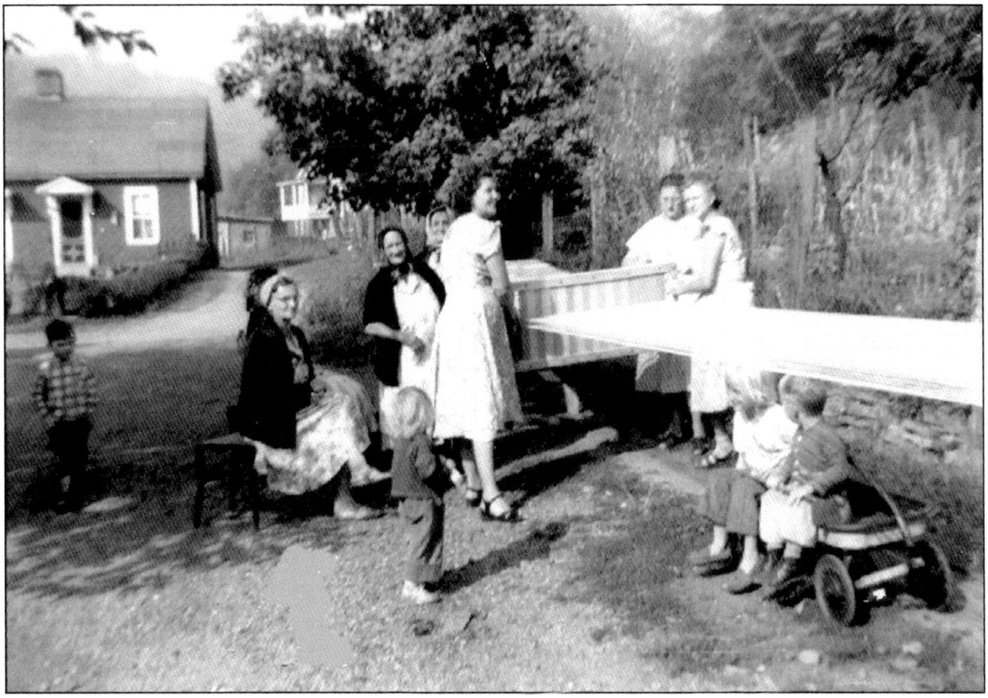

Rug Weaving. This photograph shows the women of Daisytown weaving rugs from strips of castoff clothing or fabric that have been cut into strips. Persons familiar with this Hungarian art introduced the skill to the area. The rugs were woven outdoors on looms at least 50 feet long, stretching for one continuous length between trees or posts. (Courtesy Mary Elaine Lozosky.)

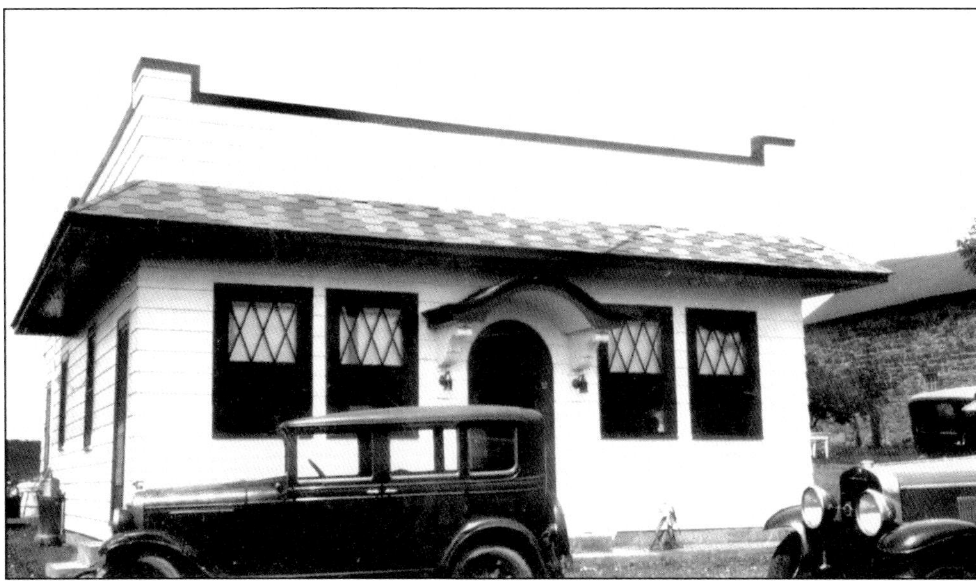

Cuppies Barbeque. This little barbeque establishment was noted for fresh ham sandwiches and was owned by J.K. and Hannah Kaupp. The hams turning on a spit were a familiar sight to customers. The popular restaurant, located on Old National Pike in the Malden area, is pictured here as it looked in 1928. (Courtesy Roger Sealy.)

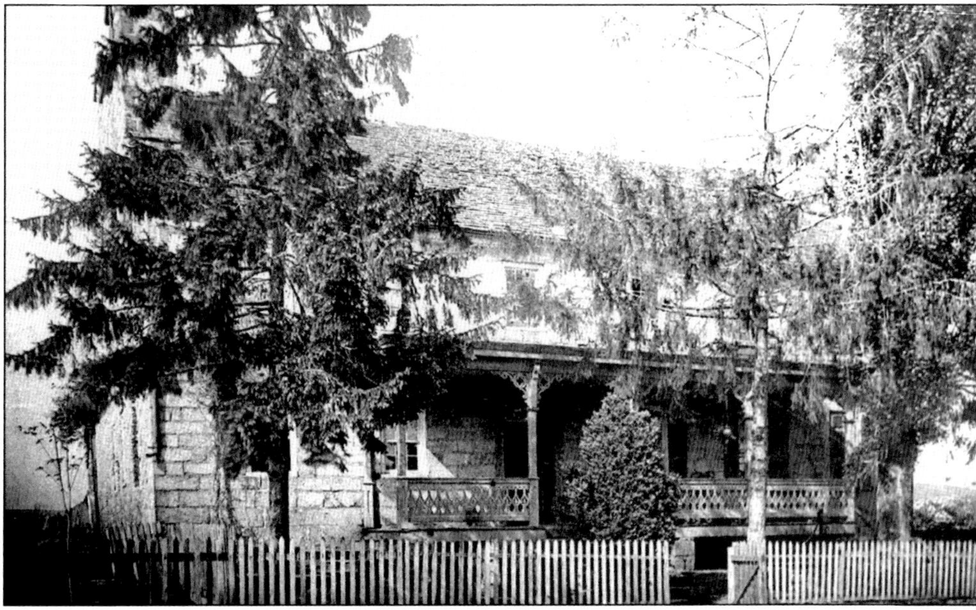

The Krepps Tavern (Malden Inn). In 1822, the Krepps family built this three-story, 12-room house of native stone with neighboring stable and outbuildings. It sat on a 220-acre site along the Old National Pike. Early travelers roomed at the inn, stabling their horses in the nearby barns. The present owner, Rose Paci, is restoring the house and has transformed the stable building into a restaurant, Paci's Lounge. (Courtesy Rose Paci.)

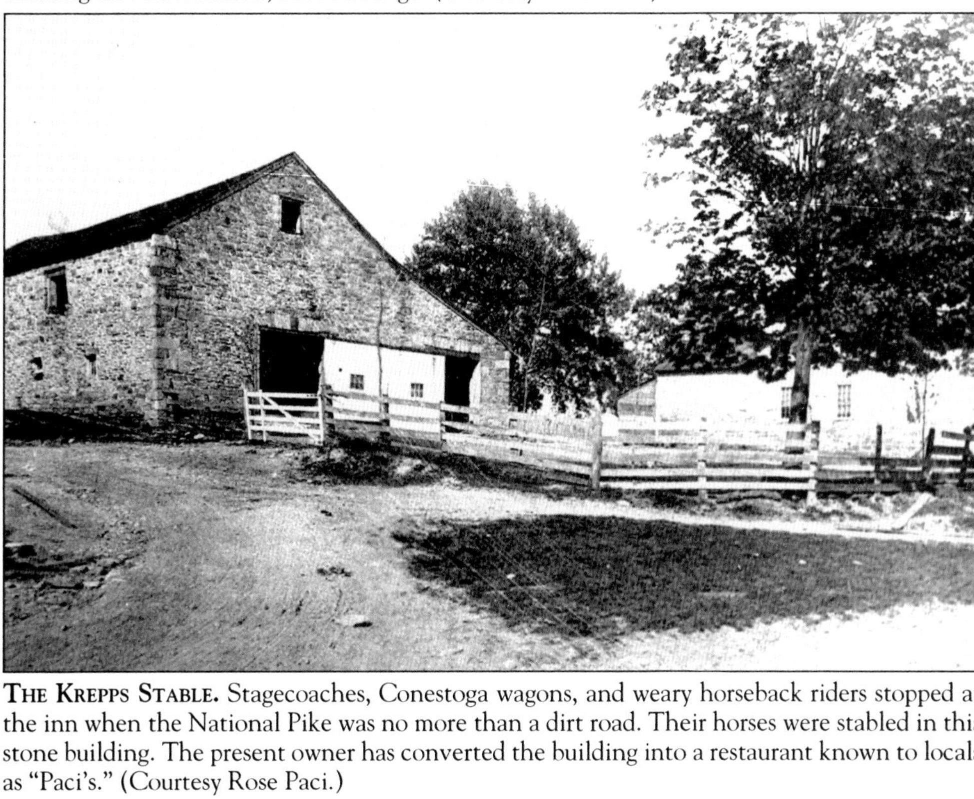

The Krepps Stable. Stagecoaches, Conestoga wagons, and weary horseback riders stopped at the inn when the National Pike was no more than a dirt road. Their horses were stabled in this stone building. The present owner has converted the building into a restaurant known to locals as "Paci's." (Courtesy Rose Paci.)

Three

Business and Industry

In 1849, the earliest citizens of California depended on local farmers and businesses in nearby communities to supply their needs. Following the example of other Monongahela River towns, a boatyard was established as California's first industry, where the hulls of riverboats were built. This industry included a sawmill and lumberyard, and the town slowly grew as skilled artisans made their way to California. Construction flourished as bricks made from the riverbank clay were used for the houses, schools, buildings, and churches that were needed by the settlers of the town.

In the span of a few short years, the town saw its first hotel and store established by Job Johnson, the beginnings of a post office, and various individual enterprises, including the first merchants, Solomon Sibbitt and Lewis Morgan. The discovery in the area of one of the largest veins of bituminous coal in the world brought an influx of immigrants to the Monongahela Valley. Hundreds of them lived and worked in California. By the turn of the next century, California had grown from a population of a mere 300 people to a self-sufficient community of more than 2,000 residents.

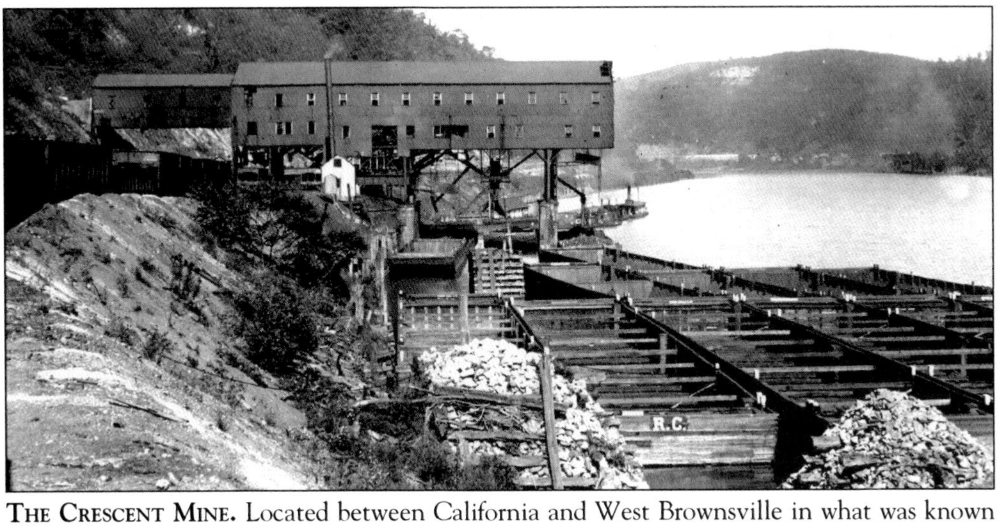

The Crescent Mine. Located between California and West Brownsville in what was known as Lilleytown, the Crescent Mine was originally owned by the Monongahela River Coal and Coke Company, before it merged with Pittsburgh Coal Company. In 1899, Joseph Underwood, a California businessman and banker, formed the California Coal Company. He owned the Crescent Mine, in addition to the Vigilant and Snow Hill coal mines.

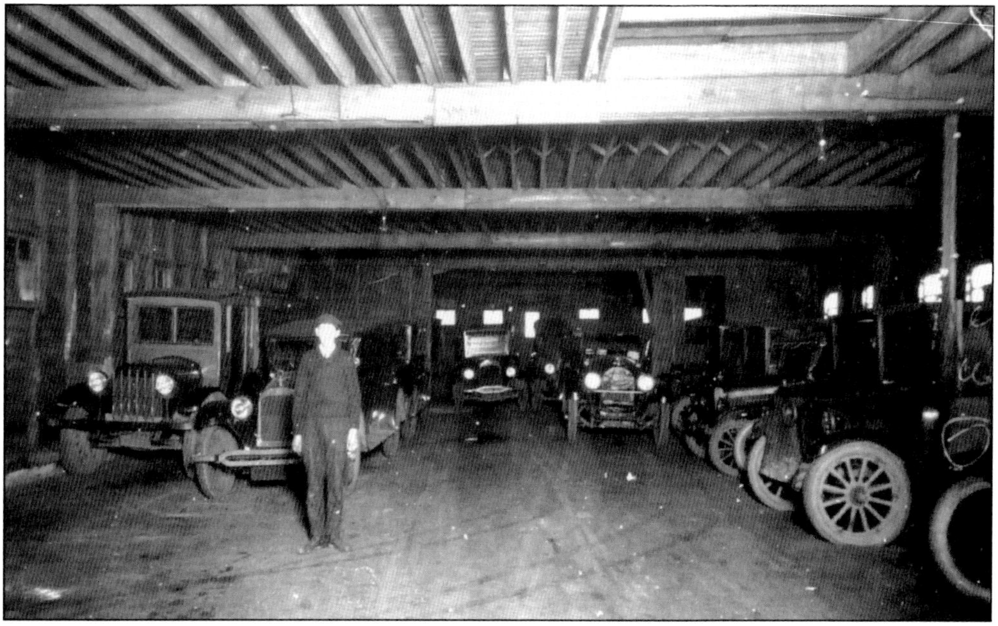

THE MAHANEY GARAGE. In the 1900s, John Mahaney, grandson of Civil War veteran William Mahaney, operated the Overland and Willys-Knight garage on Wood Street, following the close of the family livery business. Later, John Mahaney was noted for his Ford repair shop at the rear of 428 Wood Street. (Courtesy Tom and Debbie Moore Jr.)

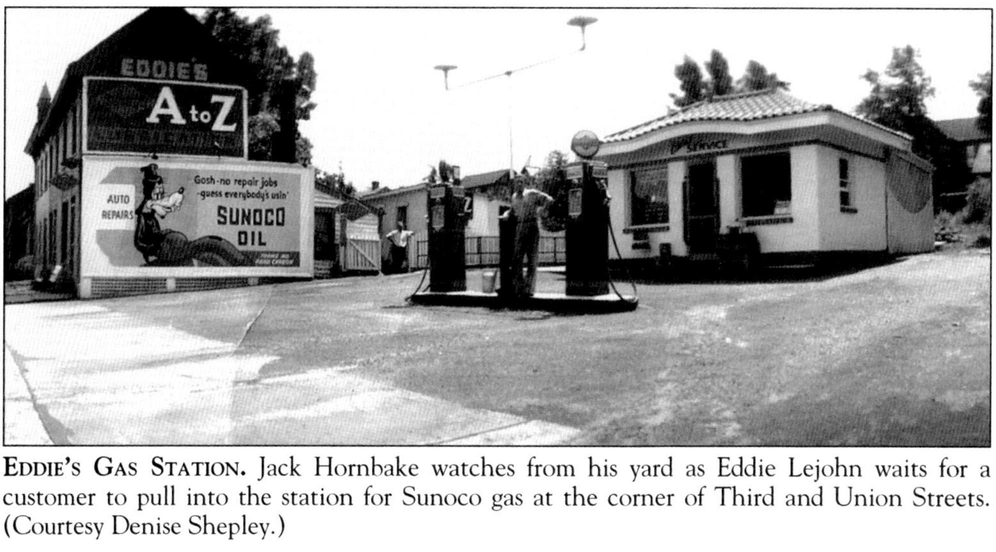

EDDIE'S GAS STATION. Jack Hornbake watches from his yard as Eddie Lejohn waits for a customer to pull into the station for Sunoco gas at the corner of Third and Union Streets. (Courtesy Denise Shepley.)

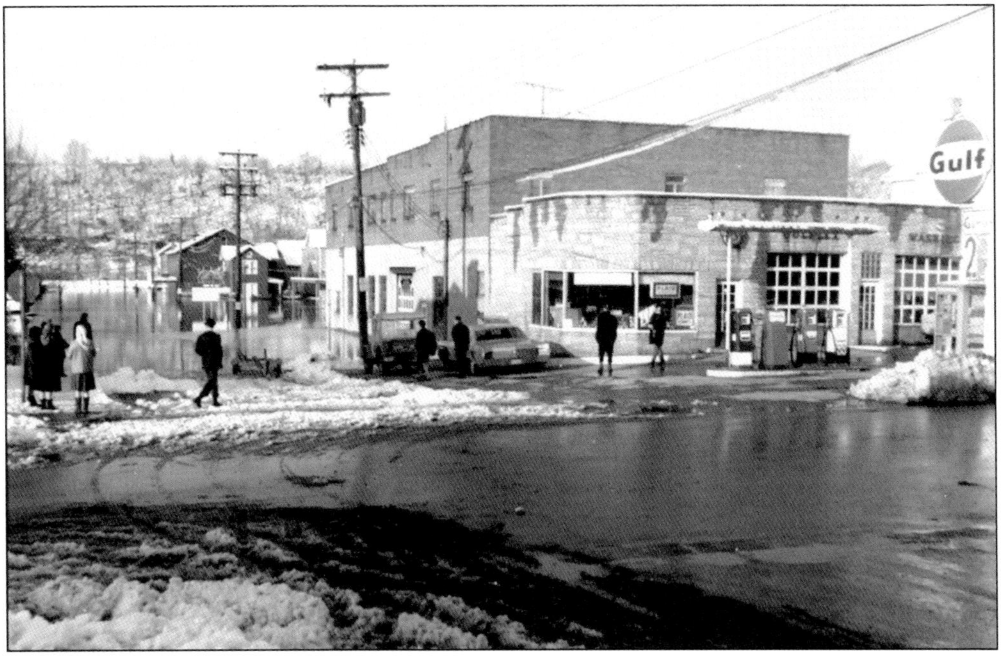

GEDDA'S GULF STATION. In 1963, the flood did not stop customers from getting gas at Tom and Frank Gedda's Gulf station, at Third and Union Streets. (Courtesy Denise Shepley.)

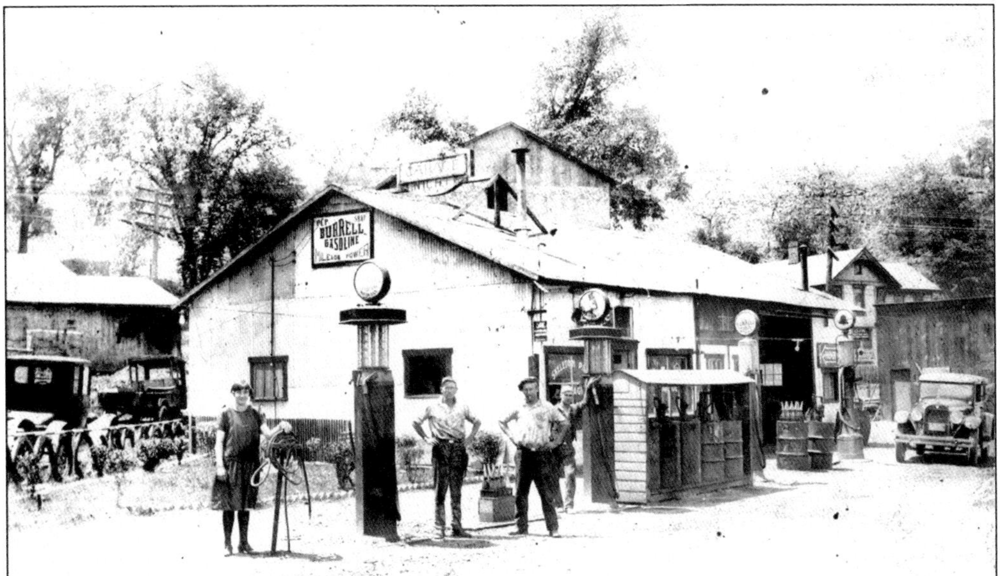

THE CASEY JONES SERVICE STATION. This familiar landmark in California opened in 1926. From 1929 to 1979, it was owned by the Layton family, before it was sold to George Powell. Powell ran it as a full-service Mobil. (Courtesy George Powell.)

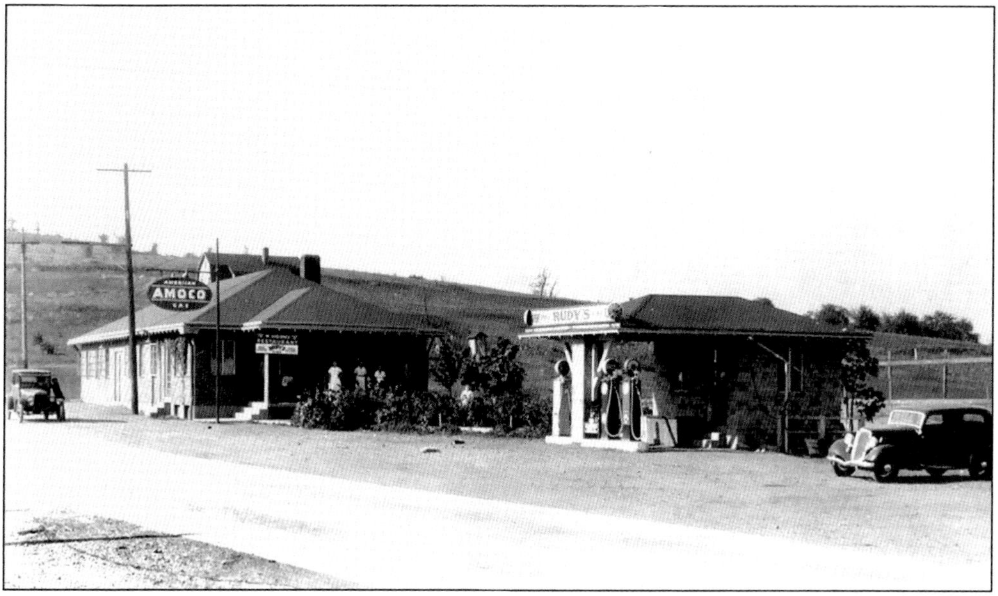

RUDY'S PLACE. Located in an ideal spot on Wood Street (Route 88), Rudy's Place was owned by Rudy Digon. People could fill up with Amoco on the way south or stop by for dinner or a baseball game in the field behind the station. (Courtesy Doris Encapera.)

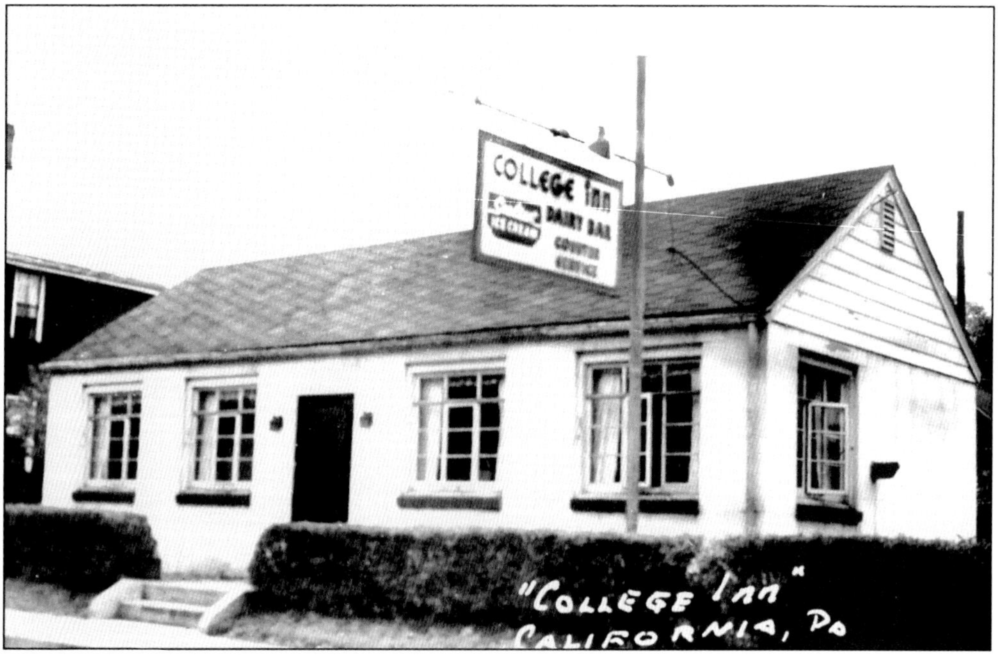

COLLEGE INN. Located on Beazell Street near California State Teachers College, this was a popular restaurant for students as well as locals. Patrons could order food from hamburgers to full meals, but the establishment was best known for its homemade doughnuts. In 1950, Bill Lancaster sold the business to Shirley and "Red" Aglio. It was razed for the construction of the Eberly Science Building. (Courtesy Louis Aglio.)

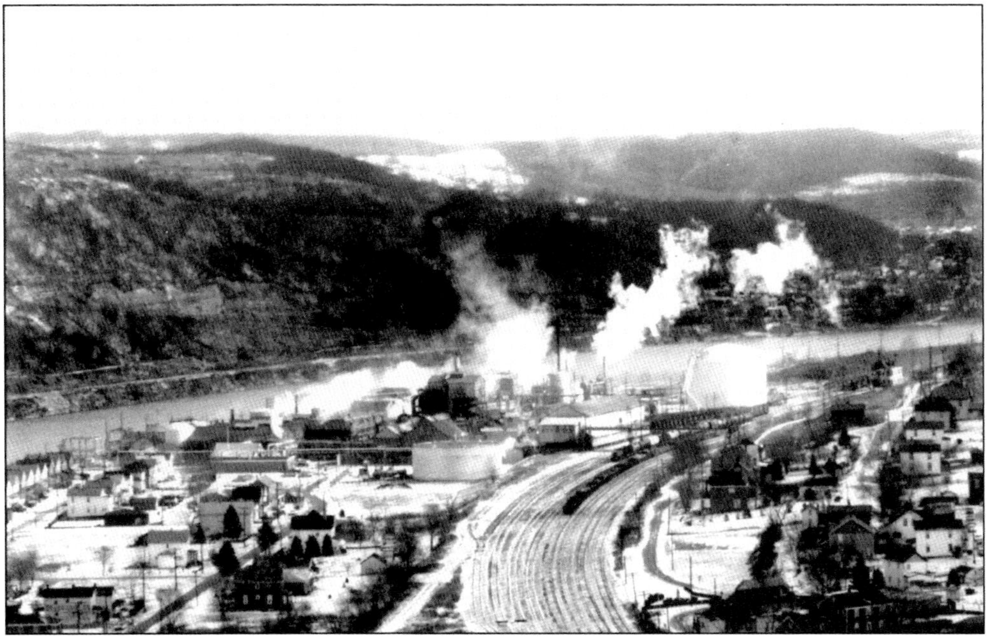

The Newell Chemical Plant. The only industry in Newell, the plant provided jobs for all the surrounding communities. During World War II, the plant made sulfuric acid, 40 percent oleum, and chemicals, providing the basis for the manufacture of powerful explosives. (Courtesy Kathryne Jankey.)

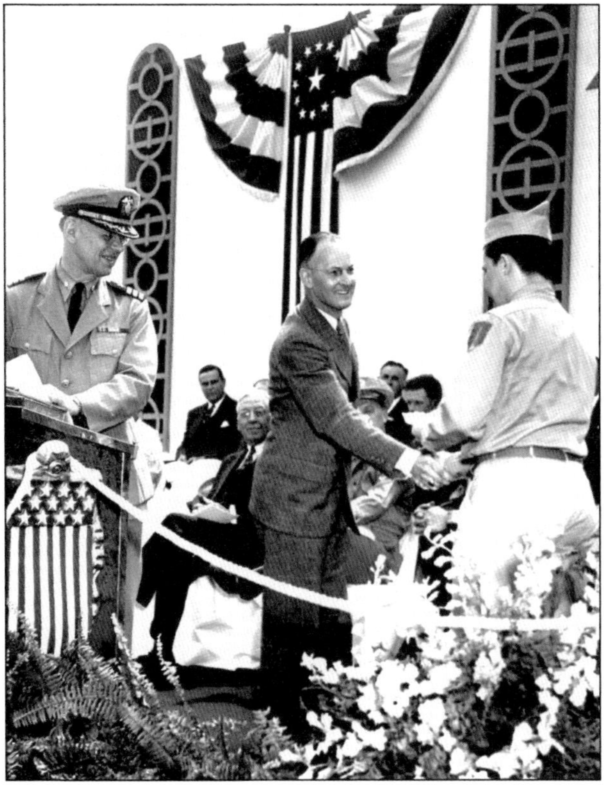

A Chemical Plant Production Award. Given the name "Soldiers of Production," the General Chemical Company, Newell Works, received the coveted Army-Navy E for excellence of production during World War II. Shown here accepting the award for his department on May 26, 1944, is Edgar G. Forbes of Office and Stores. Those attending the ceremony included schoolchildren, bands, and guests from the valley. (Courtesy Kathryne Jankey.)

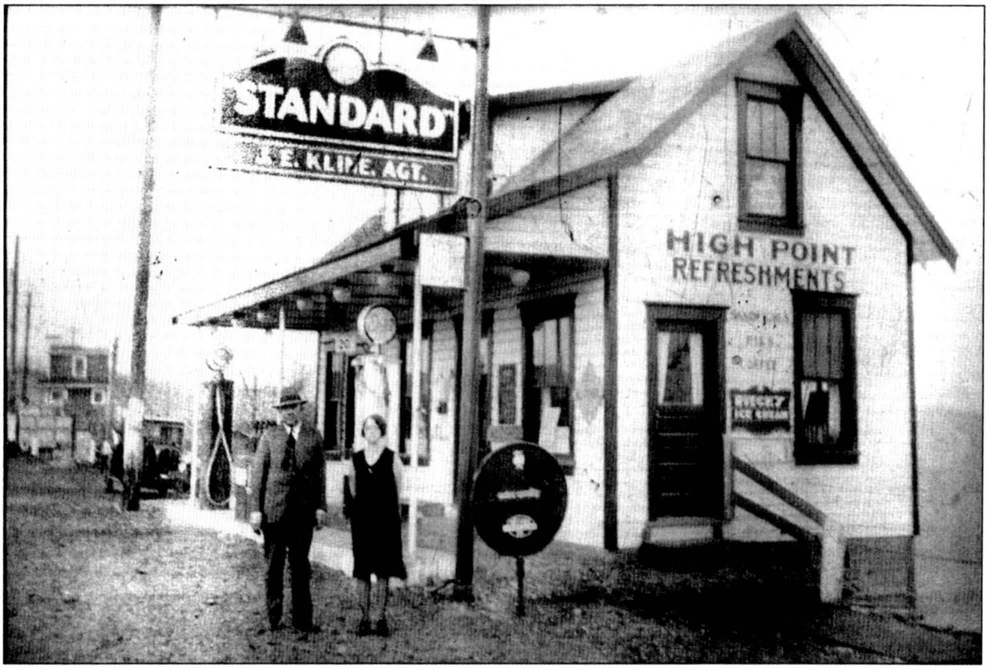

HIGH POINT. J.E. Kline, a river man, would look up to the top of the hill every time he passed the Greenfield Bend and would think, "What a nice place for a business." He bought the land, which was originally part of the Ailes farm, from L. Cophenhaver *c.* 1929. Once the site of a small gas station, it was expanded into a tavern, the High Point, so called because of its location. (Courtesy Glen Dixon.)

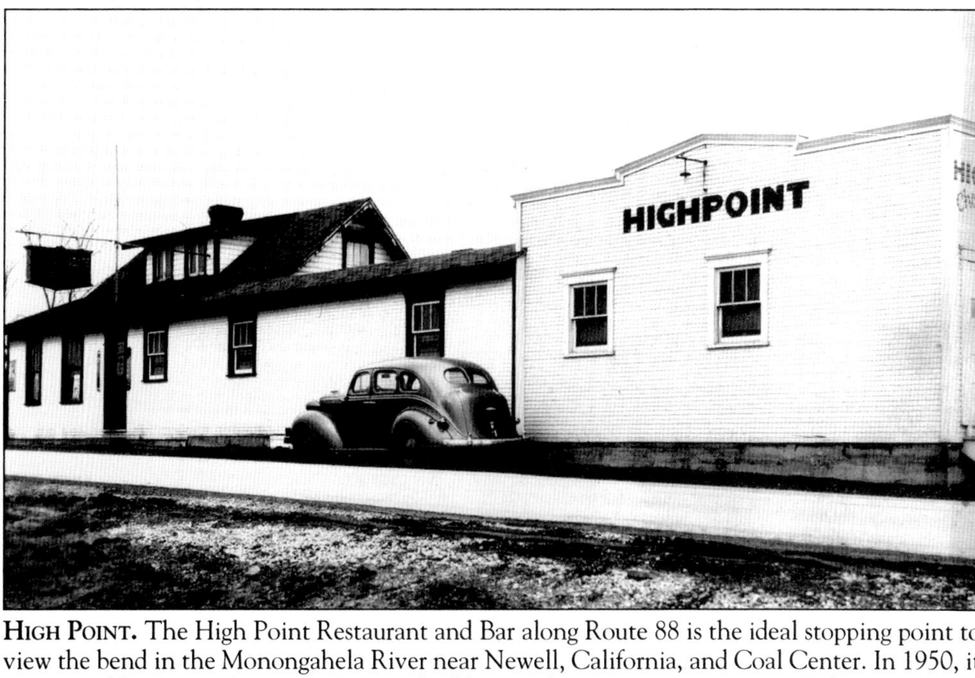

HIGH POINT. The High Point Restaurant and Bar along Route 88 is the ideal stopping point to view the bend in the Monongahela River near Newell, California, and Coal Center. In 1950, it was owned by George Hrivnak. During the filming of *Maria's Lovers*, starring Robert Mitchum, the outside of this restaurant was used for a bus-stop scene.

A Newsstand. Charles Roderick observes Third Street from the newsstand he ran for 26 years. He retired in 1947. (Courtesy Helen Rapp.)

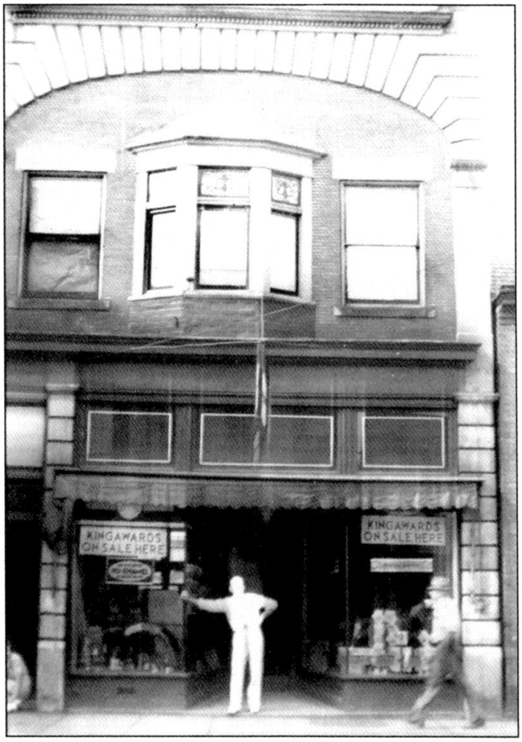

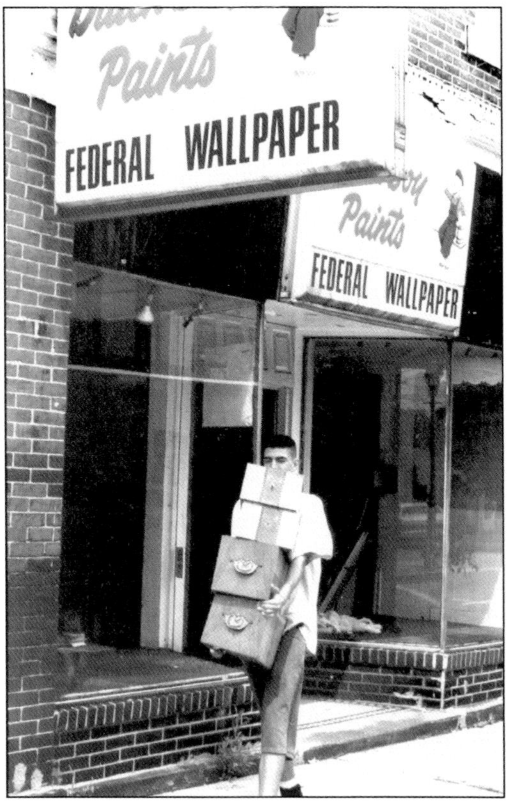

Muffy's Hardware Store. Before settling into this Third Street building in 1952, the Ruben family operated a similar wallpaper and paint store begun in Coal Center in 1921. Customers could buy anything from feather dusters to funnels, from paint to thumbtacks, and of course wallpaper. Orders could be placed for the perfect product to solve almost any household dilemma. The hardware store was always known as "Muffy's." (Courtesy Roger Sealy.)

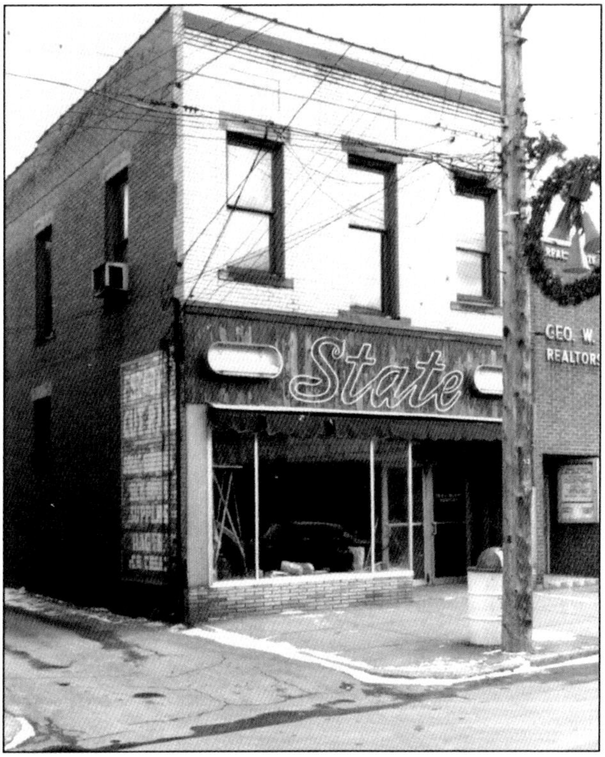

THE STATE PHARMACY. Sidney and Irwin Applebaum owned the State Pharmacy from 1946 to 1965. Then, William and Marguerite Willfong managed it until 1973. The oldest records reveal that the establishment was known as Piper's Drug Store from 1915 to 1929.

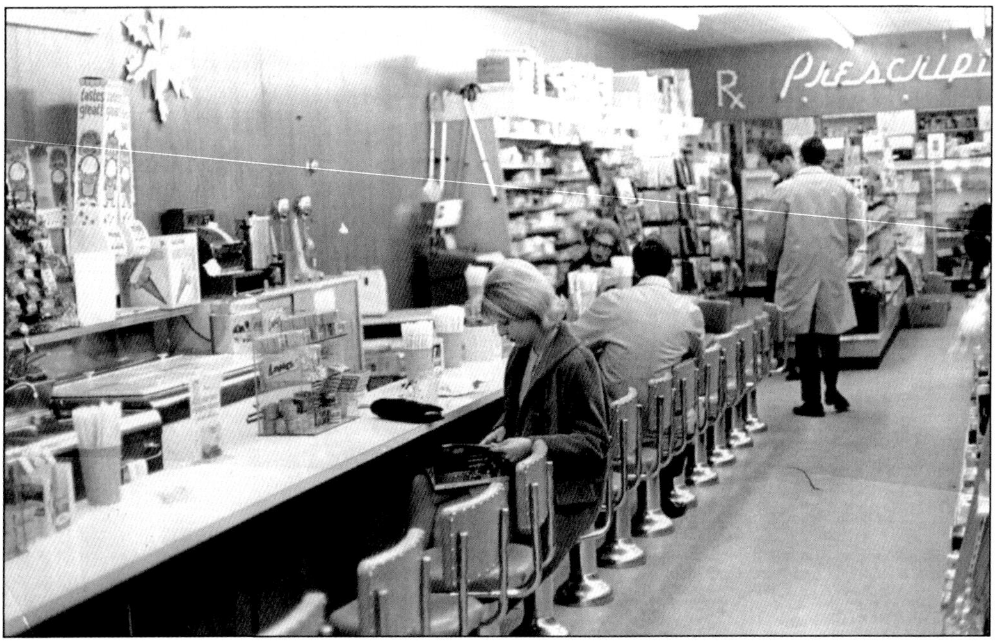

THE STANDARD PHARMACY. While waiting for prescriptions, customers could browse through magazines or could purchase greeting cards. The most popular place in the pharmacy was the soda fountain, where locals could eat a banana split, drink a malt, or enjoy the popular cherry soda. The Standard Pharmacy was located at 321 Third Street from 1950 to 1970 and was owned by Freidlander Brothers. (Courtesy Roger Sealy.)

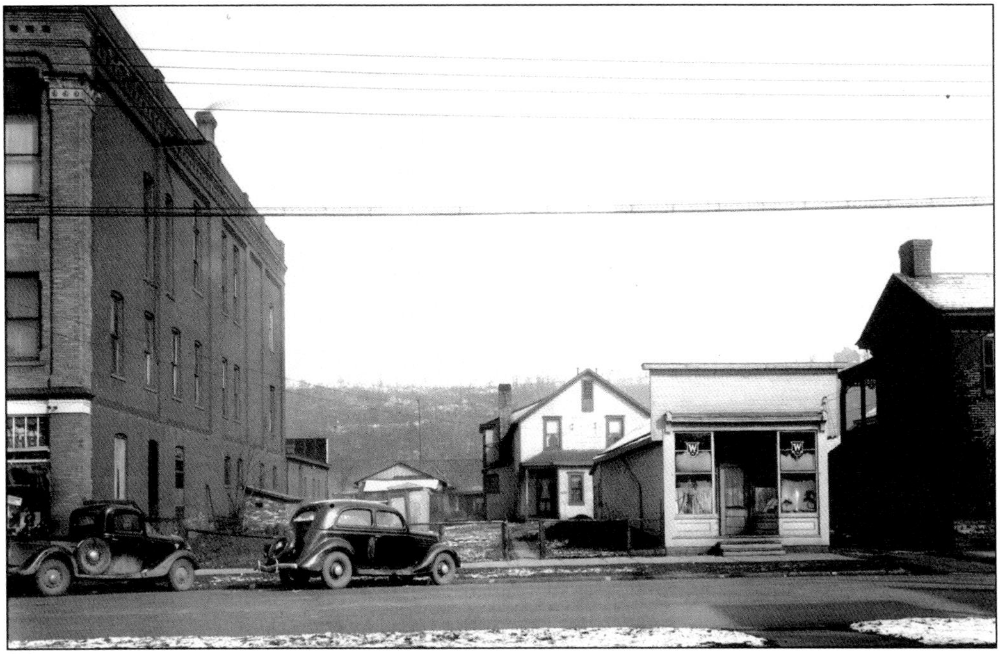

Second Street and LeMoyne Alley. This corner lot is the home of the California post office. In 1936, the property was purchased from Max Kotler for $10,000. The small building to the right (with the letter *W*s in the windows) was the home of the American Legion. The American Legion headquarters was moved to Wood and Temperance Alley and then relocated to its present location on Second Street.

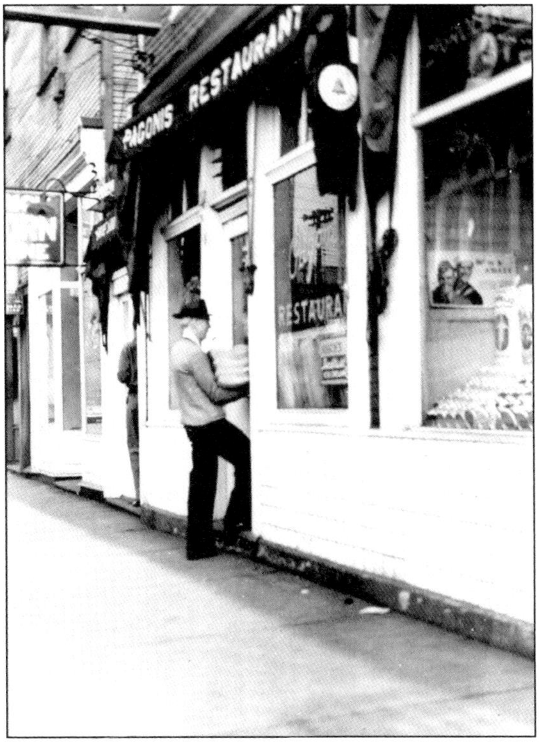

The Pagonis Restaurant. In the late 1920s, Ted Pagonis owned this restaurant on Wood Street. The popular eatery eventually moved across the street, and friendly Ted operated the same business in the new location. (Courtesy Helen Rapp.)

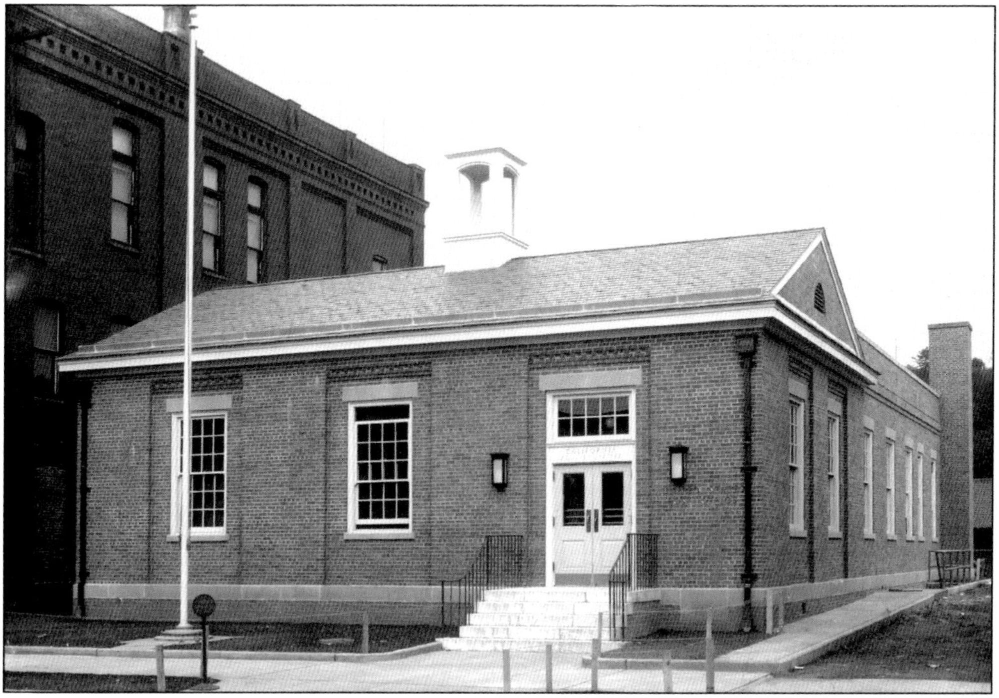

The California Post Office. The post office occupied several locations before this building was erected in 1938 on Second Street.

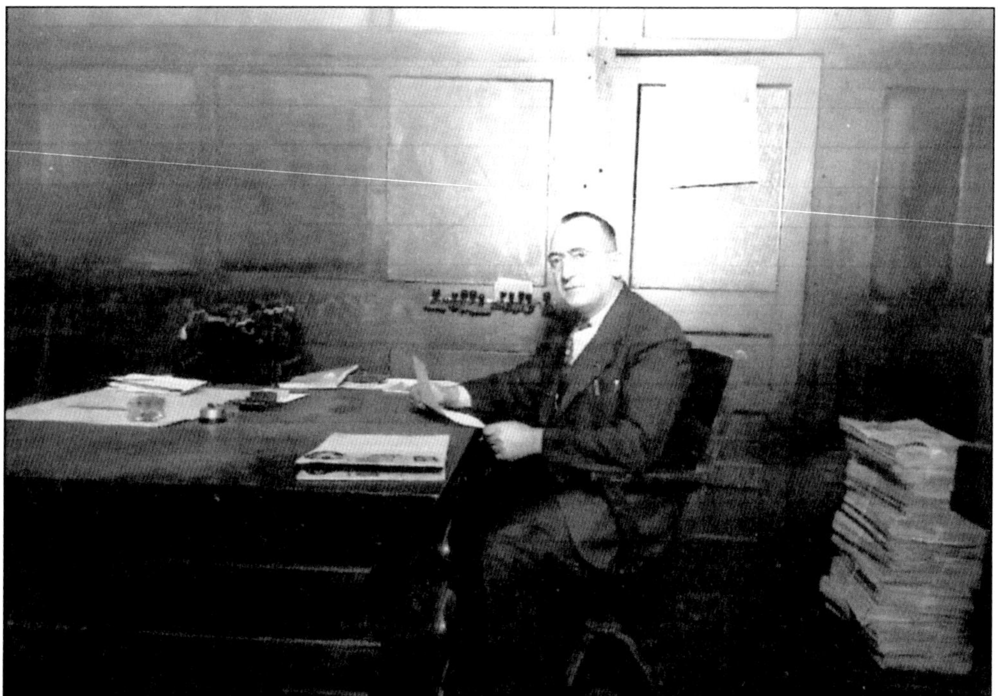

The Postmaster. Herschel C. Cowen sits at his desk in the Third Street office. He was the first postmaster in the new Second Street office. (Courtesy Gerald Cowen.)

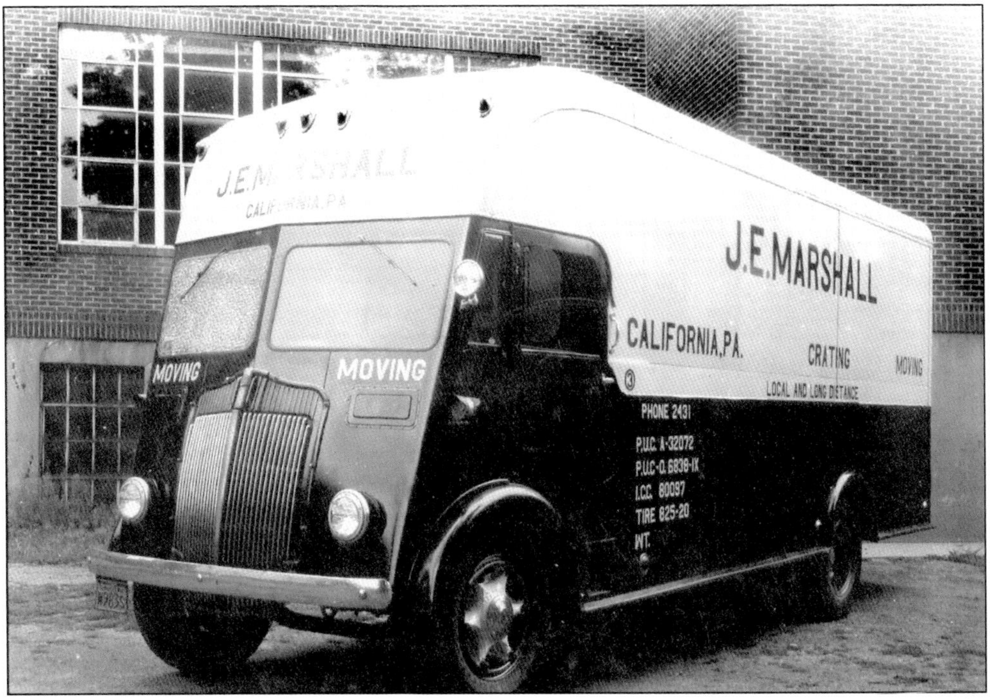

Marshall Moving. "Red" Marshall ran his moving and storage business from 1901 to 1955. This new van was the last one he used from his home at 621 Wood Street.

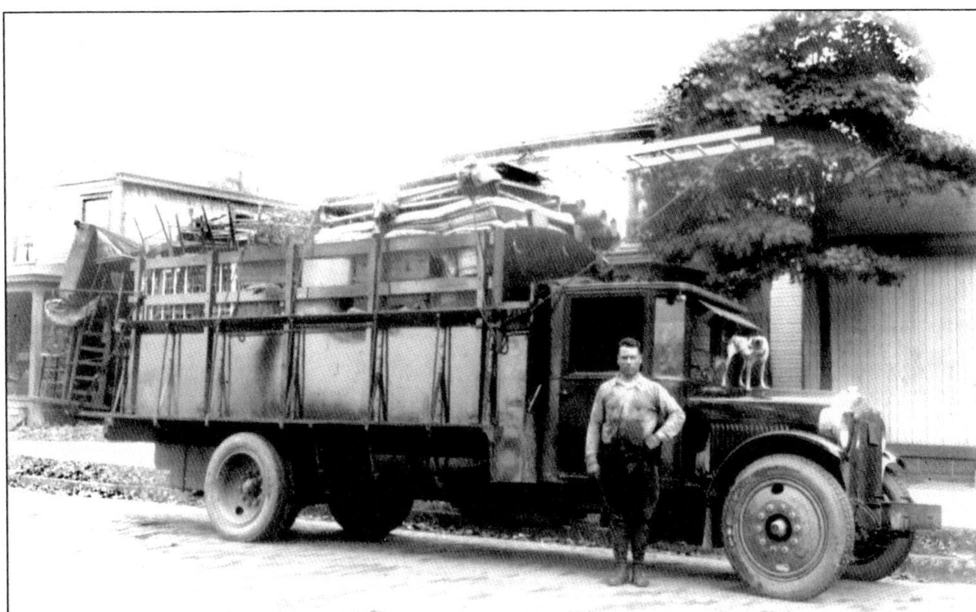

A Moving Van. In 1900, moving was as simple as packing a truck with belongings, grabbing the dog, and being ready to go.

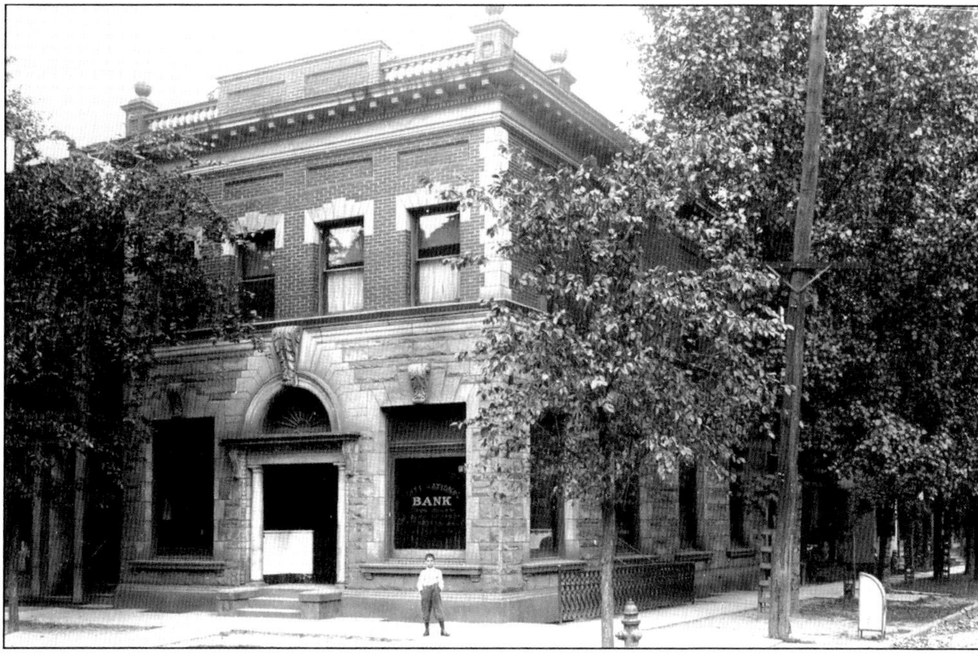

THE FIRST NATIONAL BANK. Organized in 1891, the First National Bank is the oldest chartered bank in Washington County. Originally housed in the Arlington Hotel, it moved to its Third Street location in 1902. In 1925, the building was extended to Liberty Street for additional space. Although the bank has endured six name changes and several transfers of ownership, it remains the longest established business in California. It is now National City Bank.

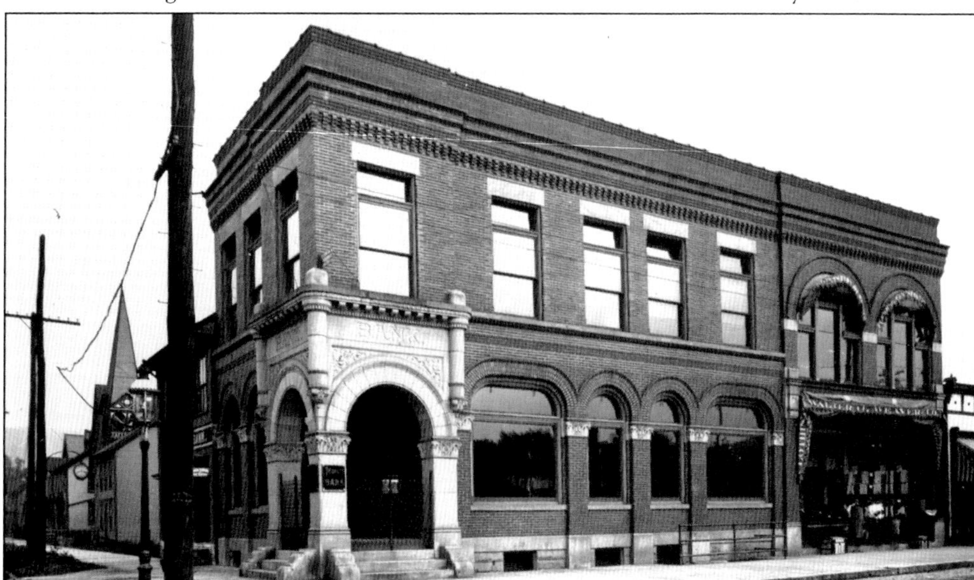

THE PEOPLE'S BANK. The People's Bank, completed on Labor Day in 1901, stands on the corner of Wood and Second Streets. It began business with capital of $75,000. A.B. Duvall was its first president. The building held offices on the second floor, a barbershop on the lower level, stores on the Wood Street side, and the telephone company on Second Street. Still in business, it is a branch of Pittsburgh National Bank. (Courtesy Harold R. Richardson.)

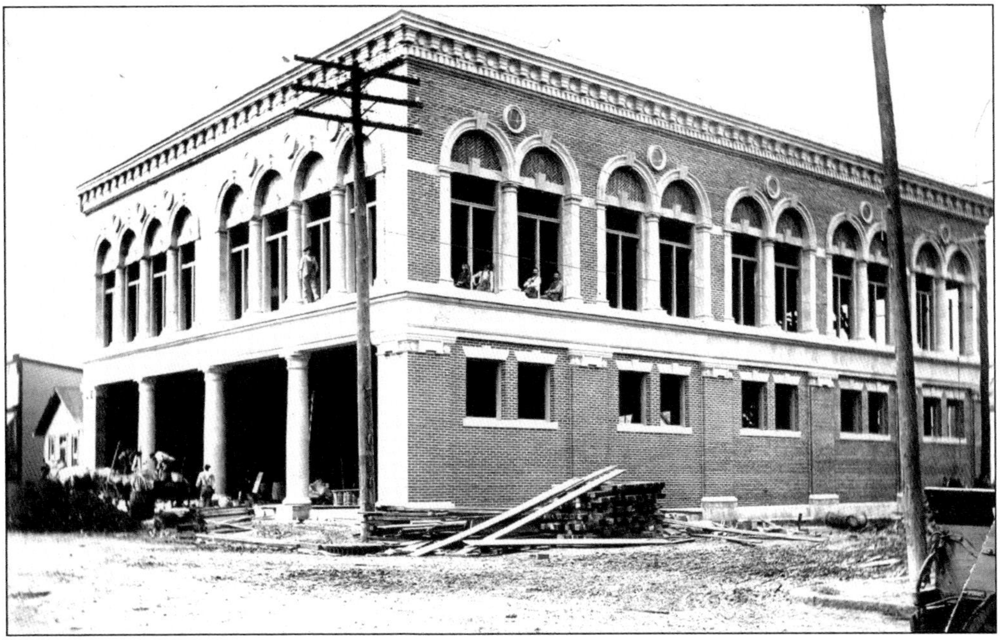

PITTSBURGH MERCANTILE. The Pittsburgh Mercantile Building is shown being constructed in 1904 as a "company store." Owned by the Jones and Laughlin Steel Company, it was used by miners who could pay with script instead of money. Later residents remember it as G.C. Murphy's.

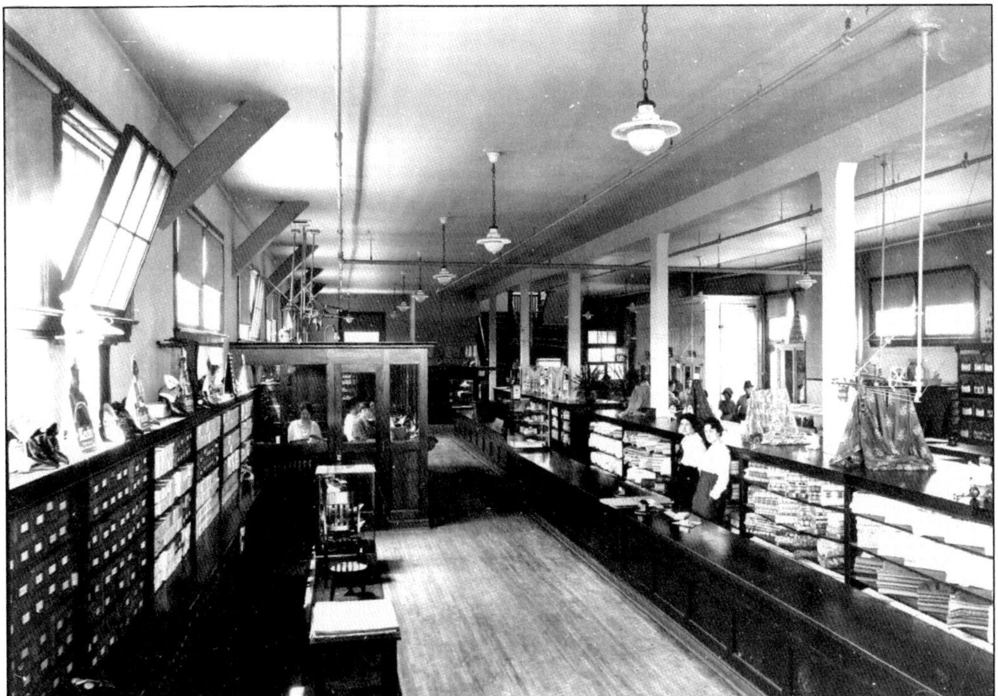

THE MERCANTILE BUILDING. The building was designed as an all-purpose department store to address the needs of the coal-mining families as well as the citizens of the town. Offerings included "men's furnishings," shoes, dress goods, groceries, and other sundry items.

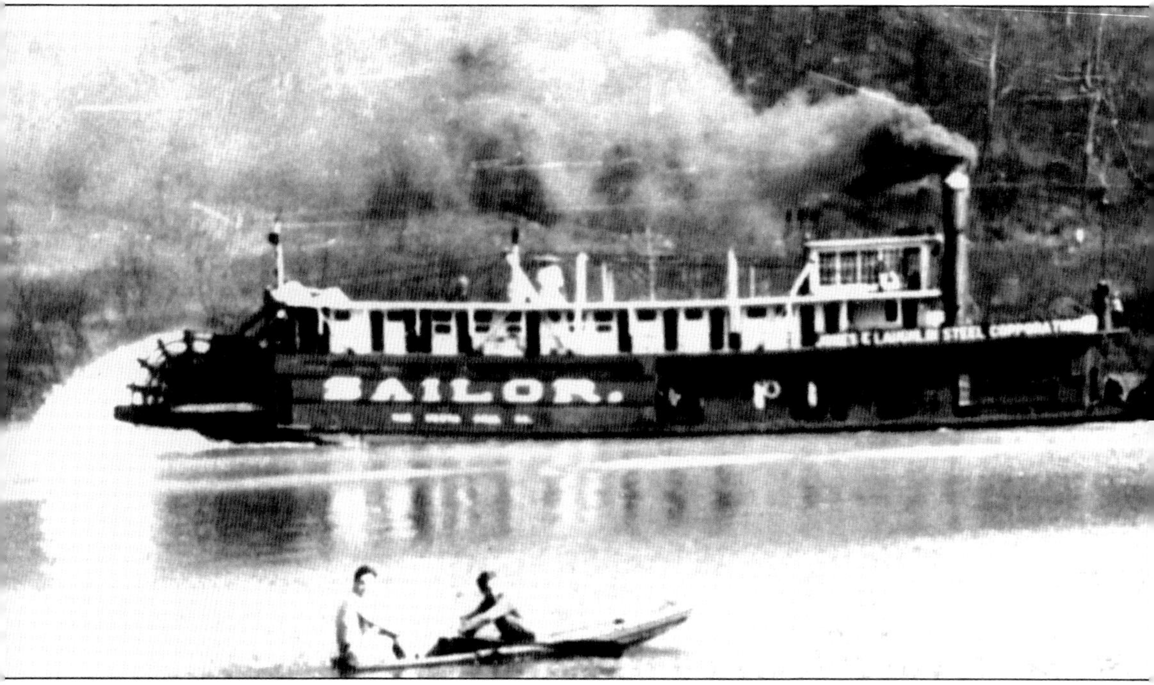

The Sternwheeler *Sailor*. The *Sailor* is typical of the sternwheelers that dominated the barge-pushing trade for 80 years. This sternwheeler, shown in the 1940s, pushed coal for Jones and Laughlin Steel Company on the Monongahela River. Many a worried parent later learned from their children what fun it was to dare each other to ride its waves in their own small boats. (Courtesy Harry Shaposka.)

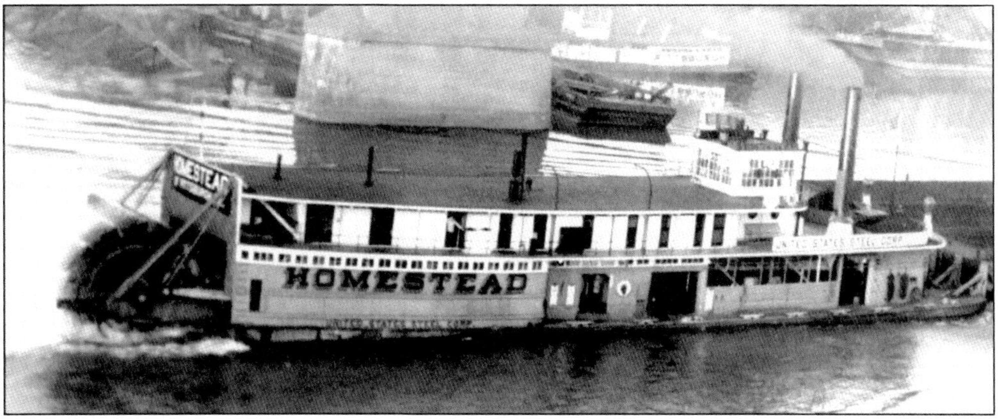

THE STERNWHEELER *HOMESTEAD*. This sternwheeler was originally the A.O. *Ackard,* built in Ambridge in 1922. It was renamed the *Homestead* in 1960 and was dismantled in 1962. The *Homestead* was 175 feet in length, with a 34-foot beam, wheel diameter of 21 feet, and a 900-horsepower engine. In the 1950s, paddle-wheelers were phased out of river use in favor of diesel-engine boats. (Courtesy Charles and Marguerite Cox.)

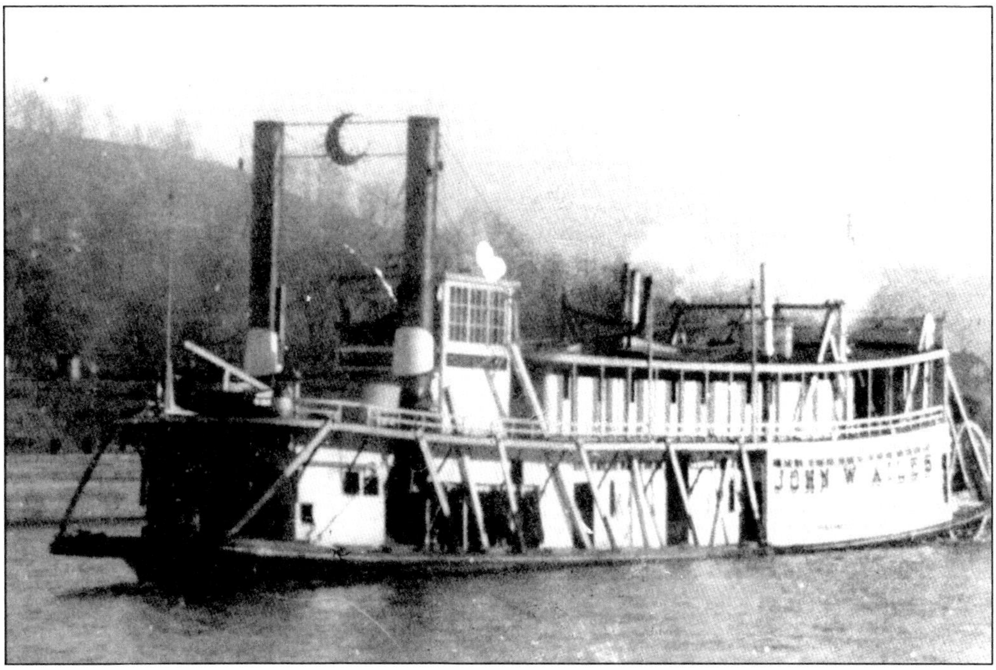

THE *JOHN W. AILES*. This sternwheeler was built in Brownsville in 1892 and was owned by the Combine Company. In February 1902, its boilers exploded, and it burned to the water. The *Ranger,* built in 1903, reused the engines from the *John W. Ailes* before being dismantled in 1935. (Courtesy Nancy Jane Conaway.)

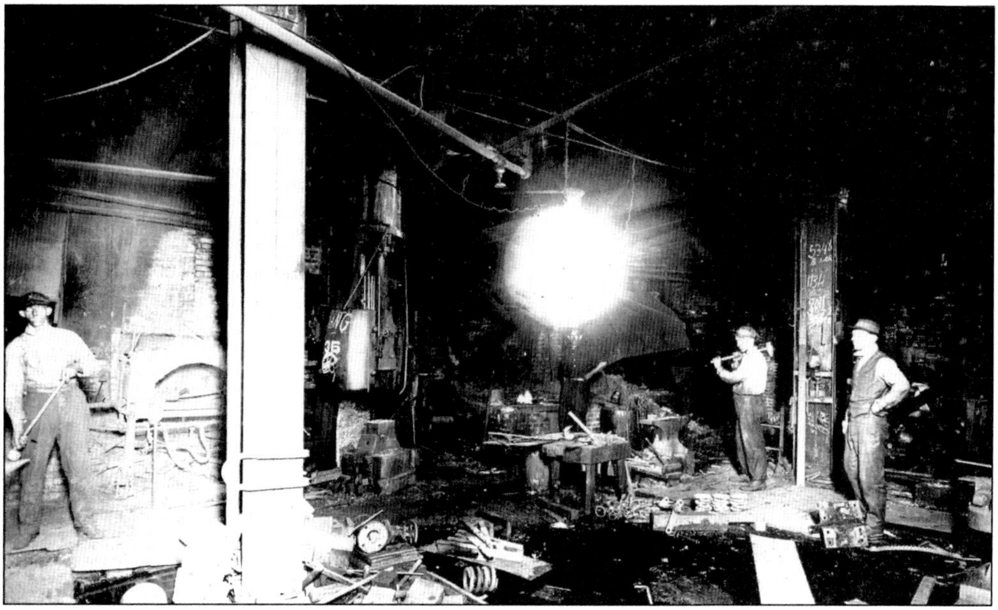

FOUNDRY AND MACHINE COMPANY. The original California Foundry, built in 1904, was managed by James R. Hill and consisted of a lathe and drill press. As time passed, gas engines replaced the steam engines. Pattern machine work was turned out of a well-equipped shop. The business was known for its extensive production of miner supplies, picks, and drills, among other things.

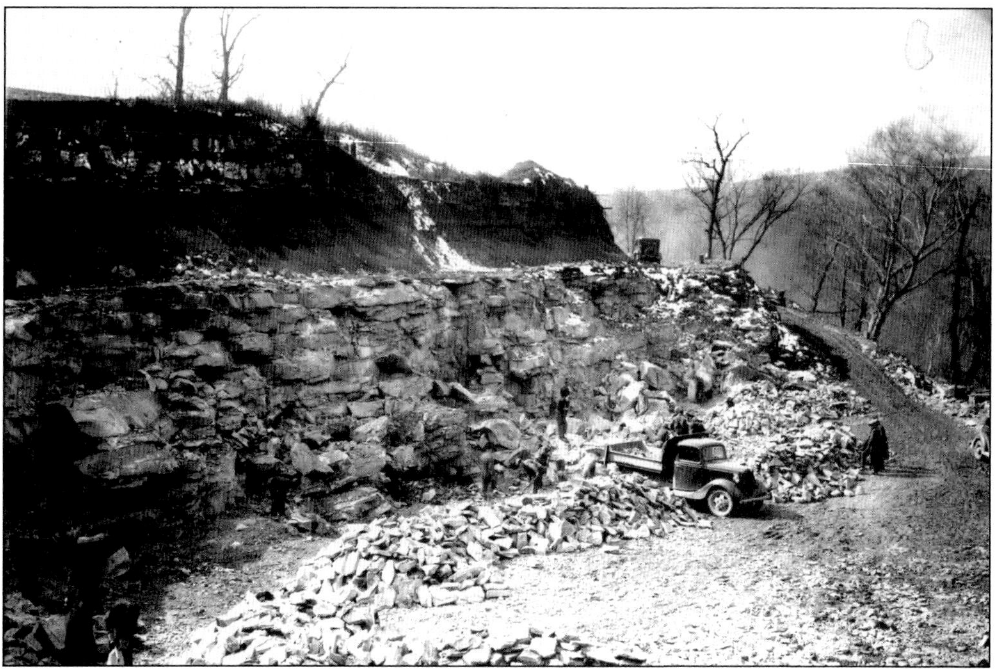

THE STONE QUARRY. In the mid-1930s, limestone was quarried from the McCrory farm by the government for use by the Work Projects Administration. Stone was used for area road repair and building of retaining walls. (Courtesy Lee Gregory.)

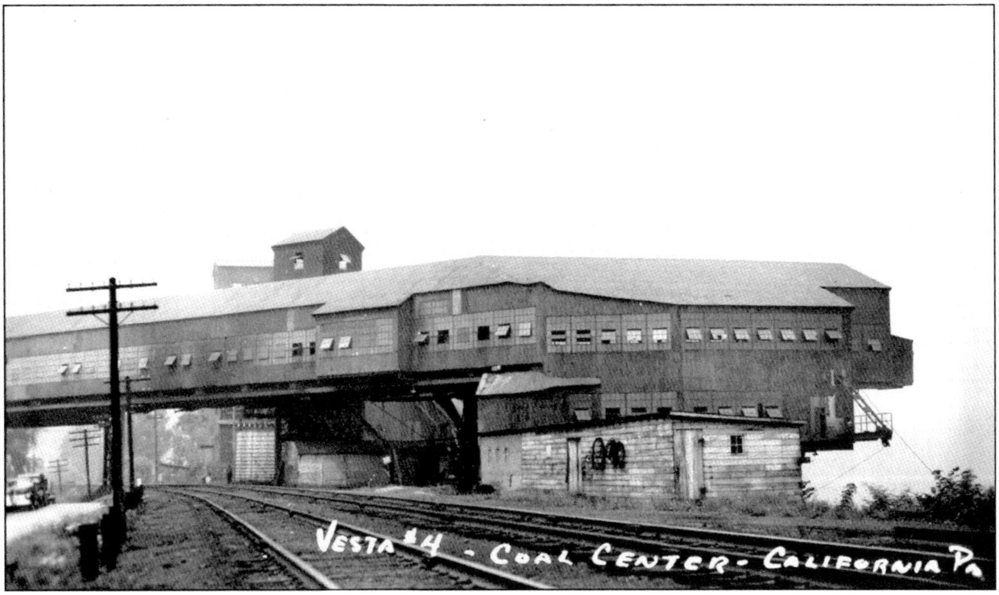

VESTA COAL TRESTLE. In 1937, the *California Sentinel* stated that Vesta No. 4 mined enough coal to cover the borough to a depth of 280 feet. More than 48.5 million tons of coal had been mined from 5,136 acres between 1904 until 1937. The mined coal was sent over the trestle to the tipple in California. (Courtesy Andrew Sentipal.)

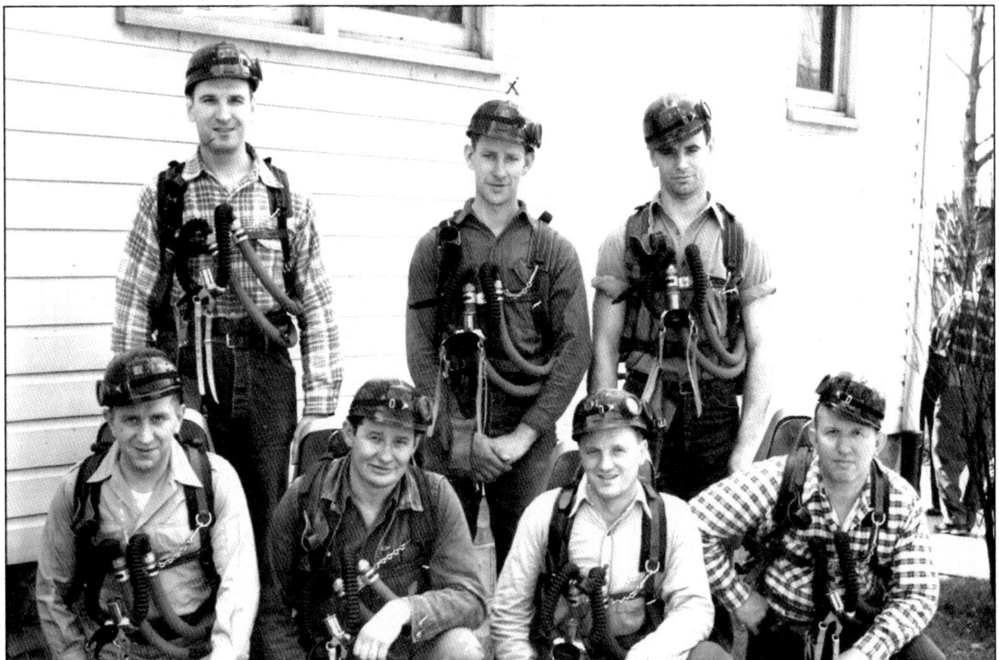

A MINE RESCUE TEAM. Mine rescue teams practiced weekly to aid in and prevent mining disasters. Shown in this 1951 photograph are, from left to right, the following: (front row) Charles Briercheck, Steve Hegedus, John Bobby, and Mike Zirgiski; (back row) Albert Colotoni, Joseph Voithofer, and Clarence McCay. (Courtesy Joseph Voithofer.)

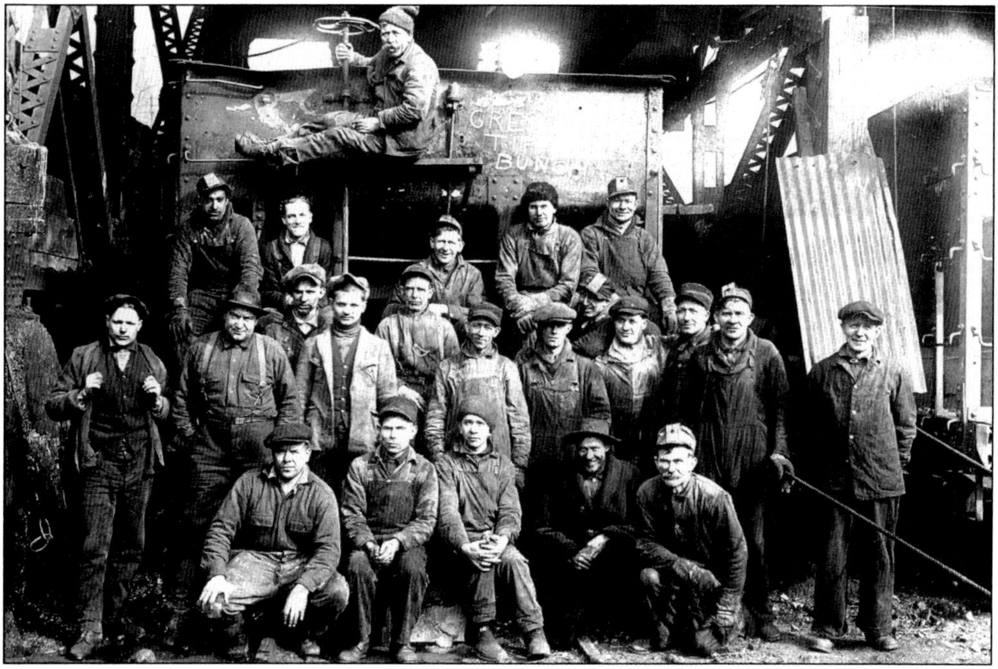

The Crescent Mine. Men from mine pose after a hard day's work. Crescent was one of the bituminous coal mines of the famous Pittsburgh seam. The mine had an average daily output of over 4,500 tons. (Courtesy Mary Jane Webber Cowen.)

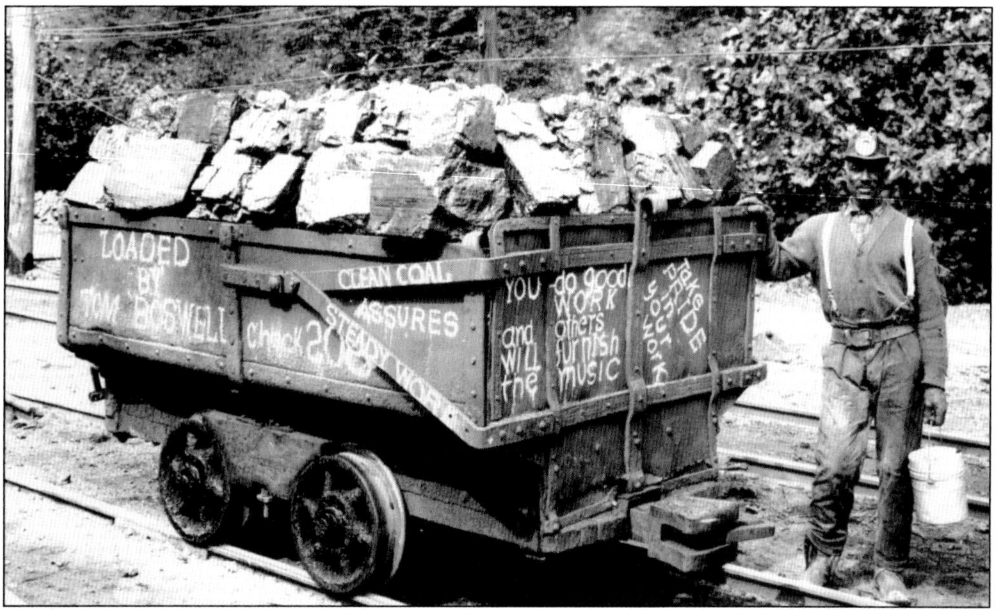

Tom Boswell. In this 1930s view, Tom Boswell is leaving the Crescent Mine after a hard day of loading his coal car. He will give his "check" No. 20 to the weigh man, who will record the amount of coal. Boswell will be paid from 50¢ to $1 per ton. Often his pay was script, which could be used only in the company store. Boswell's safety lamp and his dinner pail, containing his lunch in the top part and water in the bottom, were important essentials every time he entered the mine.

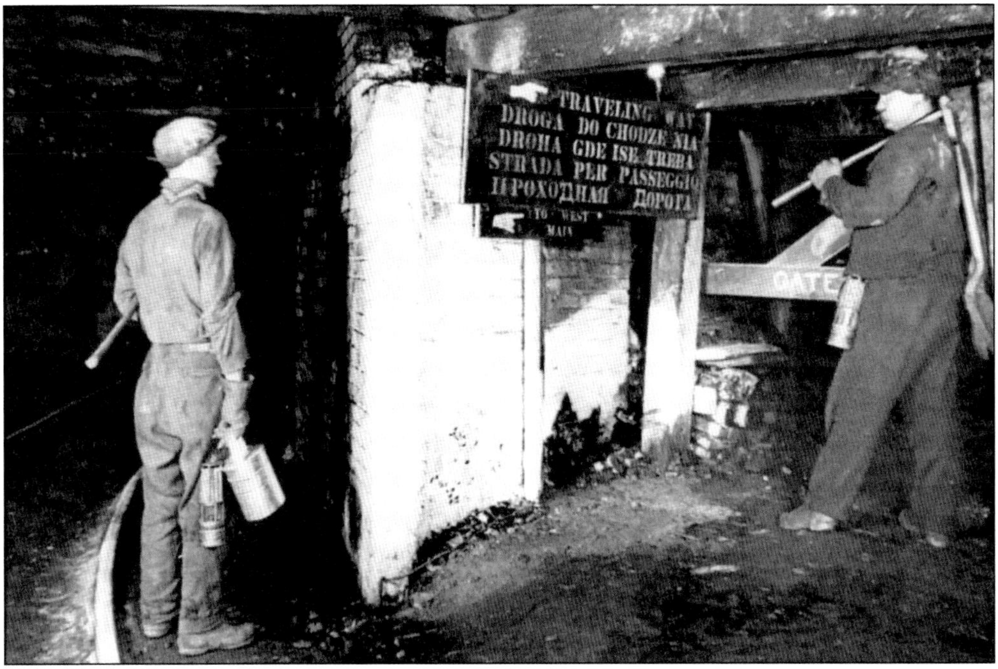

MINERS. Many miners who immigrated to the coal fields spoke only their native languages. To facilitate better communications, managers posted directional signs in the mines in several languages. (Courtesy John Konat.)

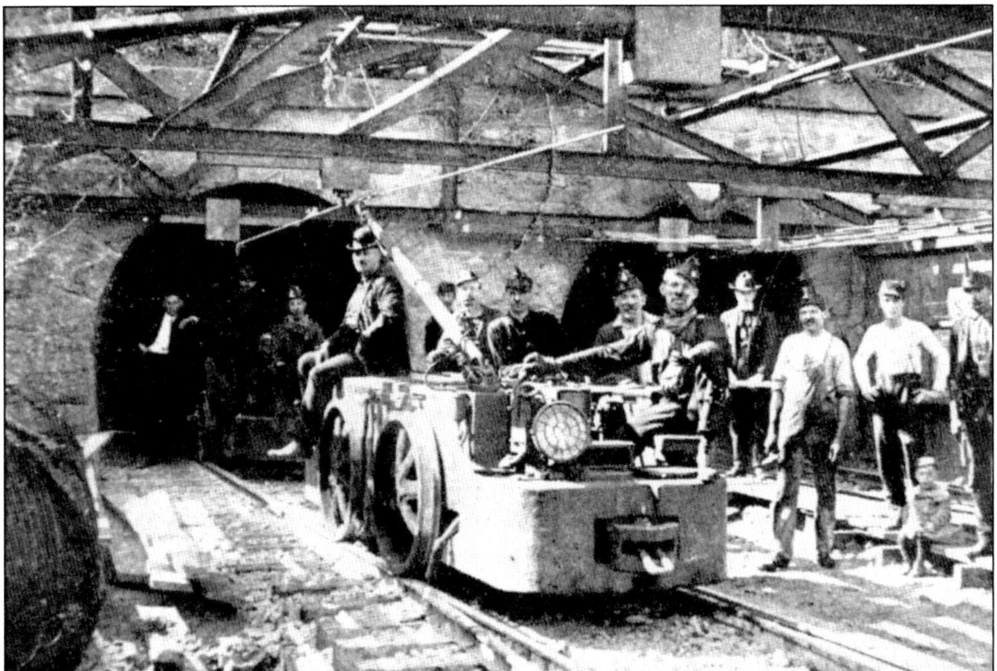

THE VESTA NO. 4 PIT MOUTH. Vesta No. 4 miners are shown here in 1903 sitting on the "man trip" car going into the No. 2 pit mouth. Wearing his bowler hat is superintendent "Charlie" Drum. (Courtesy John Konat.)

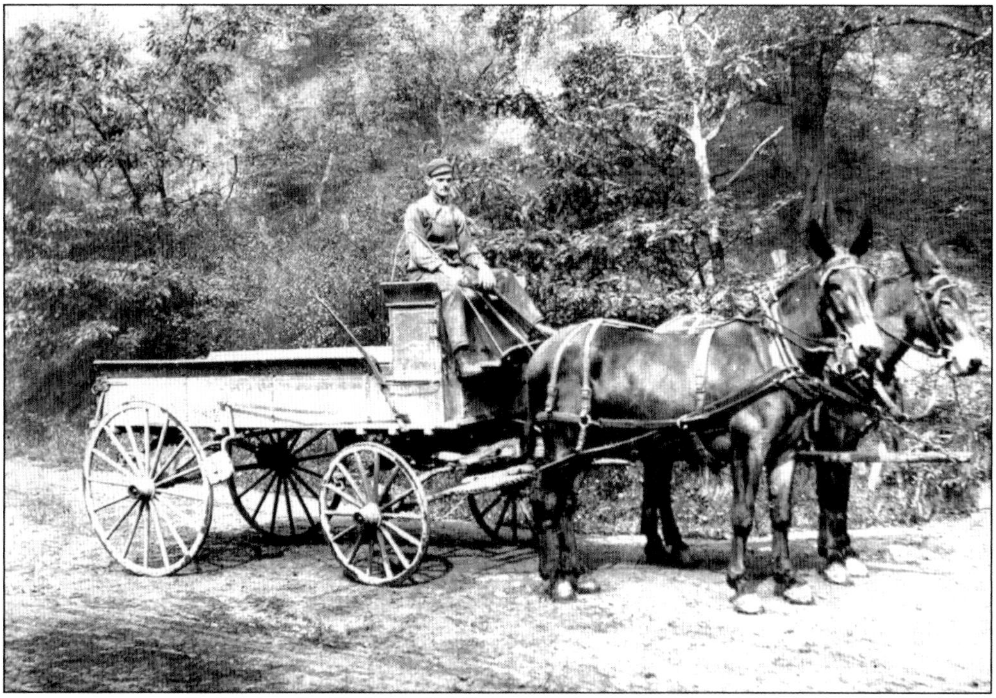

Berky's Mules. To a miner, his mule was as important as his pick and shovel. Berky drives his mules to work Supply Company No. 123.

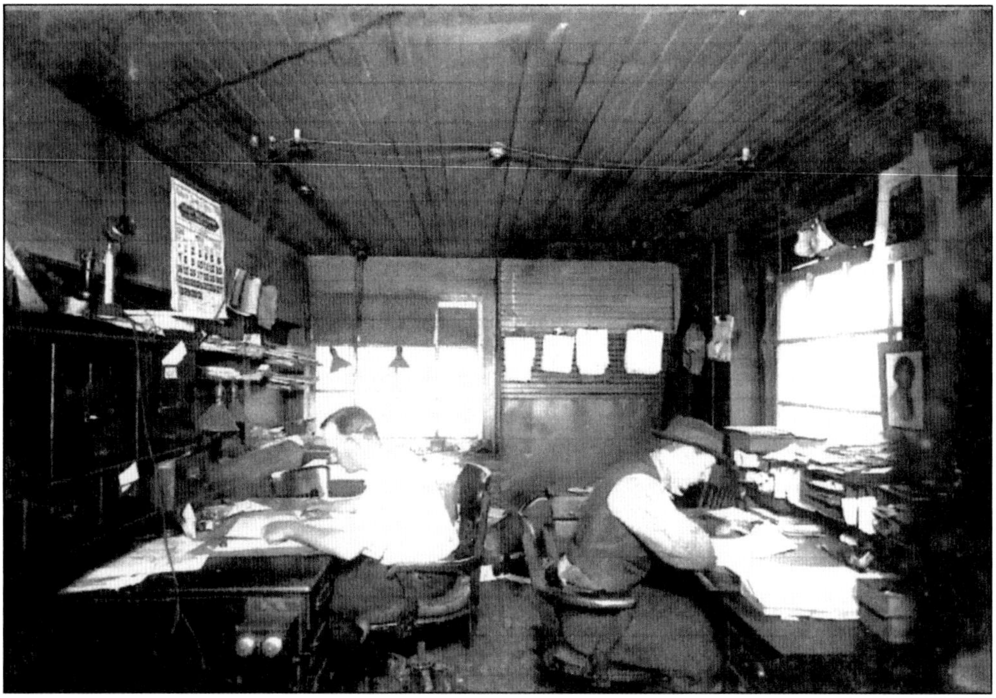

Jones and Laughlin Office. The wall calendar dates this Jones and Laughlin office photograph as 1916. On the left, Herschel Cowen sits at his desk, keeping records for the coal company. (Courtesy Gerald Cowen.)

Four

EDUCATION

The early history of California and its education institutions are so closely related that it is almost impossible to mention one without the other. The incorporators of the town were the same men who laid the foundation for the education of its citizenry. The first schools came to the community shortly after its incorporation, when in 1852 the California Seminary, also known as the Academy, was established. Five years later, the state legislature divided the state into normal-school districts, and the prescient founders of the community immediately applied to charter the Academy as the 10th Normal School District of Southwestern Pennsylvania. The charter was granted in 1865, and the cornerstone of the Southwestern State Normal School was laid in 1868. High-school students attended the normal school until 1913, when the state required a series of small community buildings in the school district.

Today's public school system, the result of a 1948 jointure between California and East Pike Run Township schools, is housed in a modern complex that serves kindergarten through grade 12. Students are bused to the central area from each of the small areas that originally had its own building. In 1929, the Southwestern State Normal School campus became California State Teachers College. In 1983, the school became what is now known as California University of Pennsylvania. Throughout its history, the growth of the borough and the university has been intertwined. California has always been known as a college town where both the local and state educational systems have grown from the insight of its original settlers.

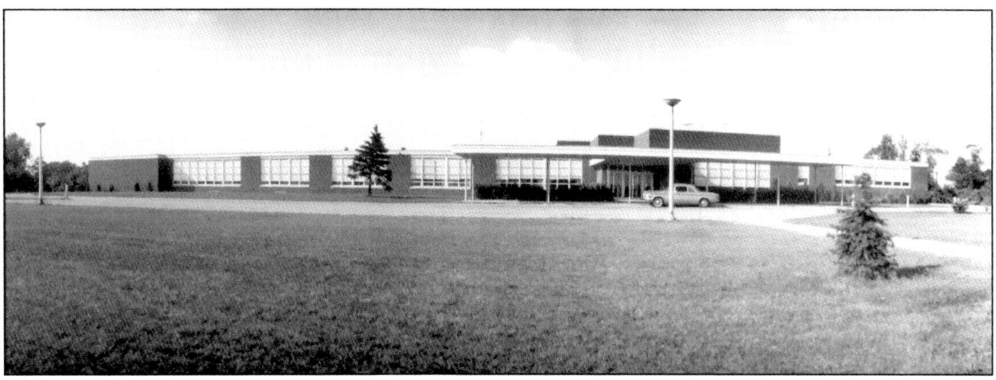

CALIFORNIA AREA SENIOR HIGH SCHOOL. The California Area School District proudly dedicated this new education complex in September 1960. Although the new facility eliminated the necessity for individual community school buildings, the older generation fondly remembers the former neighborhood schools. (Courtesy Matt Mazick.)

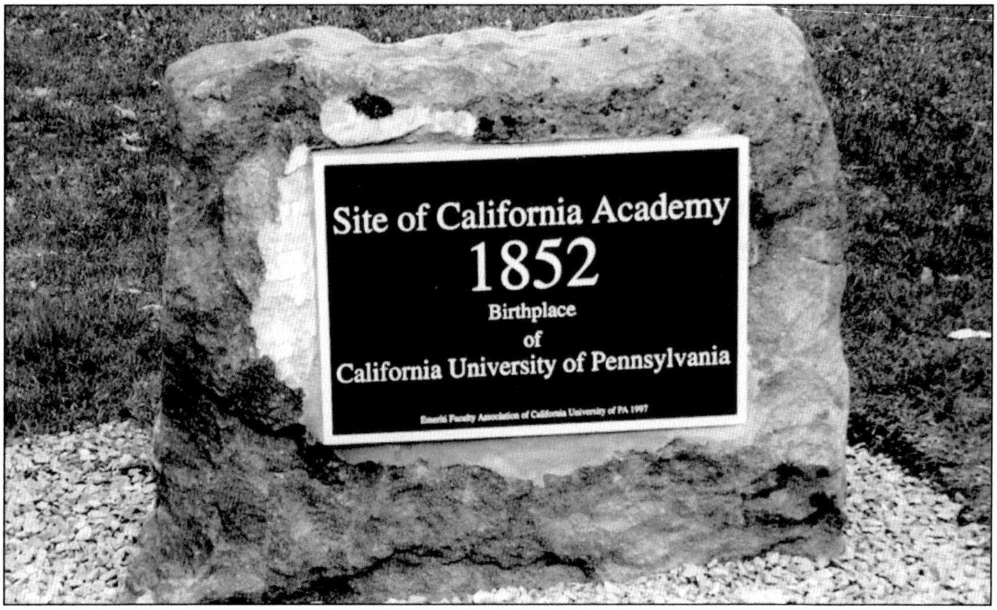

The First School. In 1852, a brick building erected on the Craft property at Fifth and Liberty Streets was the home of the first public school in California. Later, it also housed a preparatory school known as the Academy or California Seminary, the forerunner of Southwestern State Normal School. The academy operated until 1864. This stone and bronze marker now shows the location of the school.

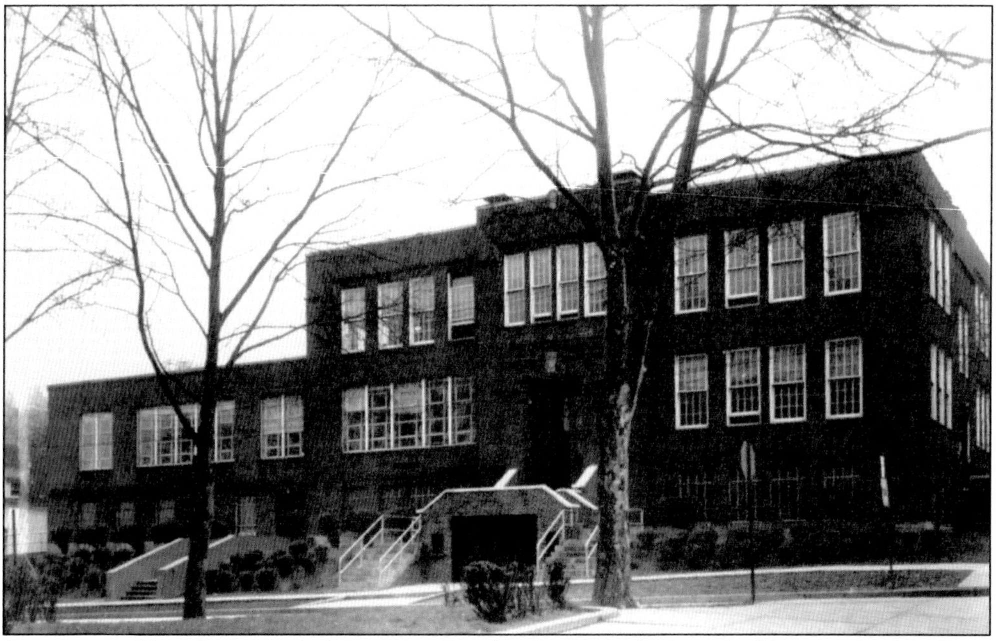

California High School. California High School consisted of two buildings on both sides of Fifth Street. Before 1945, this building housed grades seven, eight, and nine, with an art studio, home economics classroom, and gymnasium used by all grades. In the mid-1930s, grades one, two, and three were also offered in this building for California students who lived in the area from Green Street to Union Street.

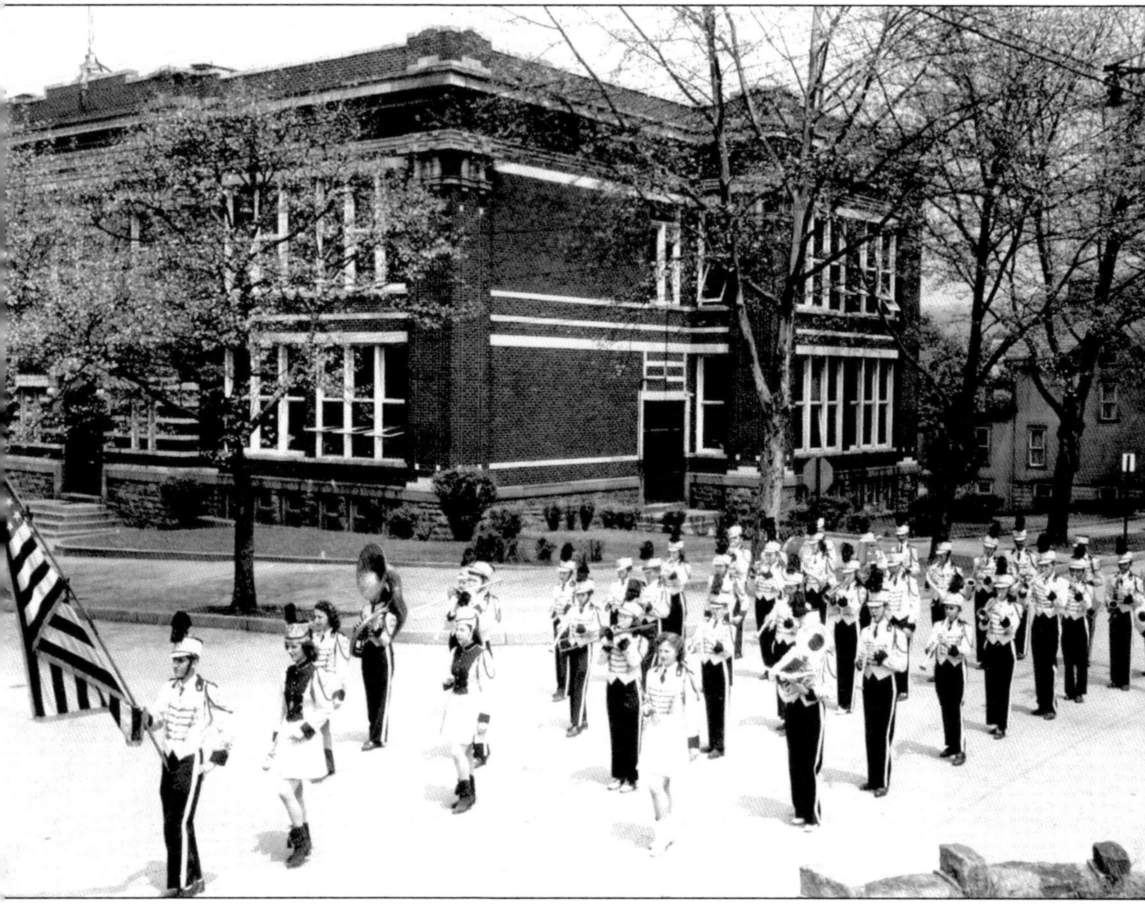

California High School. California High School (shown here in 1948) was located on the corner of Fifth and Liberty Streets. This building contained classrooms, a library, and administrative offices. In 1914, the graduating class had two members. By 1949, the 1948–1949 class of the California and East Pike Run Township High Schools had 121 graduates. Here the "Cub" band practices, dressed in the red-and-white school colors.

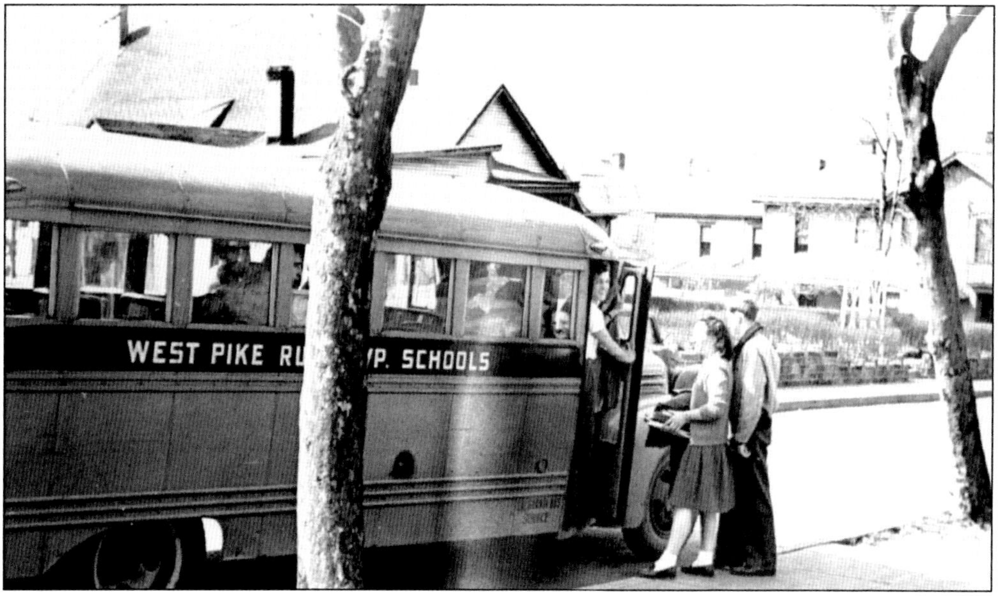

A SCHOOL BUS. After the California Area School District was created in 1949, only town students walked to school. Each outlying district sent its own students by bus to the front entrance of the senior high school on Liberty Street. Shown here, West Pike Run Township students eagerly prepare to board the bus on their way home. (Courtesy Barry Niccolai.)

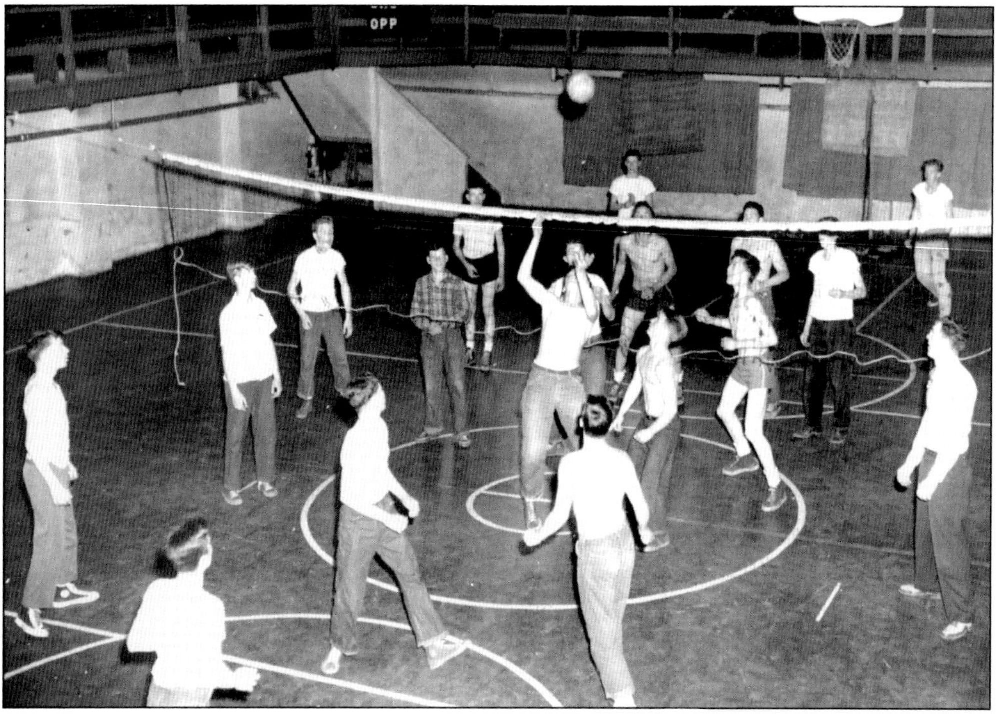

THE CALIFORNIA HIGH GYMNASIUM. The small floor space in the high-school gymnasium provided limited seating for basketball games. Adults sat on benches around a wooden balcony, while students sat on the floor. However, the space was adequate for volleyball. Coach Bob Neil is shown supervising. (Courtesy Barry Niccolai.)

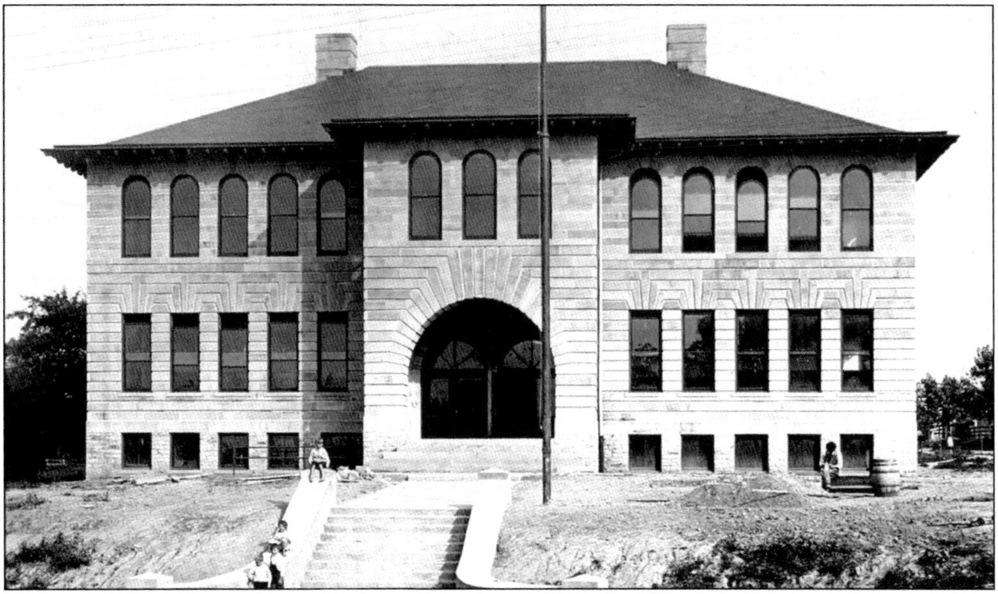

REPUBLICAN SCHOOL. Sadly missed by East Pike Run Township students, this stone building on Wood and Pennsylvania Avenue was erected in 1910. Elementary students in grades one through six attended the school, as well as students in grades seven and eight. As the population grew, it served kindergarten through grade six. The building was closed in 1976, but it is still remembered by the many students who attended the school.

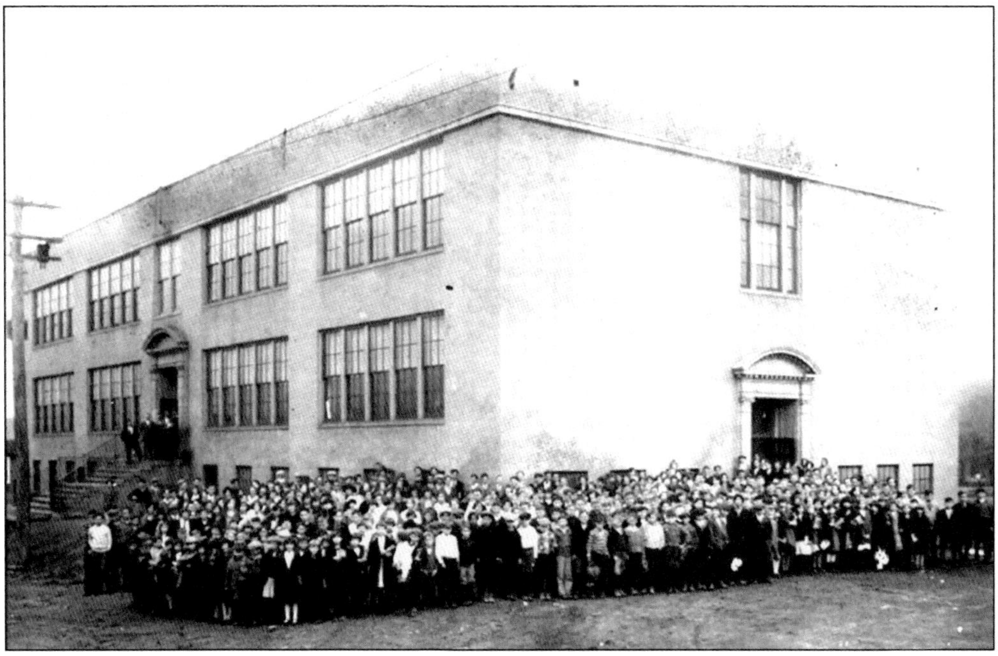

EAST PIKE RUN TOWNSHIP HIGH SCHOOL. East Pike Run Township High School was founded in 1925. Academic and general courses were offered to the students as well as sports, debate teams, music, physical training, science laboratories, and a library. After the 1949 jointure of East Pike Run Township and California, the building was used as the junior high and served grades seven, eight, and nine.

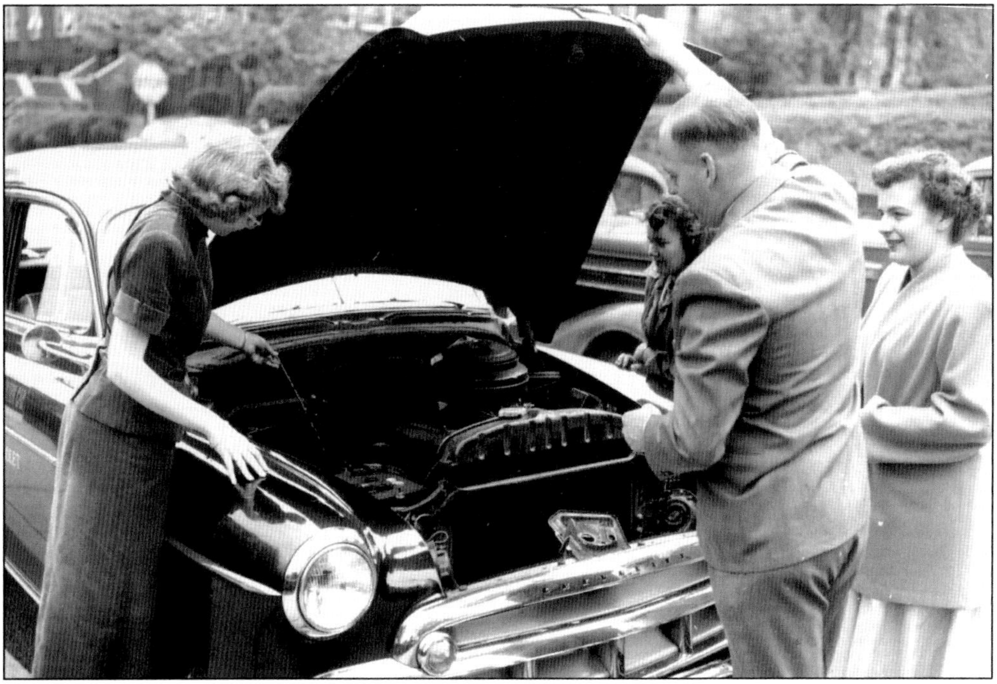

DRIVER'S EDUCATION. At California High School, the students were offered driver's education. For instructor Tom Griffin, this meant more than teaching driving skills; it also meant giving instruction on engine maintenance.

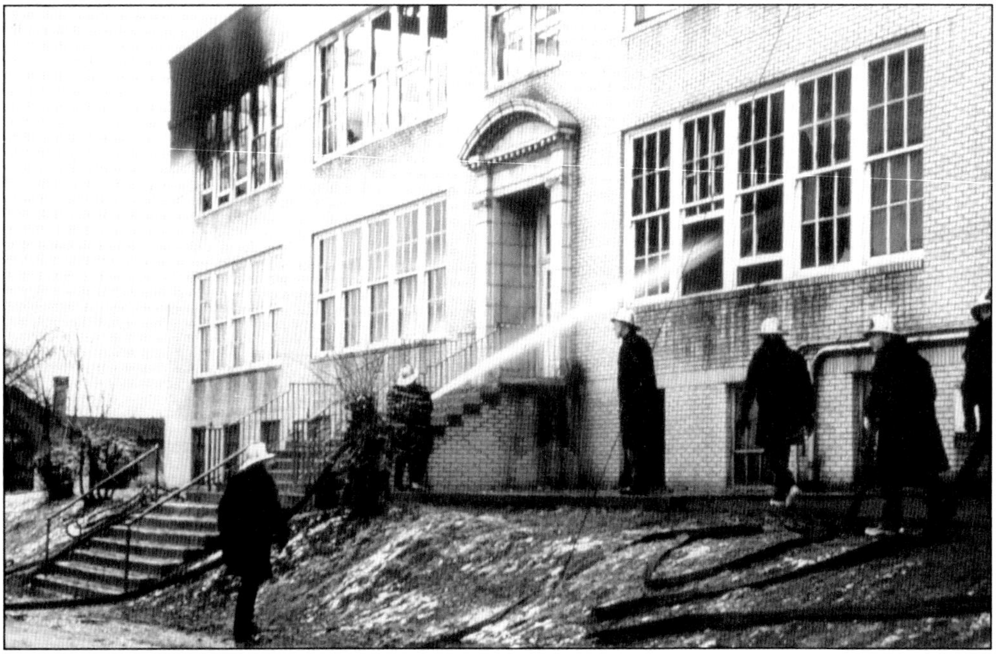

THE PHILLIPSBURG SCHOOL FIRE. Local firemen extinguish the remaining flames from a four-alarm fire at the Phillipsburg Elementary School on March 13, 1959. Although the building sustained $500,000 worth of damage, all 317 students walked to safety thanks to the teachers, who averted panic by marching the children in orderly lines from the burning building.

Coal Center School. The elementary school of Coal Center borough taught six grades in four classrooms. This photograph shows the school on Spring Street in 1936.

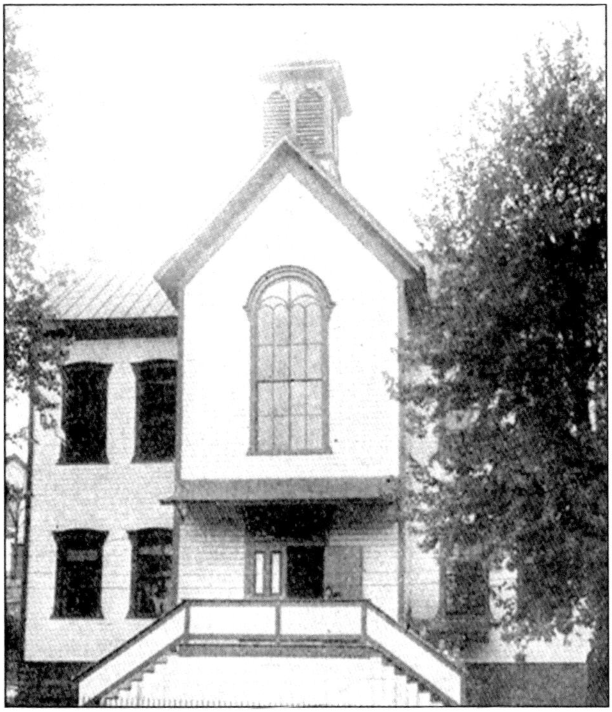

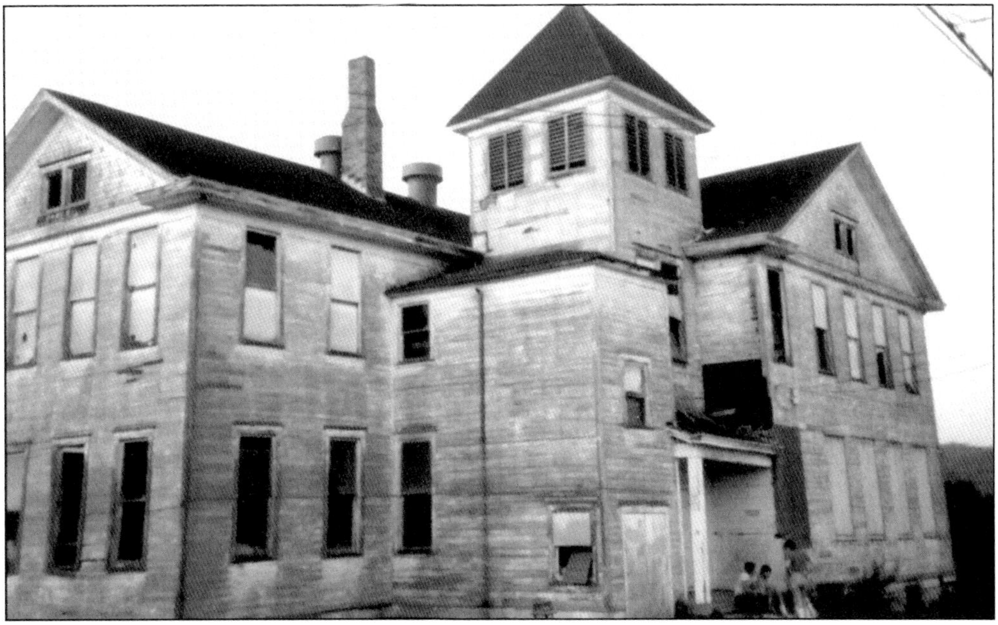

The Blainesburg School. After the closing of the Blainesburg School, the building was used by the West Brownsville Club, formed in 1964. When the upkeep became too expensive for the club, the building was donated to the Southwestern Pennsylvania Firemen's Association in 1985. The association used it as an instructional facility. As a reminder of the good old days, the school bell was given to the borough council for safekeeping. An unusual feature of the building is the fire escape, an enclosed metal slide running from the top floor to the ground. (Courtesy Dr. Stephen Pavlak.)

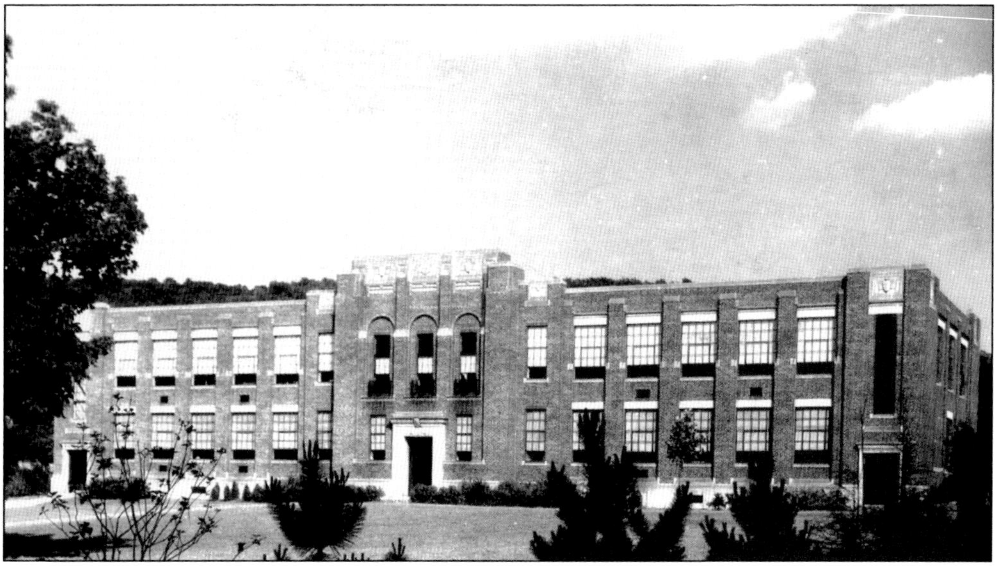

NOSS DEMONSTRATION SCHOOL. The Theodore B. Noss Demonstration School, built in 1930, was a modern training facility for its time with a series of elementary classrooms. The school offered "demonstration and observation" lessons to students studying for teaching certification.

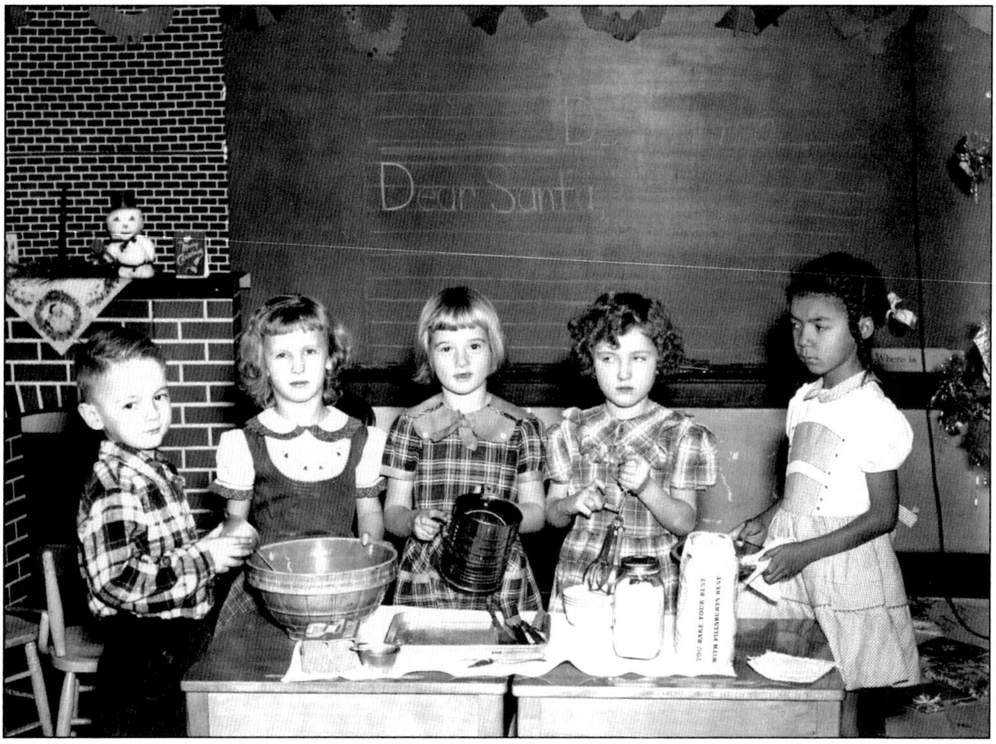

CALIFORNIA ELEMENTARY STUDENTS, 1950. First-grade students prepare Christmas cookies for a class project in the elementary department annex of California High School. From left to right are Henry Huffman, Charlotte Medency, Patty Rishert, Norma Tuman, and Sandra Thompson. Bertha Gue was the teacher. (Courtesy Estate of Bertha Gue.)

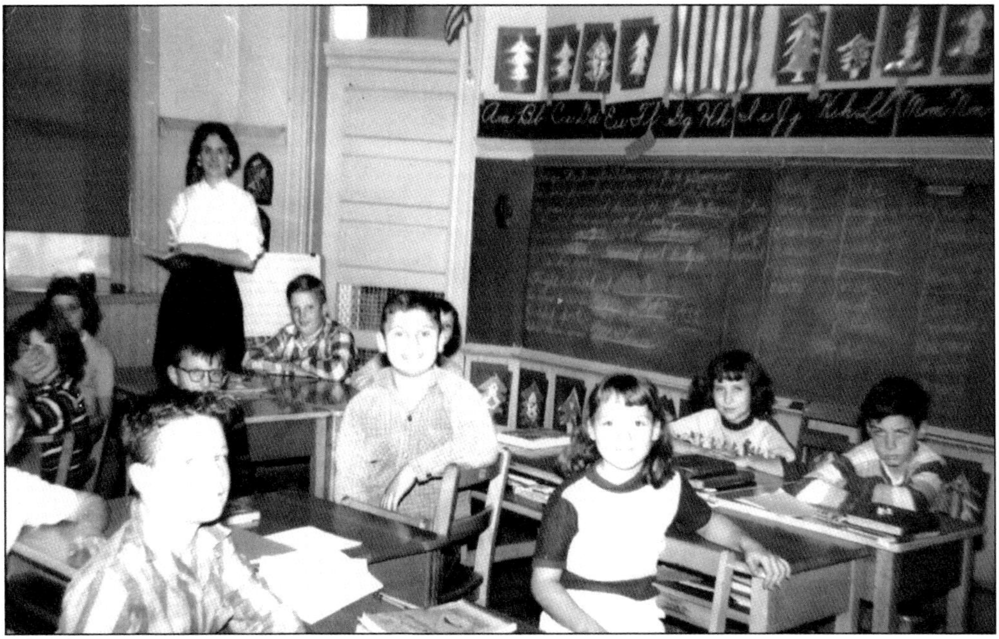

A Roscoe Class, 1956. Fourth-grade students at Roscoe School take a break from arithmetic to pose for a picture with their teacher, Patricia Cowen. From left to right are the following: (front row) Mike Scrip, Paul Rebar, Donna Zetka, and Joe Timlin; (back row) Diane Webb, B. Keminovich, Sharon Jones, Billy Joe Ray, and Cheryl Niceling.

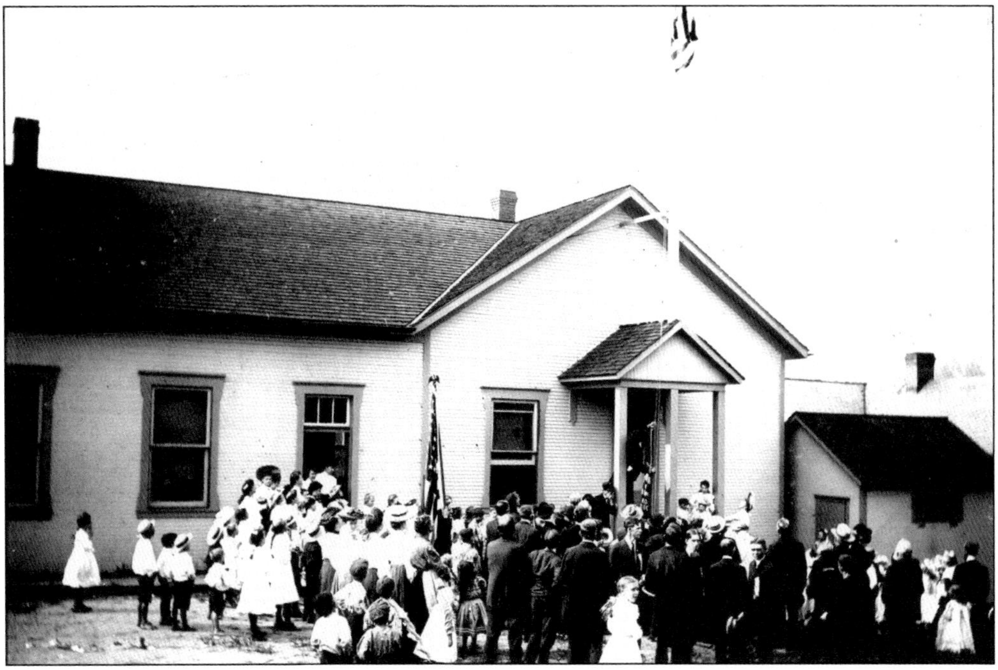

Jackman School. In 1912, Long Branch had two one-room schools. In 1922, another room was opened in the Jackman School. It was used until 1947, when all Long Branch schools were closed. Students were sent to the California School district. This Jackman building became the Grange hall and community center in 1960. (Courtesy Roland Pichard.)

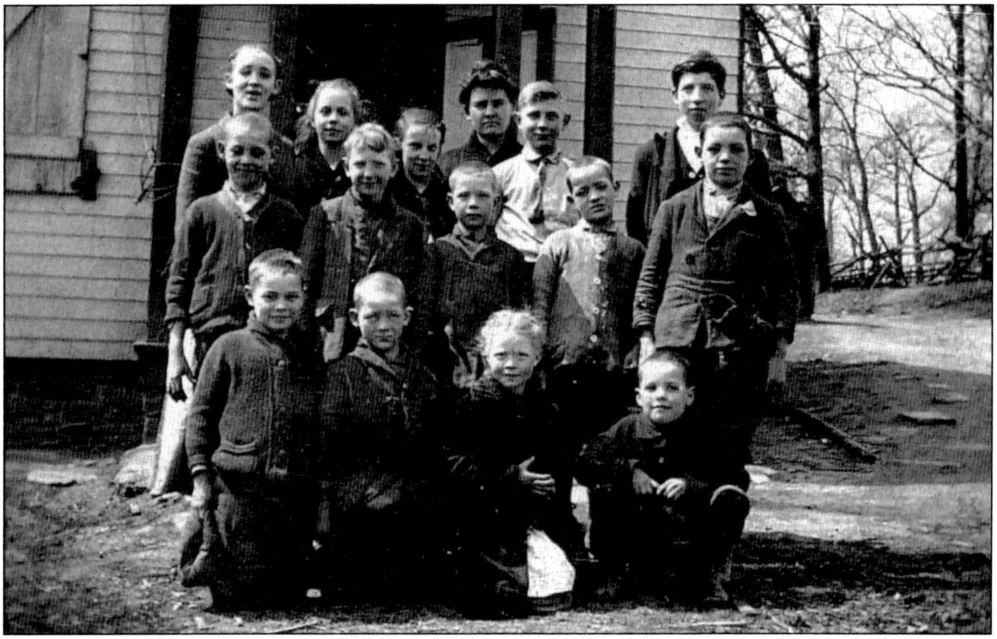

UNION SCHOOL. In 1914, Miss Manosky poses with her class at the one-room school on Highland Drive in East Pike Run Township. The children were mainly from the Staley, Gillis, and Fisher families. The property for the school was given to the school district by the Ailes family, with the stipulation that the property be used only for the building of a school. (Courtesy Jeannie Gillis King.)

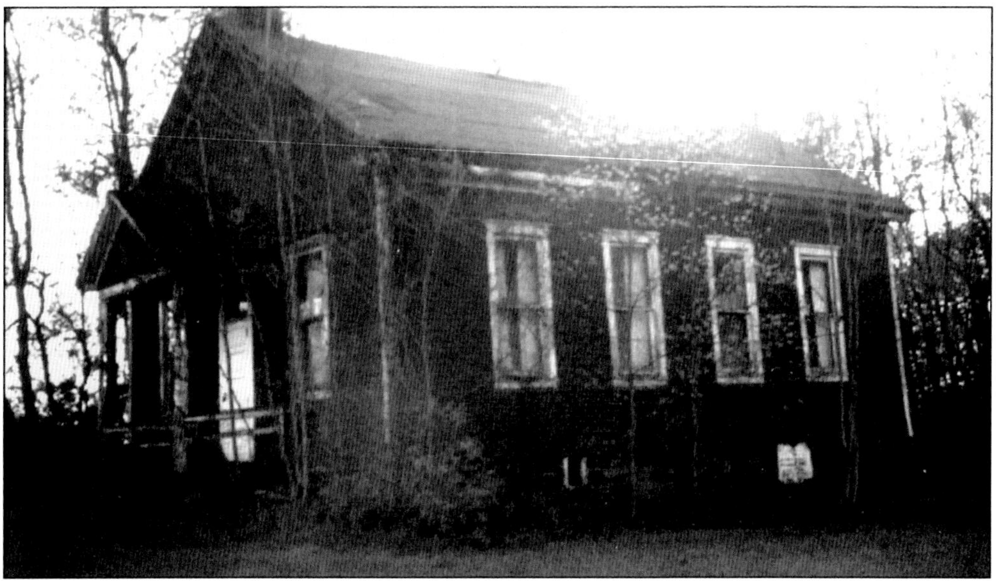

HOWE SCHOOL. Howe School was built *c.* 1900 in East Pike Run Township. This one-room school housed grades one through eight and had on average 30 to 35 students during its time of operation. The large bell on the roof called students to the beginning of class. A cistern and hand pump provided water. The teacher's desk in front was flanked by a piano to the side. Two coatrooms held storage shelves. A raised platform with drapes provided space for plays and programs. All this was contained in a little one-room school, which closed in 1952.

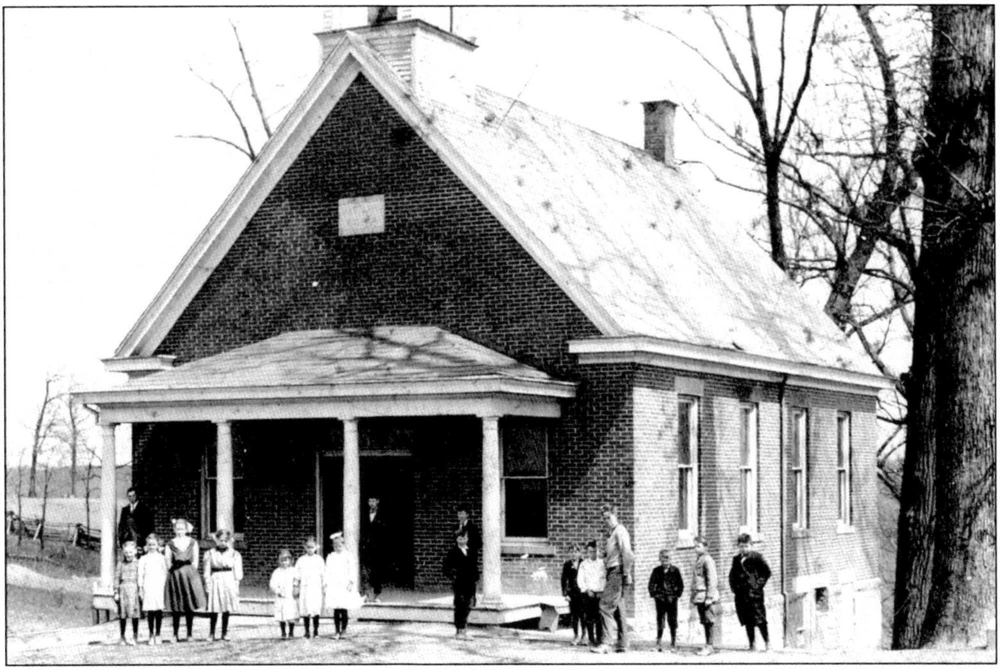

WESTLAND SCHOOL. Records show that a school was organized at Westland in 1786. Thought to be one of the first schools in the area, it was sponsored by the Society of Friends (the Quakers). (Courtesy W. Floyd Gillis.)

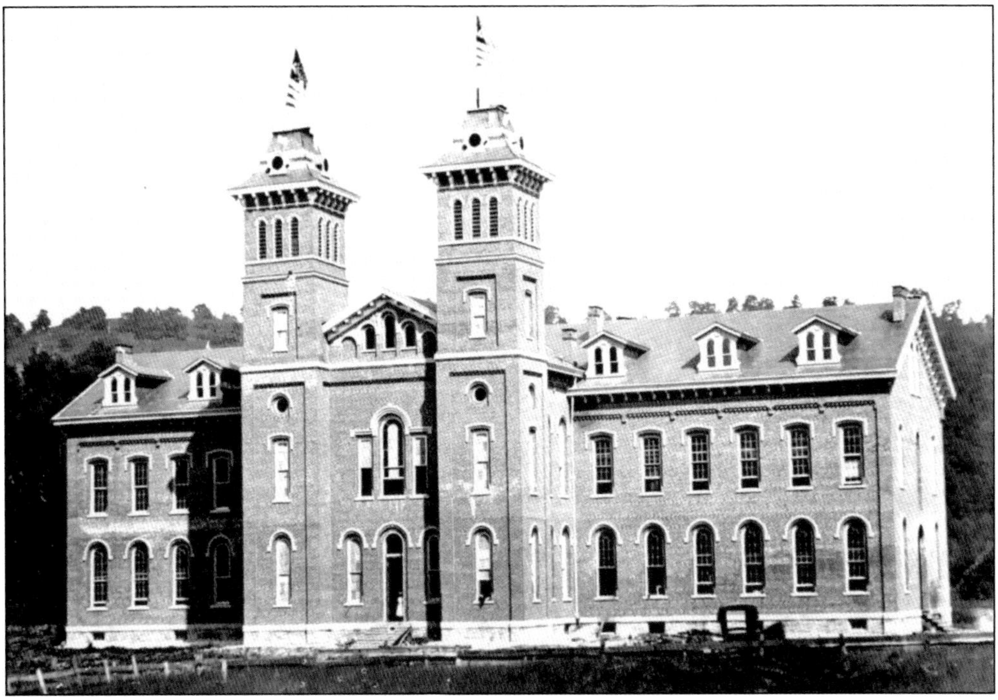

THE SOUTHWESTERN STATE NORMAL SCHOOL. The cornerstone for the first complex of the Southwestern State Normal School was laid on August 26, 1868, and included the central building (Old Main) and two dormitories (North and South Hall).

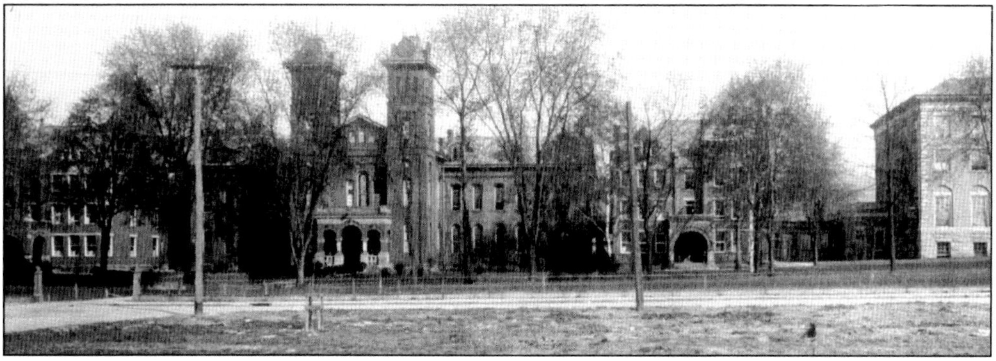

California State Teachers College. Now known as California University of Pennsylvania, the main campus of California State Teachers College consisted of Old Main with its identifying twin towers. South Hall is to the left of the tower, and North Hall and Dixon Hall are to the right. The homes on College Avenue have not yet been constructed in this 1908 picture.

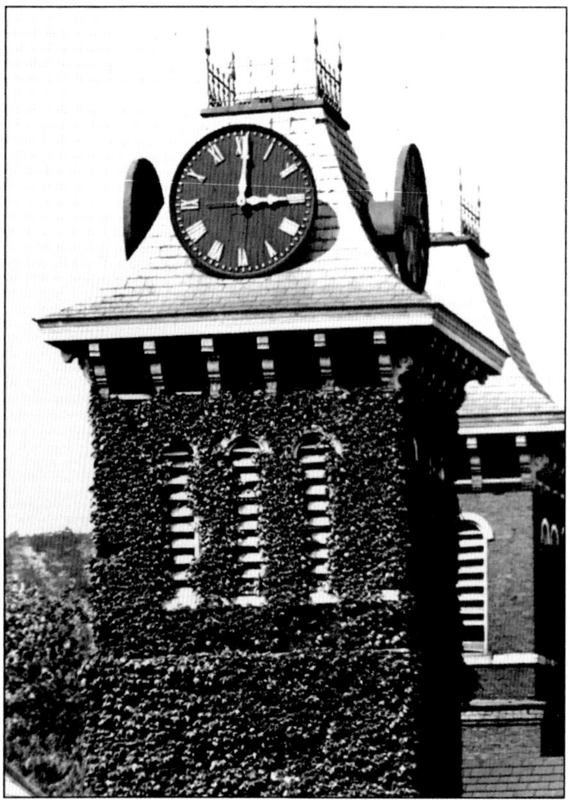

The Tower Clock. The clock located at the top of the South tower at California University of Pennsylvania was not part of the original tower but was added in 1869. The original hands were wooden, powered by an iron pendulum weight. The modern clockworks was built in 1943 by the college electrician Earl R. Hornbake.

The Old Main Bell. One of the interesting items in the towers of Old Main (California University of Pennsylvania campus) is the tower bell. Received as a gift in 1869, it was cast in Pittsburgh by Andrew Fulton, one of the leading manufacturers of bells in the United States. Held up by oak and metal supports, the bell has been silent for many years.

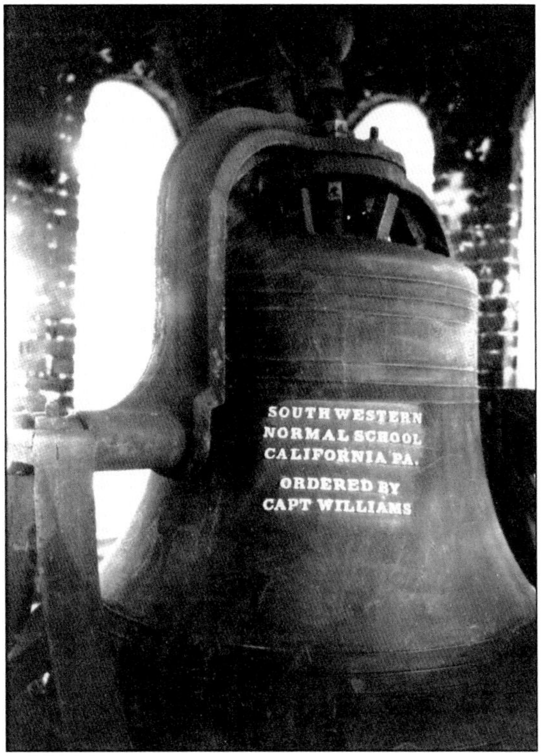

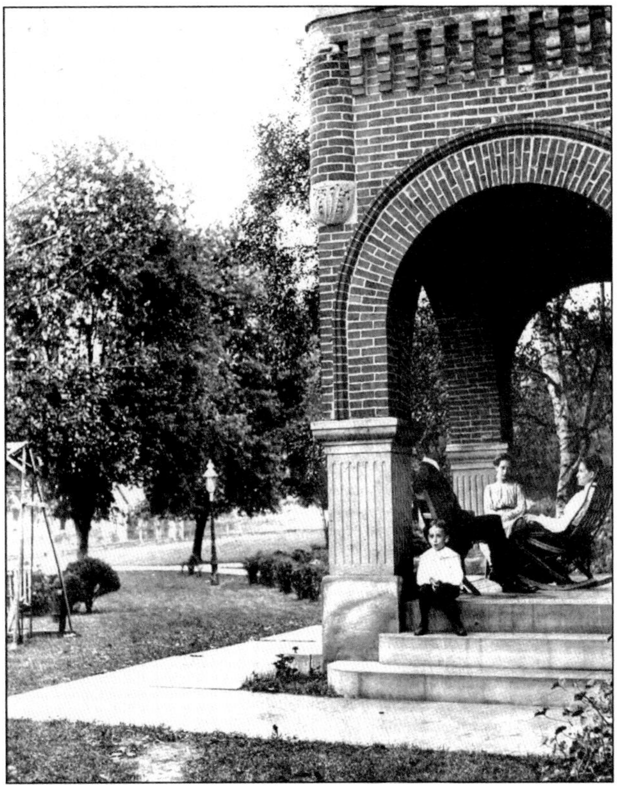

Old Main, the Noss Family. The cool breeze from the river and the artistic view of the campus and College Avenue made a relaxing spot for the Noss family. On the porch are Dr. Theodore Noss, principal at Southwestern State Normal School, and wife Mary (Graham) Noss, with children Mary and young Theodore. (Courtesy Special Collections, California University of Pennsylvania.)

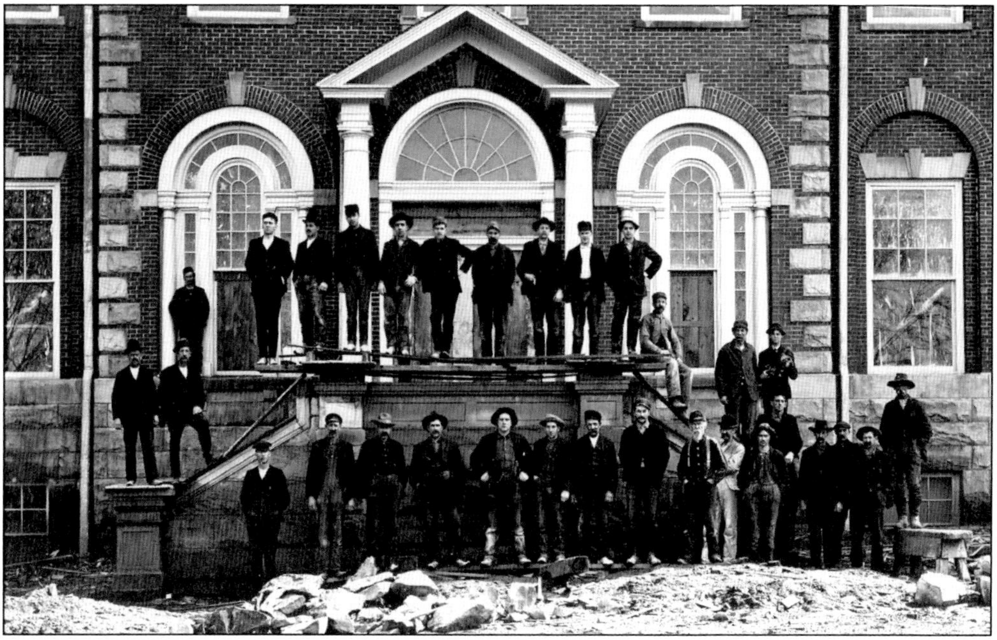

Dixon Hall Construction. When completed in 1907, Dixon Hall (California State Normal School campus) was 70 by 134 feet and four stories high. Named after then-president of the board of trustees, John N. Dixon, it contained dormitories for 100 students, a dining hall for 450, and a kitchen.

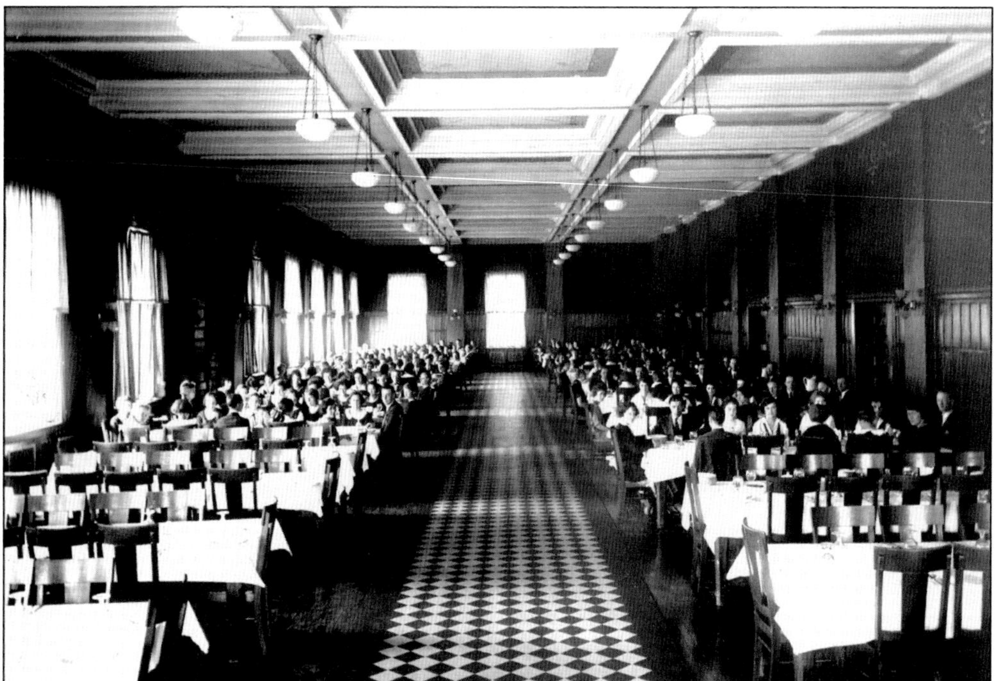

The Dining Room, Dixon Hall. Normal-school students ate in the Dixon Hall dining room. Men came in shirts, ties, and suits. Women wore dresses, hosiery, and dress shoes. Today's student diners are markedly less formal in appearance.

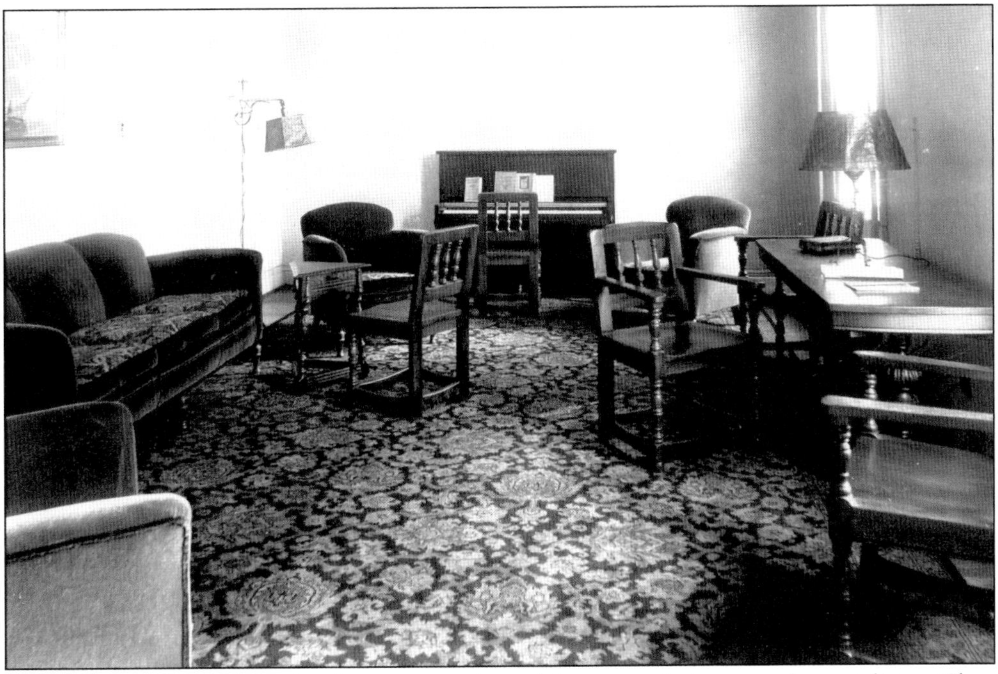

A PARLOR. During the 1900s, dormitory students did not use their rooms for socializing. They needed a parlor or social room for visiting and meetings, such as those of the YMCA. Here they could talk to friends or gather around the piano for musical enjoyment.

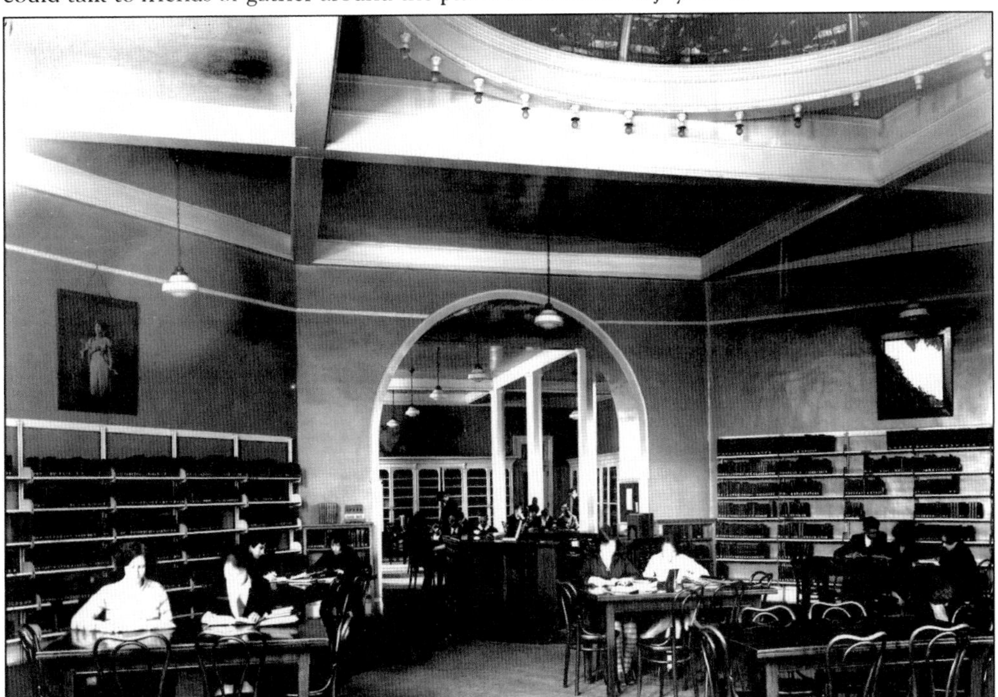

THE LIBRARY, OLD MAIN. Students are shown here studying in the library of Old Main. Today it is known as "the Dome Room" because of the huge stained-glass ceiling.

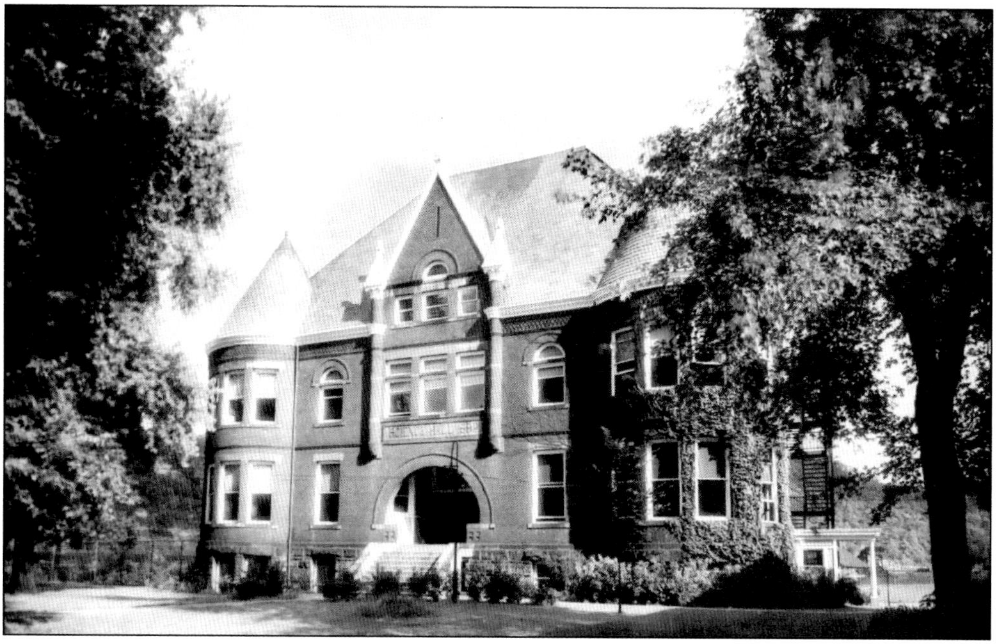

SCIENCE HALL. Built in 1892, this campus training school in Science Hall played an important part in providing firsthand observation as part of the future teachers' training. Teaching seniors participated in the education and activities of "real" children in classroom settings. Later the building was used for science classes.

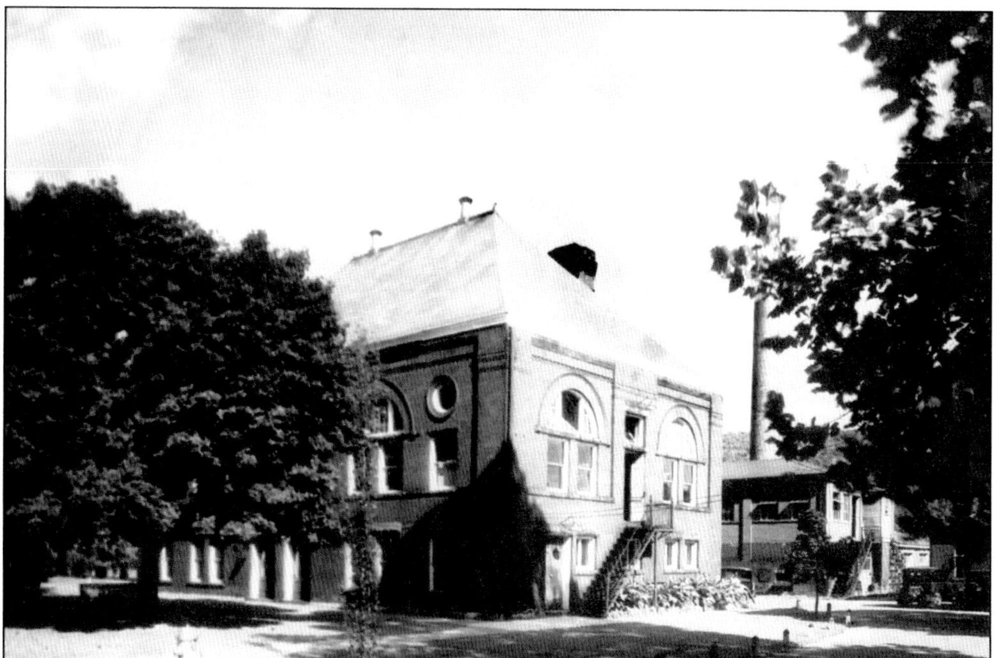

VULCAN HALL. Located in the center of the Southwestern State Normal School campus, Vulcan Hall was the gymnasium for boys' and girls' basketball from 1893 to 1931. The small floor area necessitated the use of a balcony for spectators.

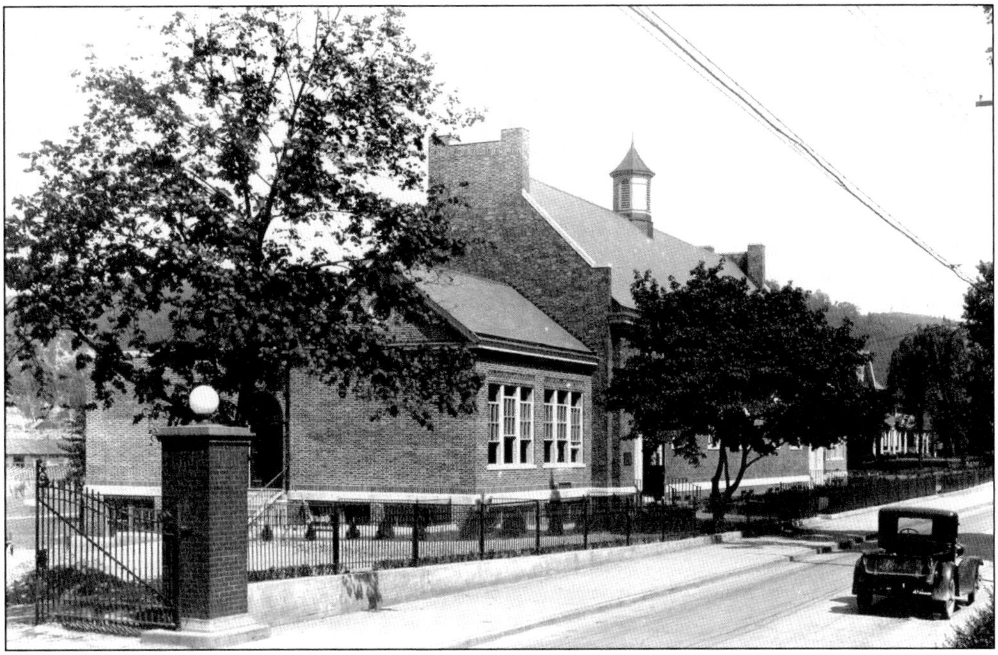

HERRON HALL. Herron Hall was completed on the California State Teachers College campus in 1932. Considered a modern facility at the time, it contained a new gymnasium with locker rooms, a swimming pool, and additional space for offices and classrooms. The building replaced the Vulcan Hall gymnasium.

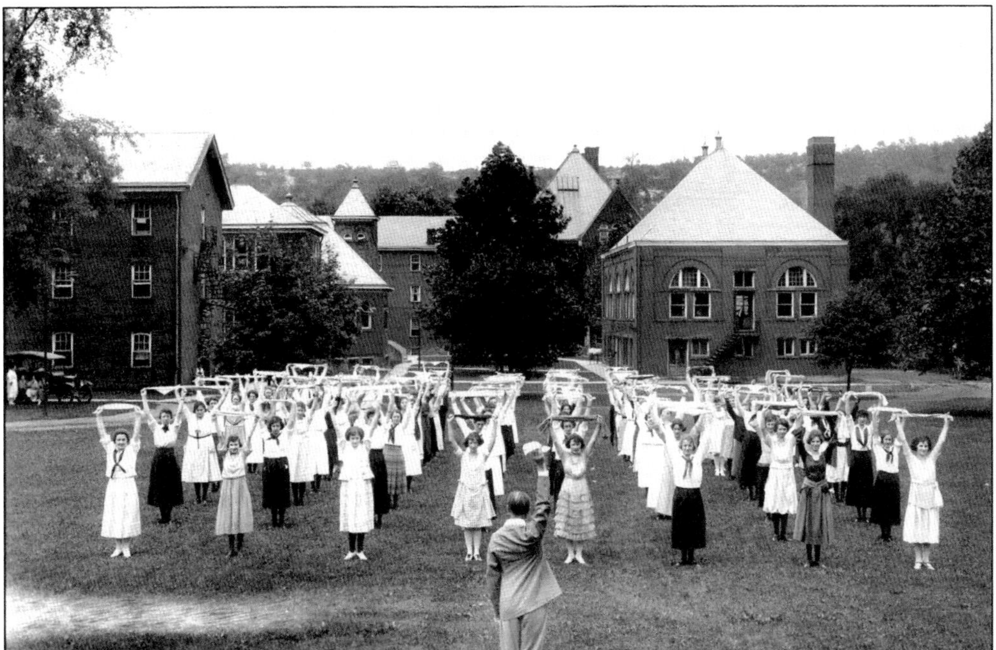

HEALTH EDUCATION CLASS. Elmer Schreiner is shown here conducting a health education class at the Southwestern State Normal School in 1922. Classes featured dance and aerobic exercises, done by students wearing their everyday clothes.

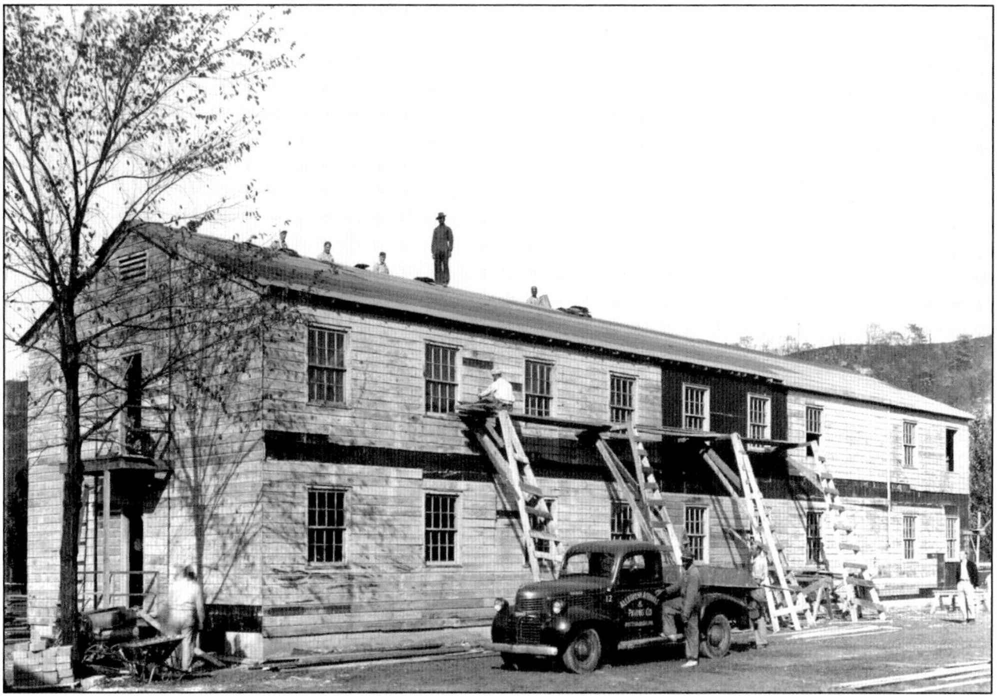

College Dormitories. In 1946 and 1947, Fayette, Greene, Somerset, and Washington Halls were constructed on the campus of California State Teachers College to provide temporary housing for the large increase in student enrollment. Of the 846 registered students, 498 were war veterans, of whom 170 were an overflow of engineering freshmen from a Pennsylvania State College cooperative program.

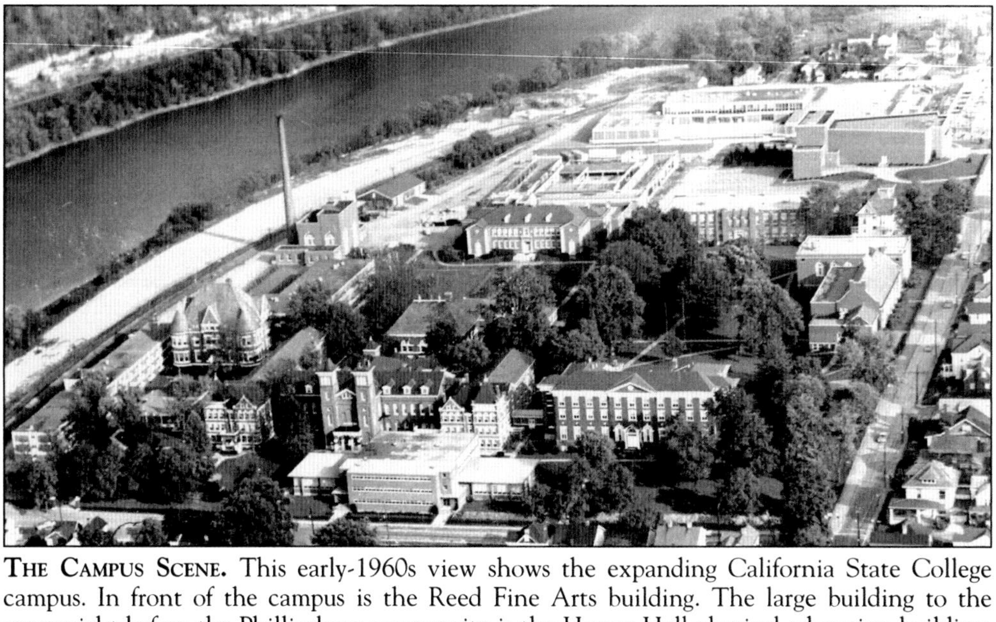

The Campus Scene. This early-1960s view shows the expanding California State College campus. In front of the campus is the Reed Fine Arts building. The large building to the upper right before the Phillipsburg community is the Hamer Hall physical education building. (Courtesy Matt Mazick.)

Five

RELIGION

The early settlers who immigrated to the California area from different countries brought with them their religious heritages as well as their native languages. Protestant, Roman Catholic, and Jewish faiths are represented in many places in the community. Houses of worship were built throughout the area, with the first Roman Catholic, Presbyterian, and Methodist churches originating in Greenfield (Coal Center). As the congregations grew in number, California built houses of worship in town. Some of the original houses of worship still exist, although many have since been relocated or remodeled. The desire for freedom of worship and of choice in matters of faith still exists in the California of today.

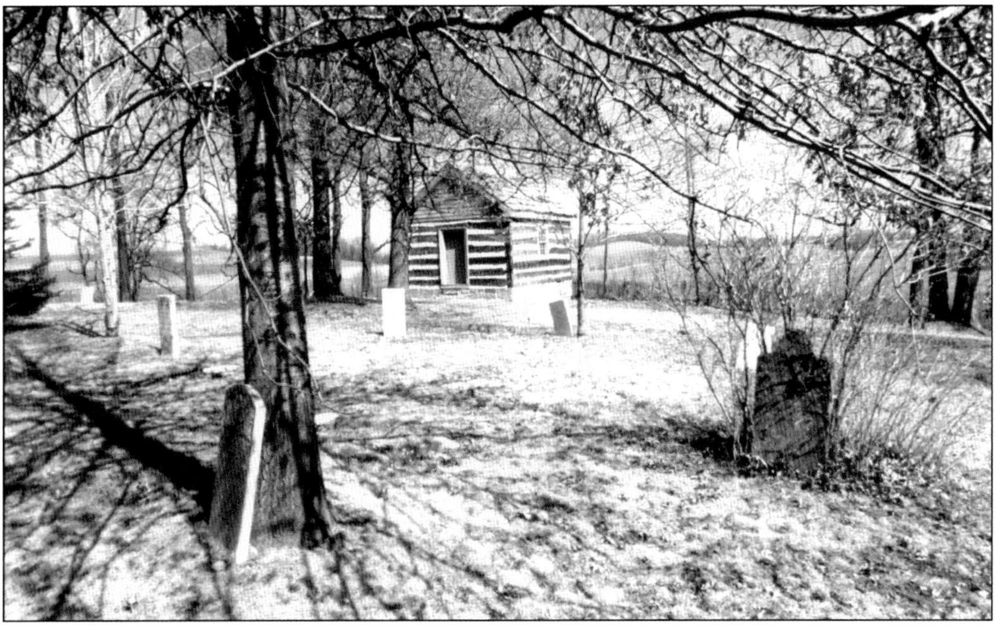

THE OLD WEST CHURCH. The St. Thomas Anglican Episcopal Church, in West Pike Run Township, was established in 1777. Edward West (1729–1812) donated land for the Old West Church, which may have been named in honor of Sir Thomas West, Lord DeLaWarr, the first Colonial governor of Virginia. The building was 27 by 30 feet and made of squared logs. (Courtesy Roger Sealy.)

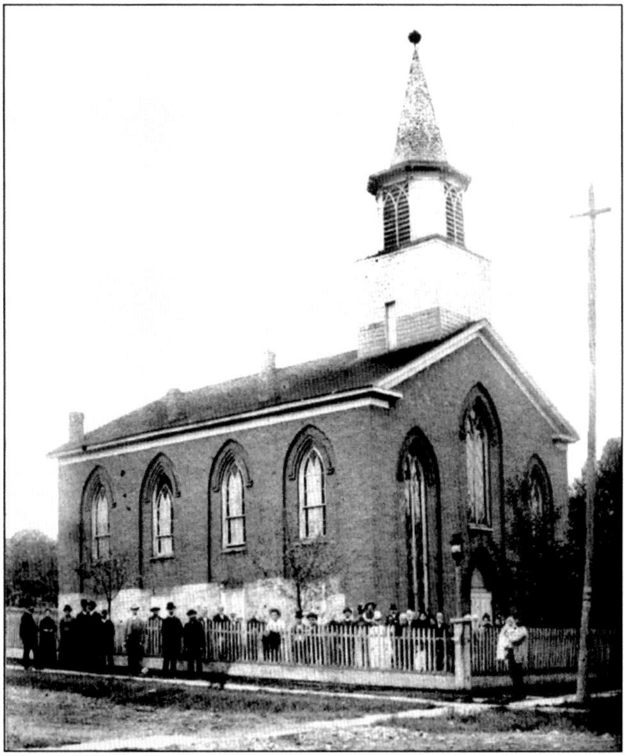

The Methodist Church, California. The Methodist congregation first gathered in Coal Center. As it grew, the congregation moved to California and met in Kiers Chapel, dedicated in 1860. Today, the church is known as the United Methodist Church. The building has expanded, and the congregation still attends this oldest church in California, located on Third and Liberty Streets.

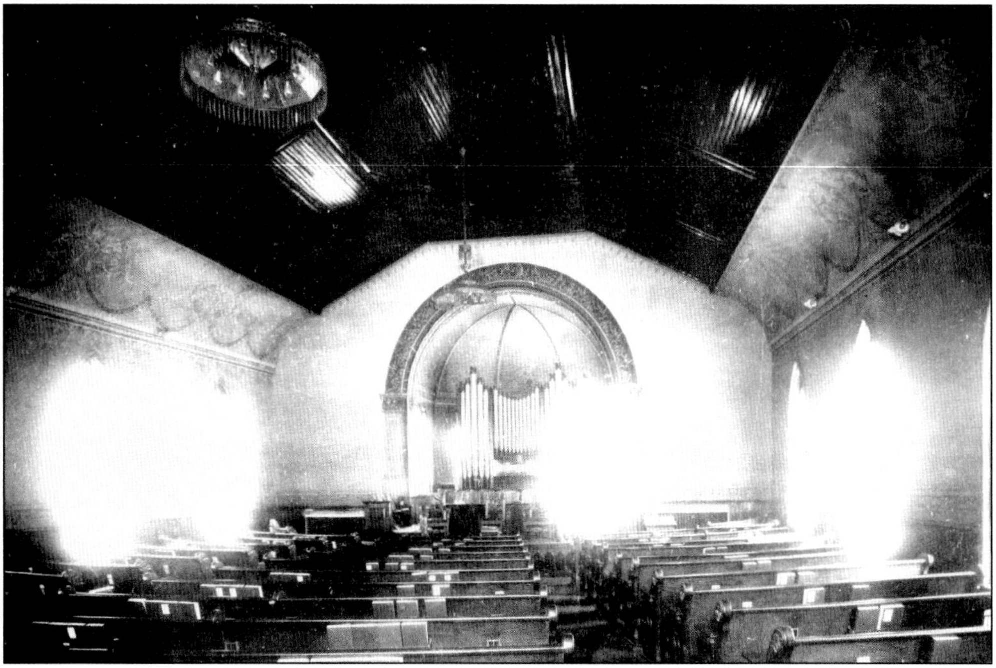

The Methodist Church Sanctuary. In 1905, Andrew Carnegie gave $1,000 toward the acquisition of a water-powered pipe organ, the sum to be matched by the congregation. It was replaced in 1958 with a Hammond electric organ. The lights, pews, and windows shown are the original ones.

THE METHODIST PARSONAGE. In 1894, during the tenure of Pastor Crissman, the parsonage of the Methodist church was built on Liberty Street next to the church. It was the home of the minister and his family until 1983, when it was razed, leaving the church with a large grassy lawn now used for outdoor activities.

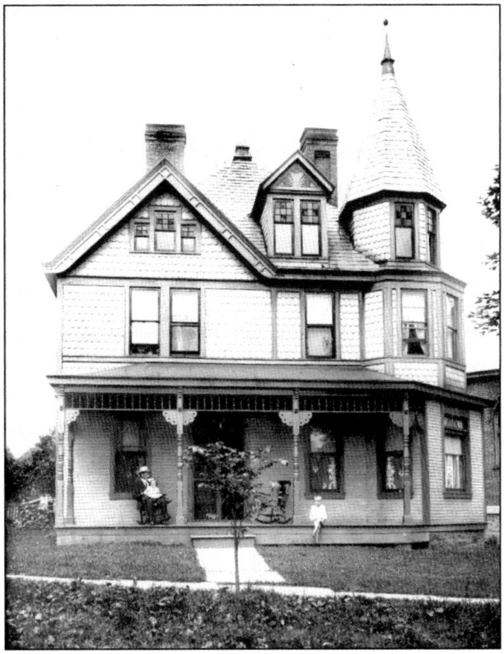

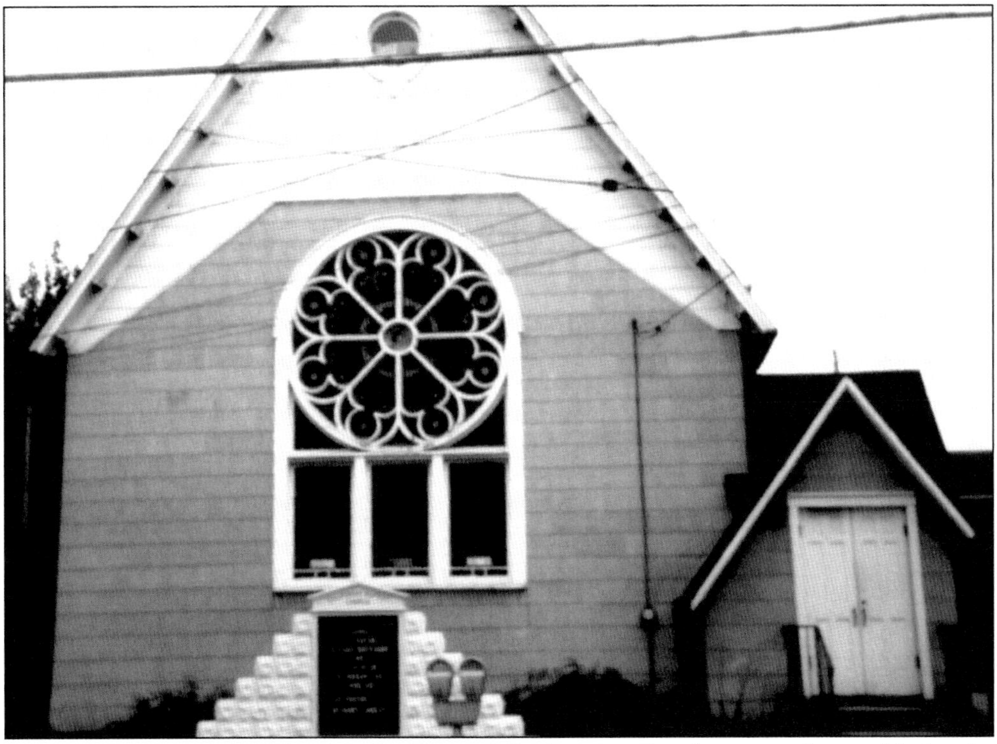

THE BAPTIST CHURCH. The first building of the Baptist church was made possible by the dissolution of the First Presbyterian Church in 1887. The property was transferred by trustee James Van Dyke. A church front was purchased from a Uniontown Baptist church *c.* 1895 and erected by the members. The church was closed from 1910 to 1922, when it reopened. It is still active today. (Courtesy Margaret Sheets.)

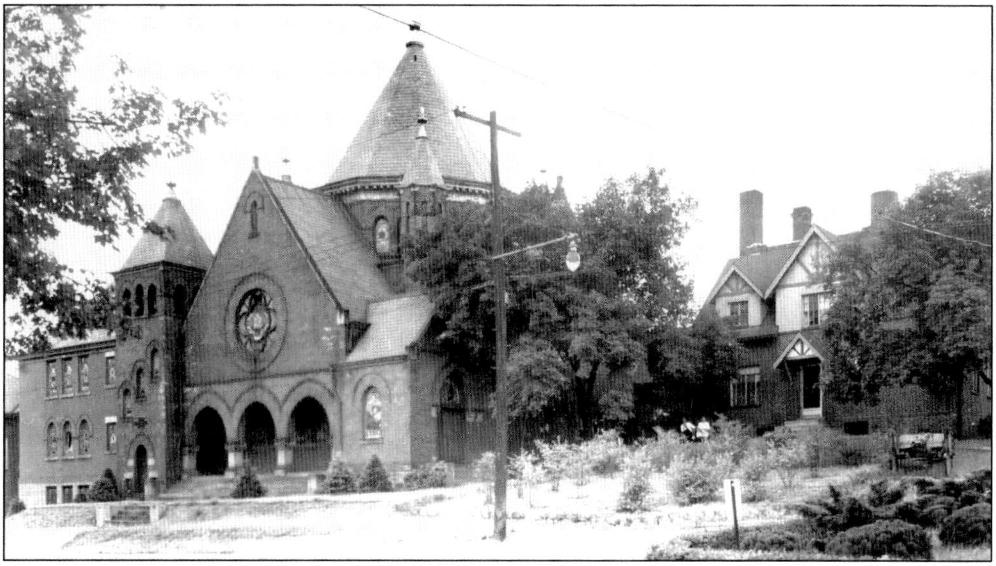

The Presbyterian Church, California. Rev. J.R. Lamb, while pastor of the Cumberland Coal Center Church, conceived the idea of a Cumberland Presbyterian Church in California. When the Coal Center Church burned in 1897, plans were escalated to complete a new church in California. The cornerstone was laid on September 22, 1900. The church is known today as the First Presbyterian Church of California. (Courtesy First Presbyterian Church of California.)

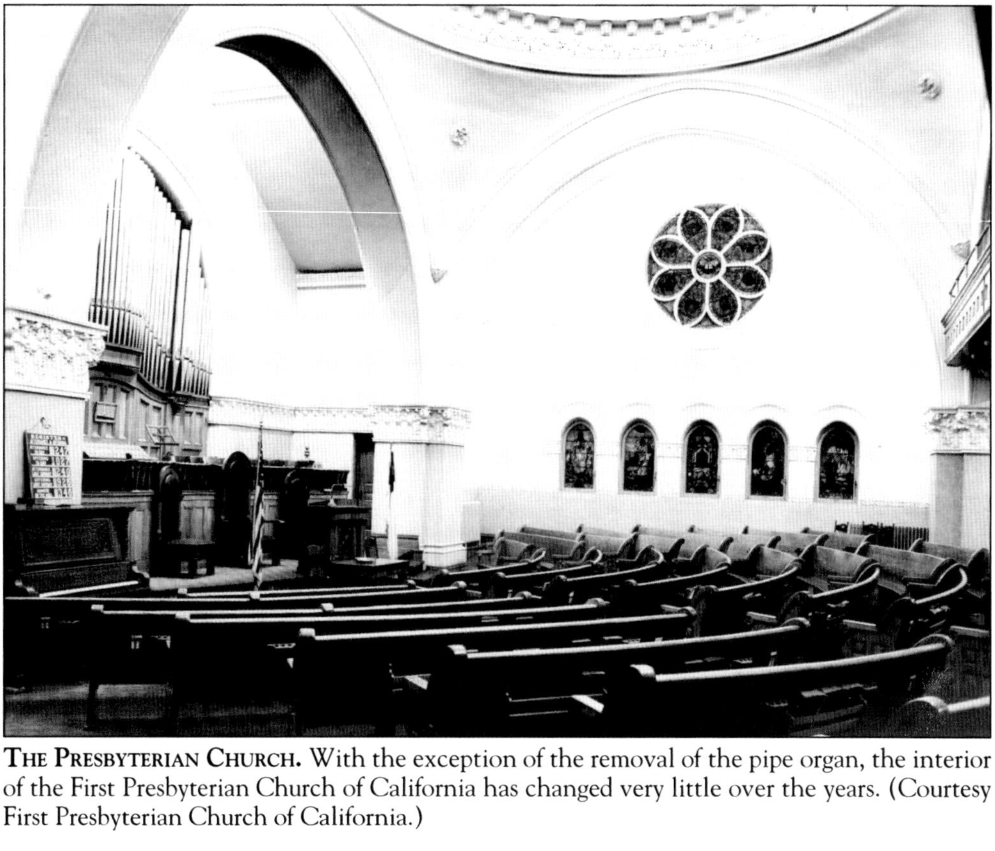

The Presbyterian Church. With the exception of the removal of the pipe organ, the interior of the First Presbyterian Church of California has changed very little over the years. (Courtesy First Presbyterian Church of California.)

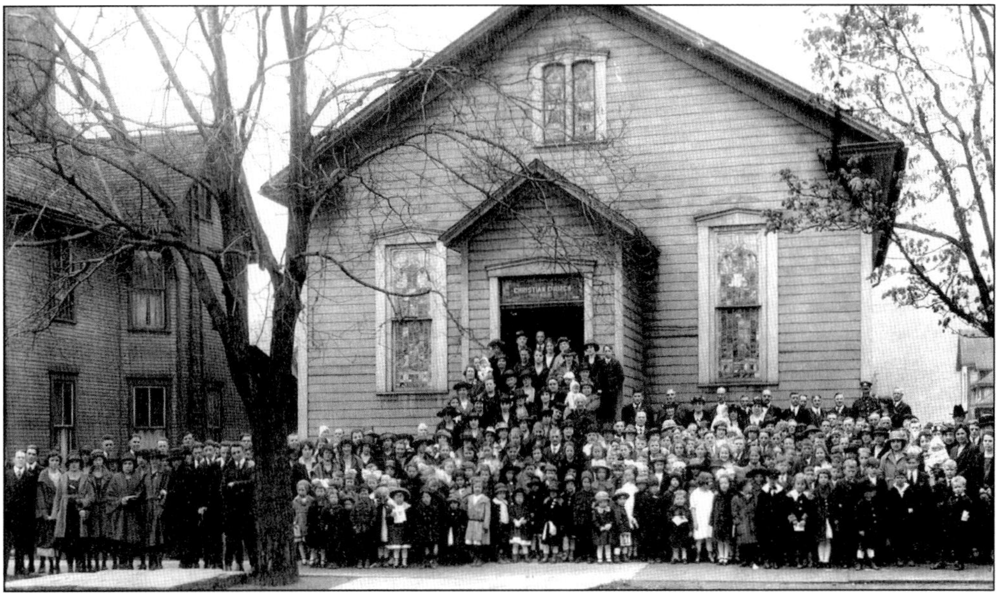

CHRISTIAN CHURCH, CALIFORNIA. The first service for the Disciples of Christ was held in 1859 in the red-brick home of Edward Riggs on Fifth Street. The congregation began to erect its own first building in 1869, using timbers from Granville Hollow brought into town by oxen teams. It was not until 1899 that records show the congregation meeting in this Second Street building. (Courtesy Gerald and Patricia Cowen.)

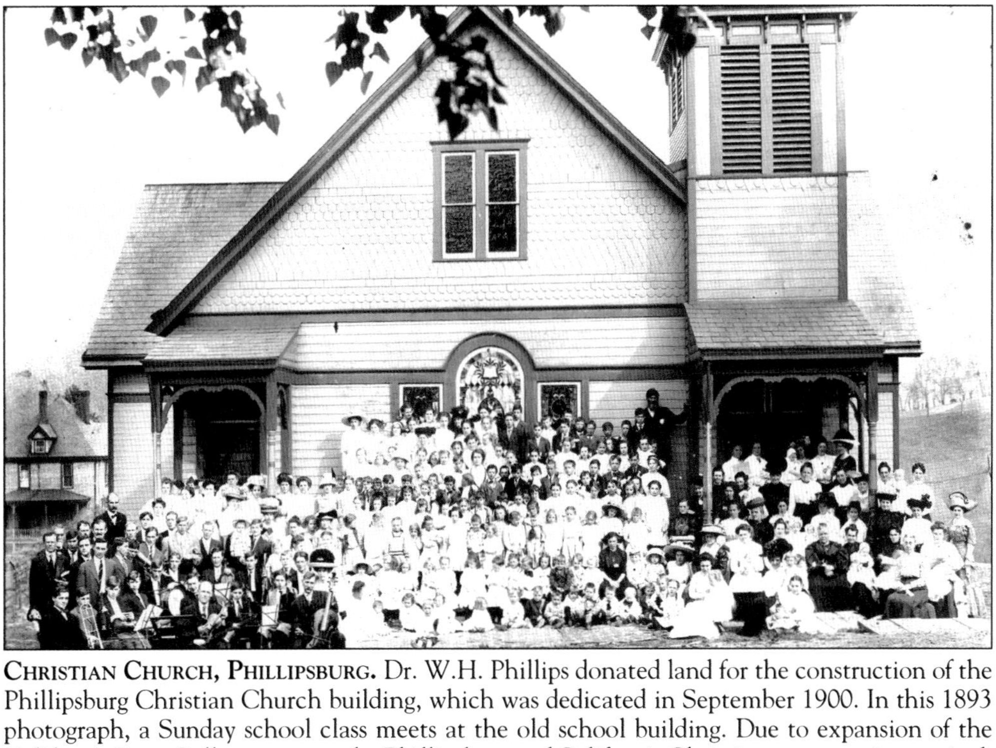

CHRISTIAN CHURCH, PHILLIPSBURG. Dr. W.H. Phillips donated land for the construction of the Phillipsburg Christian Church building, which was dedicated in September 1900. In this 1893 photograph, a Sunday school class meets at the old school building. Due to expansion of the California State College campus, the Phillipsburg and California Christian congregations united. In 1966, the Phillipsburg Christian Church building was razed. (Courtesy Alva Harris.)

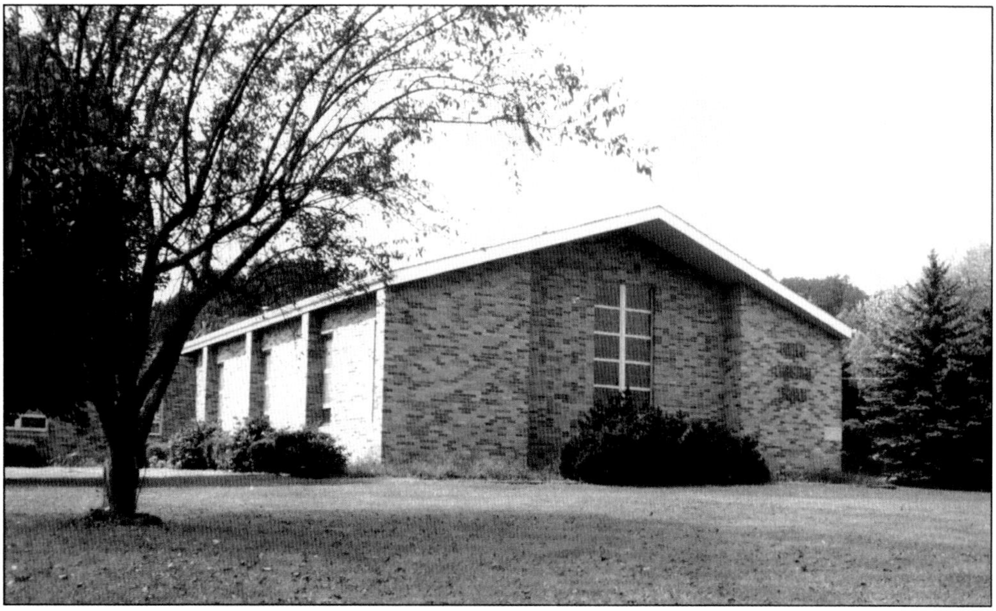

United Christian Church, California. In response to increased membership and congregational activities, a new United Christian Church building with eight classrooms, social hall, kitchen, and sanctuary was built for the combined membership of the California and Phillipsburg Christian churches. Today, members of the congregation continue to worship at this East Malden Drive location. (Courtesy Joseph Dochinez.)

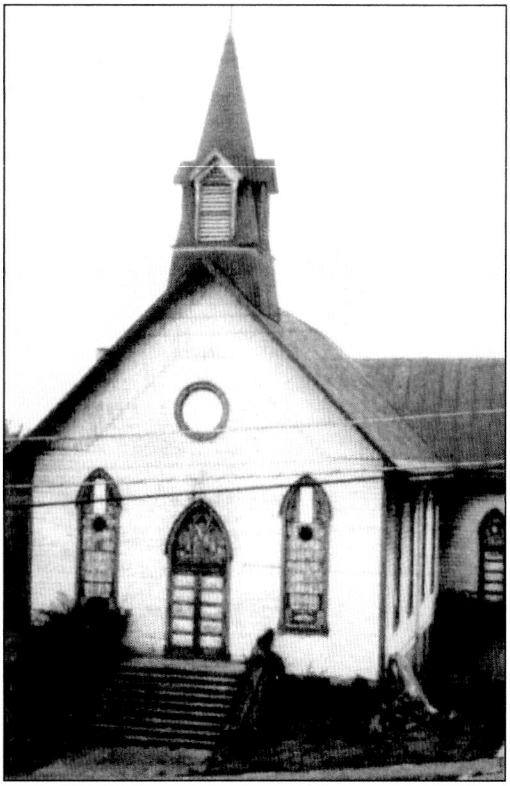

St. Thomas Aquinas, Coal Center. The Roman Catholic St. Thomas Aquinas Church congregation gathered in Coal Center. Mass was celebrated in this old wooden structure from 1888 until its new California church was built in 1956. The little white church then stood empty, until it burned in November 2001. (Courtesy Andrew Sentipal.)

HOLY TRINITY RUSSIAN ORTHODOX CHURCH. The Russian Orthodox congregation purchased the residence of Dr. Phillips, overlooking Phillipsburg, for its place of worship. The home then became the residence for its pastor and provided facilities for a chapel. In 1955, an entire church building had been completed. (Courtesy Joseph Dochinez.)

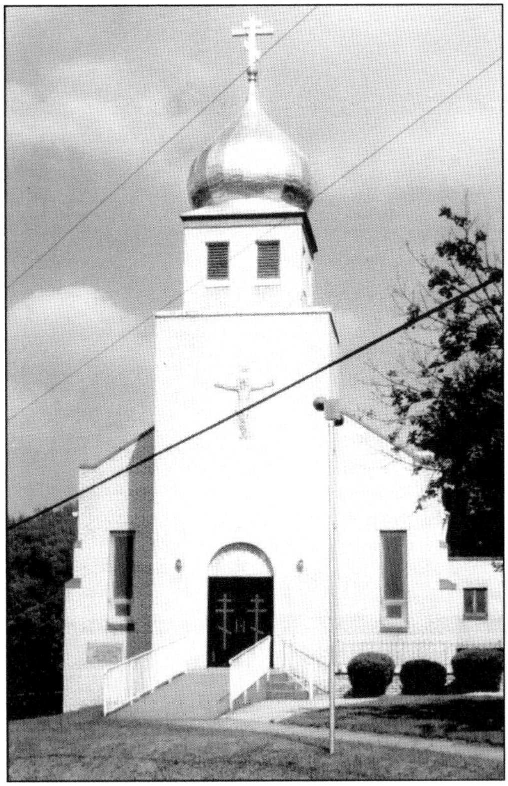

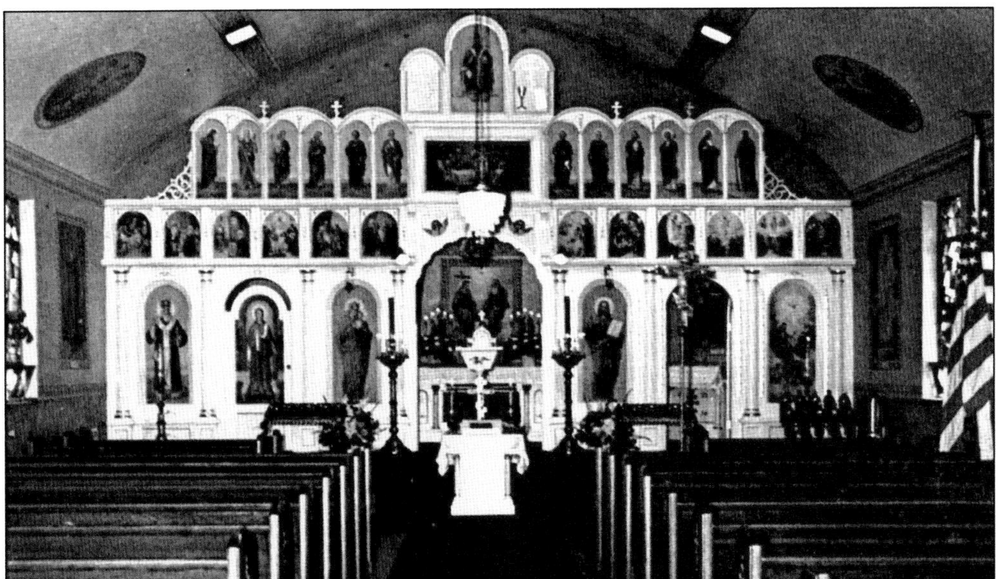

THE INTERIOR OF THE RUSSIAN CHURCH. This postcard picture shows the interior of the Holy Trinity Russian Orthodox Church, where Rev. Edward A. Sadvary was pastor. (Courtesy Barry Niccolai.)

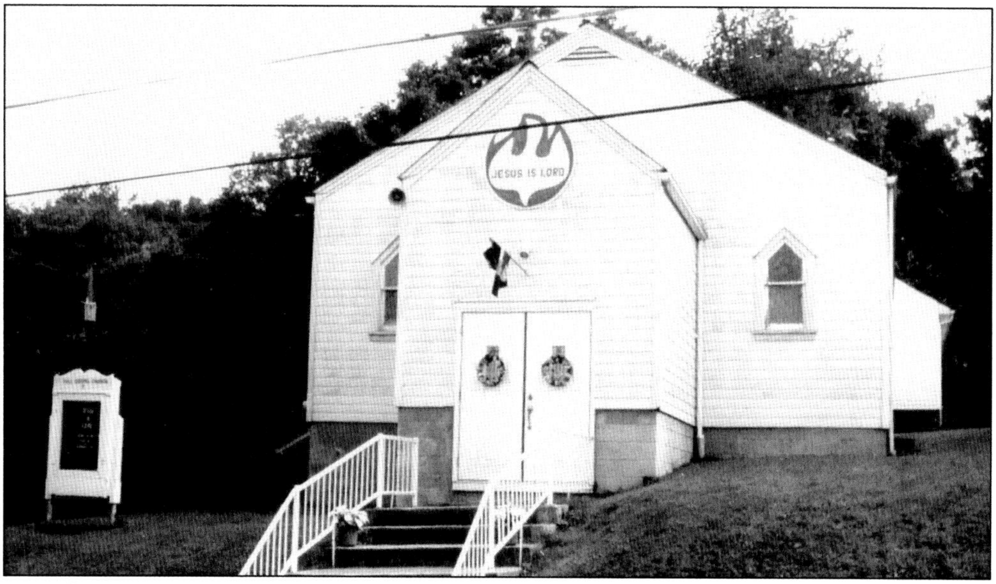

FULL GOSPEL CHURCH. One of the newer churches of California is located on Fifth and Green Streets. Dedicated in January 1949, it was known as the First Italian Christian Church. Later, the name was changed to the Full Gospel Church because of the multiple nationalities in the congregation. It is a part of the Christian Church of North America denomination. (Courtesy Joseph Dochinez.)

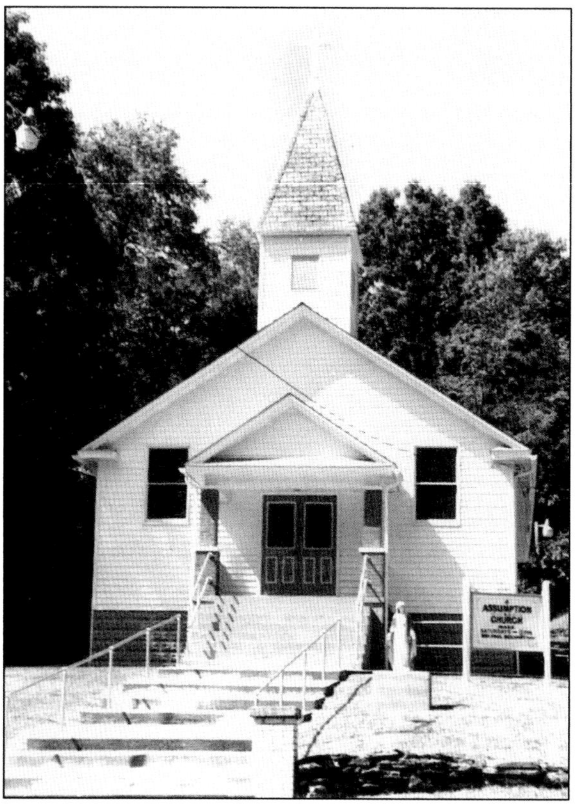

ASSUMPTION ROMAN CATHOLIC CHURCH. This one-story frame church was dedicated in 1937. Located in Daisytown on Pike Run, many residents attended the church until its closing in 1994. Today, the building is used by the Catholic church for religious instruction classes. (Courtesy Helen Ridge.)

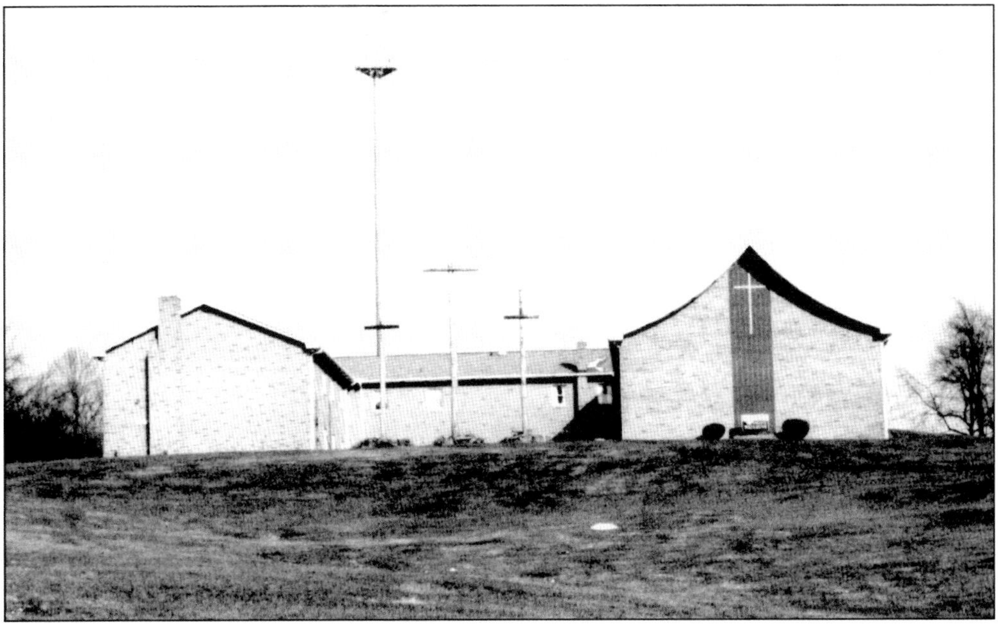

The Nazarene Church. A seven-acre tract of land was given to the Nazarene congregation by Hallie Taylor in 1974. The church is located on Promise Land Drive off Malden Road. (Courtesy Gina Mohney.)

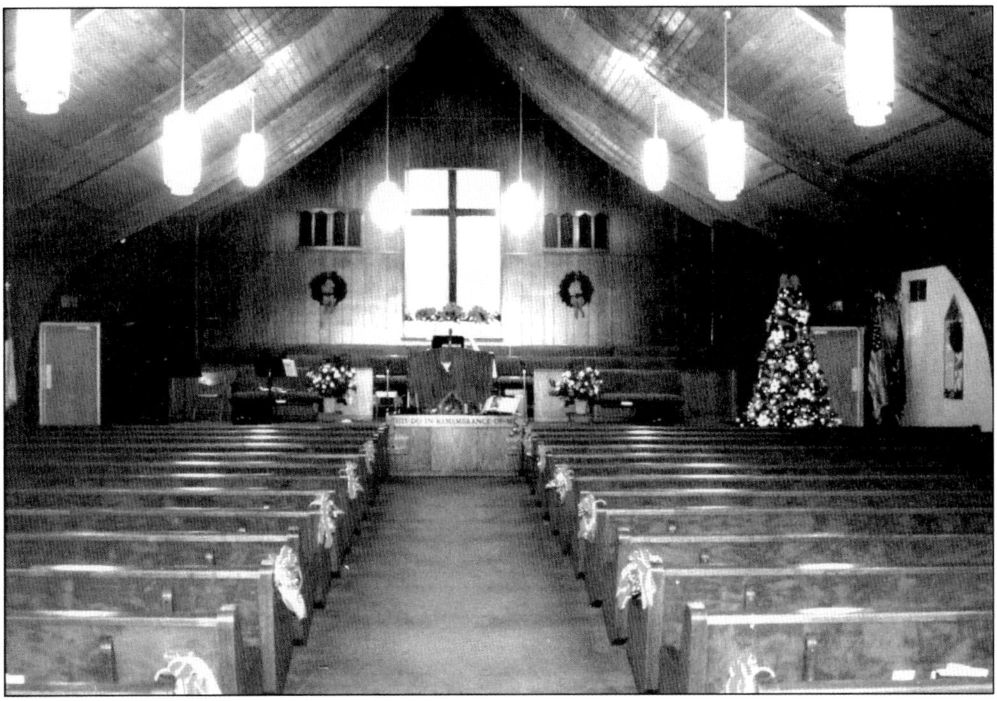

The Nazarene Church. This interior view reflects the spirit of the Nazarene congregation's Christmas celebration. (Courtesy Gina Mohney.)

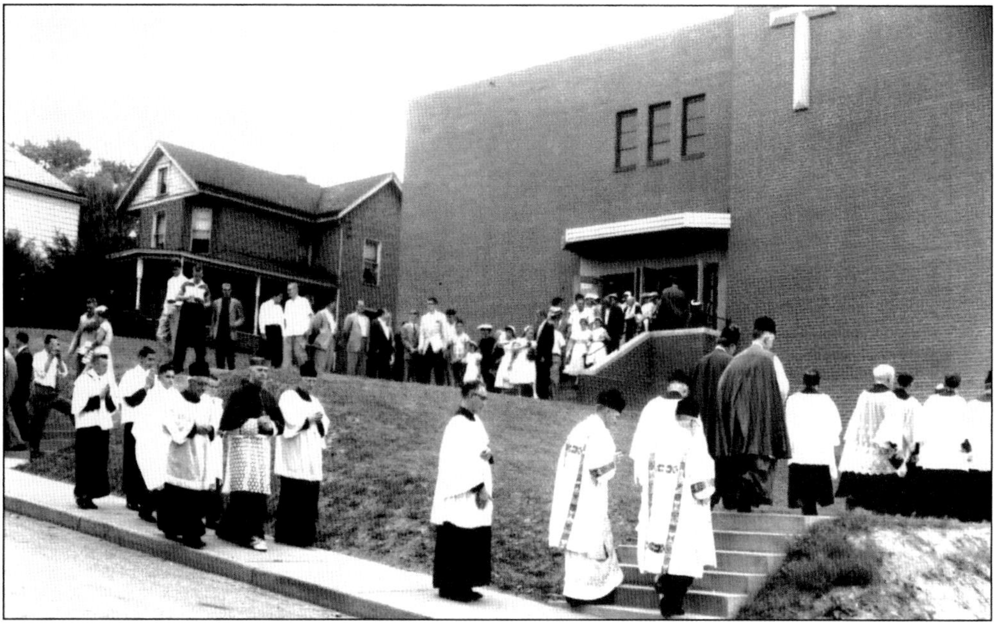

St. Thomas Aquinas, California. Originally built to be a church school, this red-brick building is the current place of worship for St. Thomas Aquinas Roman Catholic Church parishioners. The 1956 dedication ceremonies are shown here, when the congregation relocated from its former Coal Center place of worship. (Courtesy Barry Niccolai.)

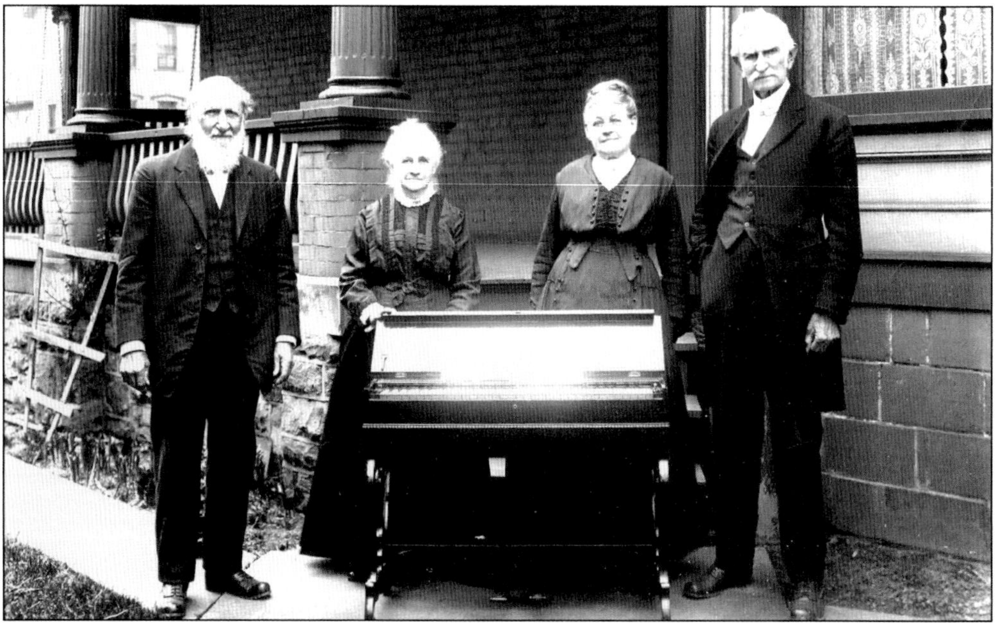

The Methodist Quartet. Many from the Methodist Episcopal congregation c. 1870 felt it was improper to have a musical instrument in the sanctuary. Nevertheless, Lewis W. Morgan, an influential member of the town and Sunday school superintendent, purchased this melodeon to use in the Methodist Episcopal Sunday school. The instrument was played by music director Samuel Craft, shown on the left with Mrs. Harris, Alberta (McFall) Forsythe, and Lewis Morgan, who formed an adult quartet for singing in Sunday school and at community functions.

Six

Recreation and Sports

Before television, computers, and organized sports leagues, the youth of California spent much time playing pickup neighborhood games. The best of these athletes went on to play sandlot baseball, and some of the best of those went on to play baseball at the professional level. Clubs, churches, and groups of miners also formed teams for competition. Watching these amateur teams compete was a favorite pastime of local families.

In addition to spectator sports, citizens took advantage of commercial entertainment offered in town. Four movie theaters, a bowling alley, and pool halls were once located in California. Local bands and a drum and bugle corps provided musical entertainment. On a hot summer day, families enjoyed sitting near the water's edge, watching river traffic as tugboats and riverboats cruised by. To this day, boating, swimming, and fishing remain popular activities along the banks of the Monongahela River.

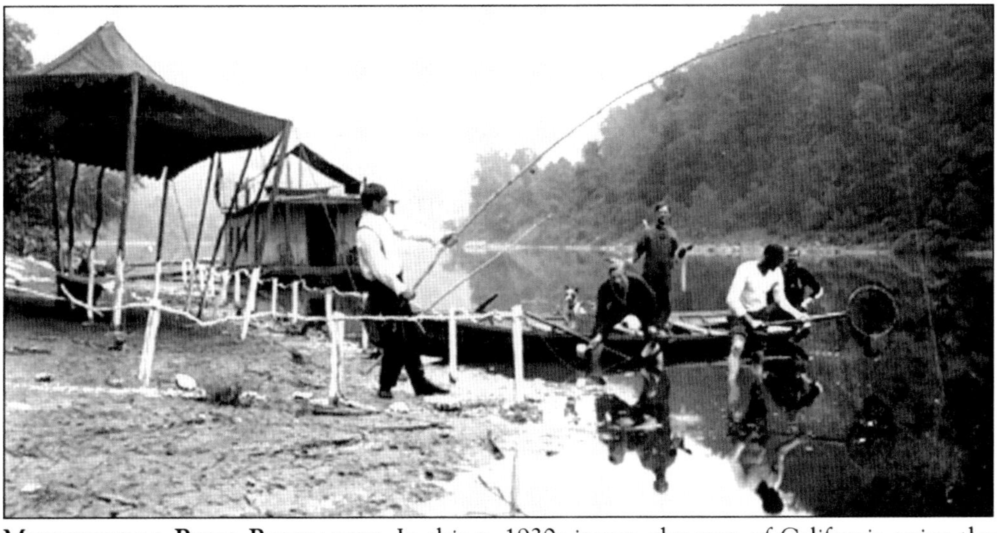

Monongahela River Recreation. In this *c.* 1930s image, the men of California enjoy the Monongahela River from their houseboat. Swimming, boating, and fishing were favorite activities along the water's edge. (Courtesy Stella Gallagher Gillingham.)

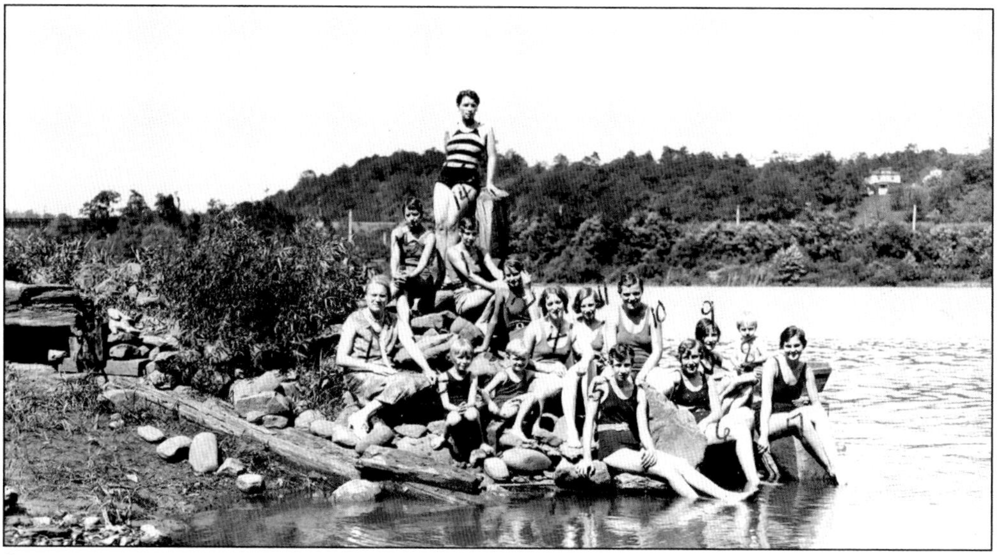

SWIMMING IN THE MONONGAHELA. Sandbars along the Monongahela River were popular spots to pose for the photographer after a good day's swim. This photograph was taken *c.* the 1930s. (Courtesy May Kay Parkinson Prosser.)

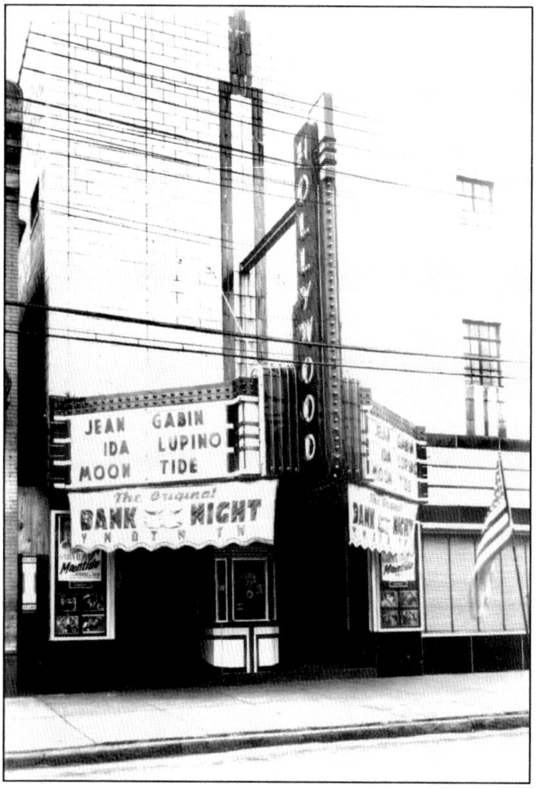

THE HOLLYWOOD THEATER. This theater opened in 1938. It was considered one of the most beautiful theaters in the Monongahela Valley. Children under age 12 had to pay 10¢ for admission and could sit only in the first 10 rows. In this 1940s photograph, the marquee indicates a "Bank Night" when prizes were given by drawing winning numbers from ticket stubs.

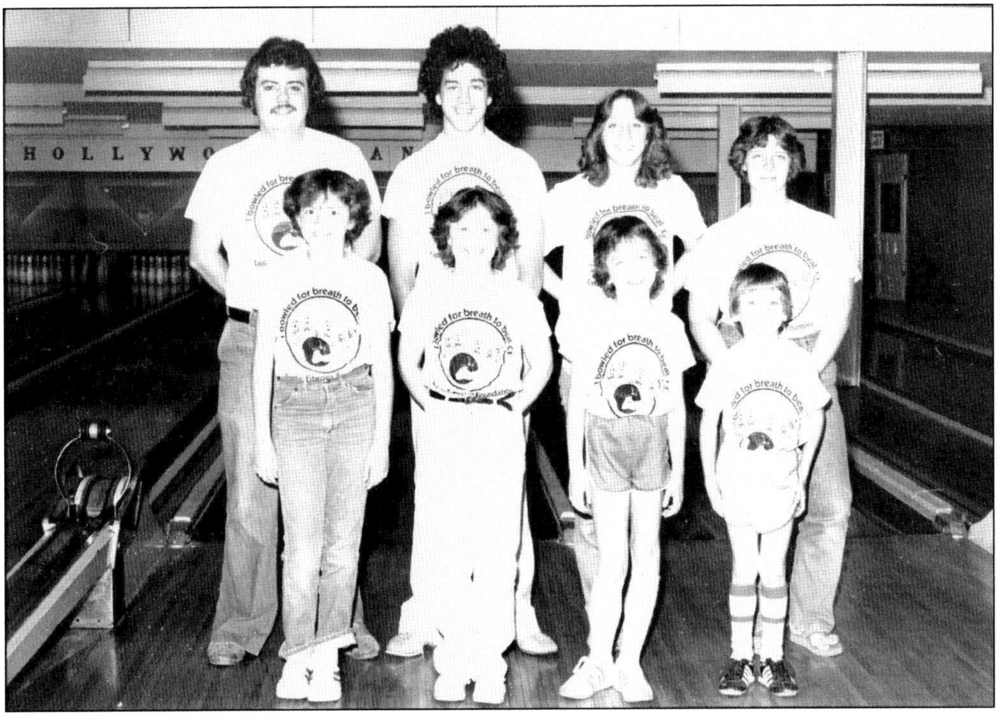

THE HOLLYWOOD BOWLING ALLEY. From the 1940s through the 1970s, bowling lanes were located beneath the Hollywood Theater and were operated by successive managers, more recently by the Bullet, Campbell, and Cole families. Bowling leagues for all ages were very popular. (Courtesy Delaine Campbell Edwards.)

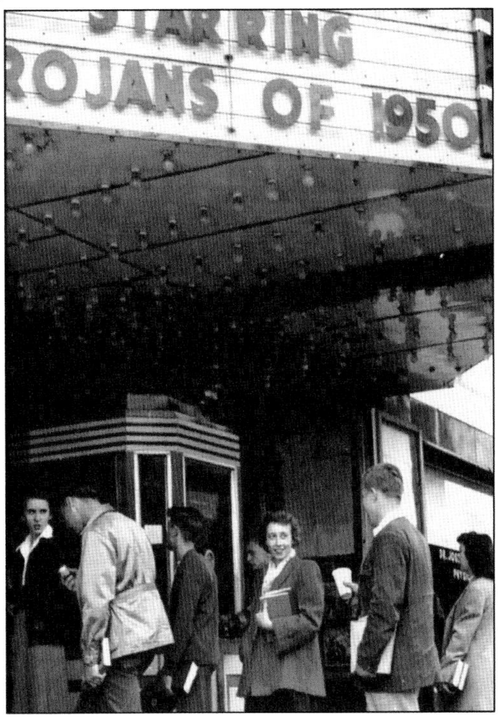

HIGH-SCHOOL GRADUATION, 1950. The Hollywood Theater was a multipurpose facility where locals could go to the movies, have a dance revue, or bowl in the lower level. Here, the California Area High School Class of 1950 is getting ready for commencement exercises.

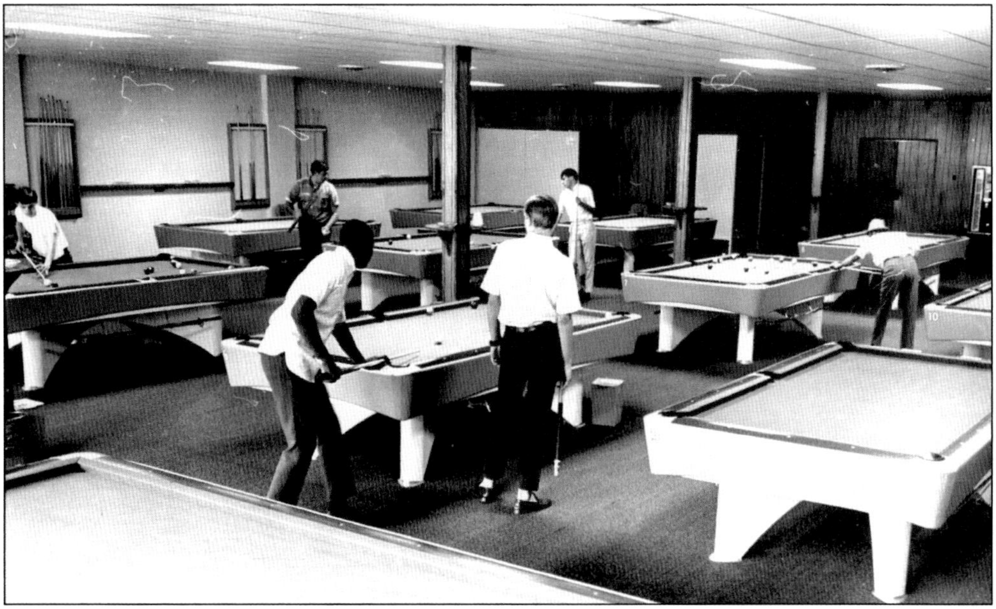

MODERN CUE. In the 1960s and 1970s, this pool hall owned by Pete Fideli and Jim Liggett, was a family-oriented place. Located on Third Street across from the Methodist church, it was attractive and well lit, a change from early incarnations of the protypical pool hall. (Courtesy Rhonda Liggett.)

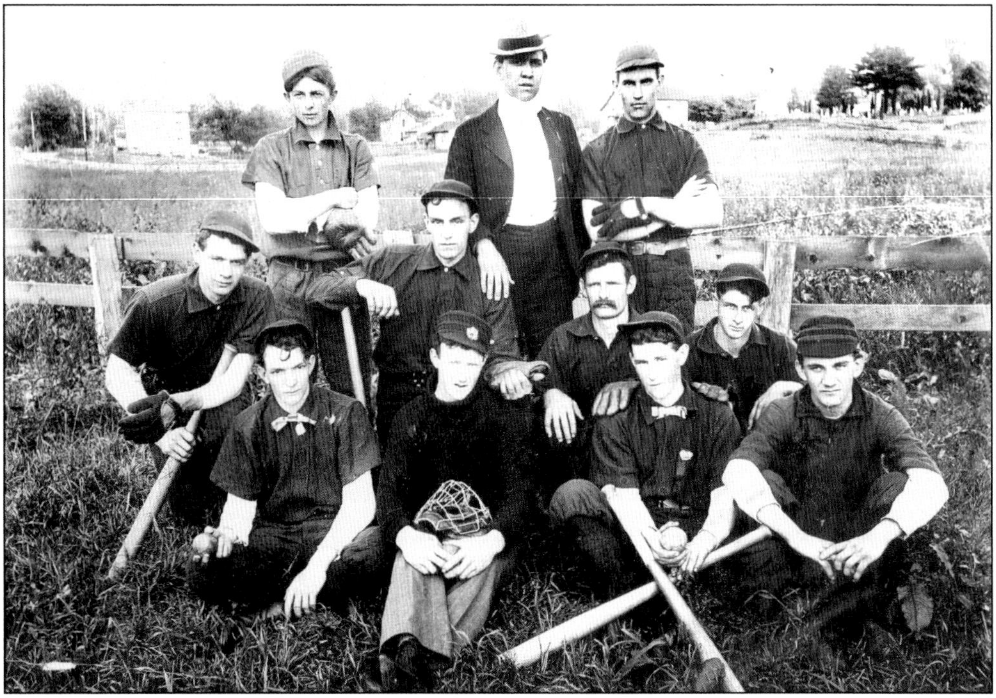

HUMPHRIES BASEBALL. The Humphries brothers played sandlot ball and are shown here at the old normal-school baseball field. Catcher "Cricket" Humphries is shown in the front row, and pitcher Bert Humphries holds the bats. Bert Humphries pitched the opener at Cincinnati's Crosley Field on April 11, 1912. His team won 10-6 over the Chicago Cubs.

Bruce DalCanton. Born and raised in California, Bruce DalCanton began his baseball career as a right-handed pitcher with the California State College Vulcans team. He was recruited while playing sandlot baseball in Uniontown and was scouted by the Pittsburgh Pirates. He then went on to play with the Kansas City Royals, the Atlanta Braves, and the Chicago White Sox. Since 1982, he has been a pitching coach for the Atlanta Braves. (Courtesy Iva DalCanton.)

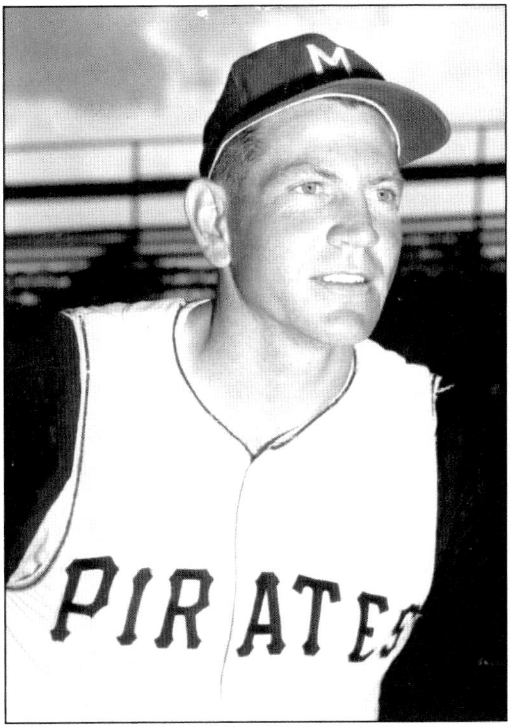

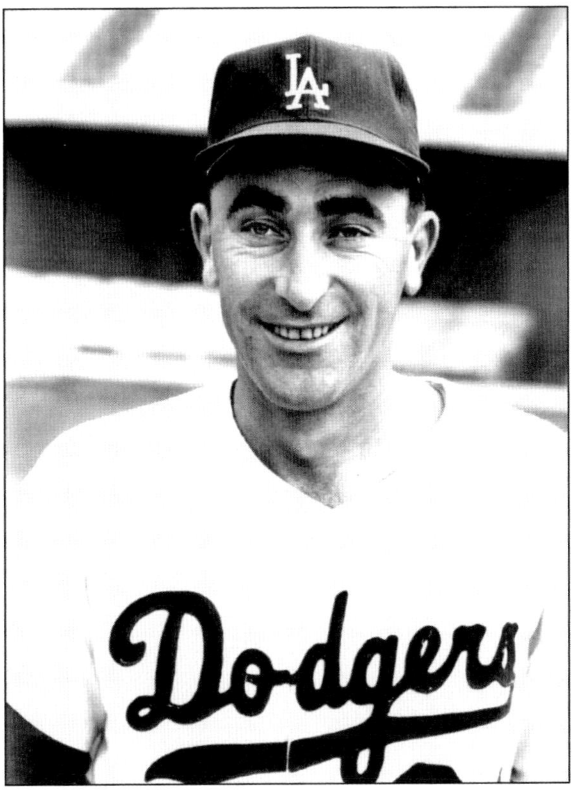

Don LeJohn. A graduate of California High School, Don "Ducky" LeJohn played local sandlot ball for the American Legion and high-school Trojan team. He started his professional career with the Los Angeles Dodgers in 1954. He was a player, coach, and minor-league manager and scout for 41 years. Some of the most memorable moments of his career were the plays he made in the 1965 Dodgers World Series championship game. (Courtesy Don LeJohn.)

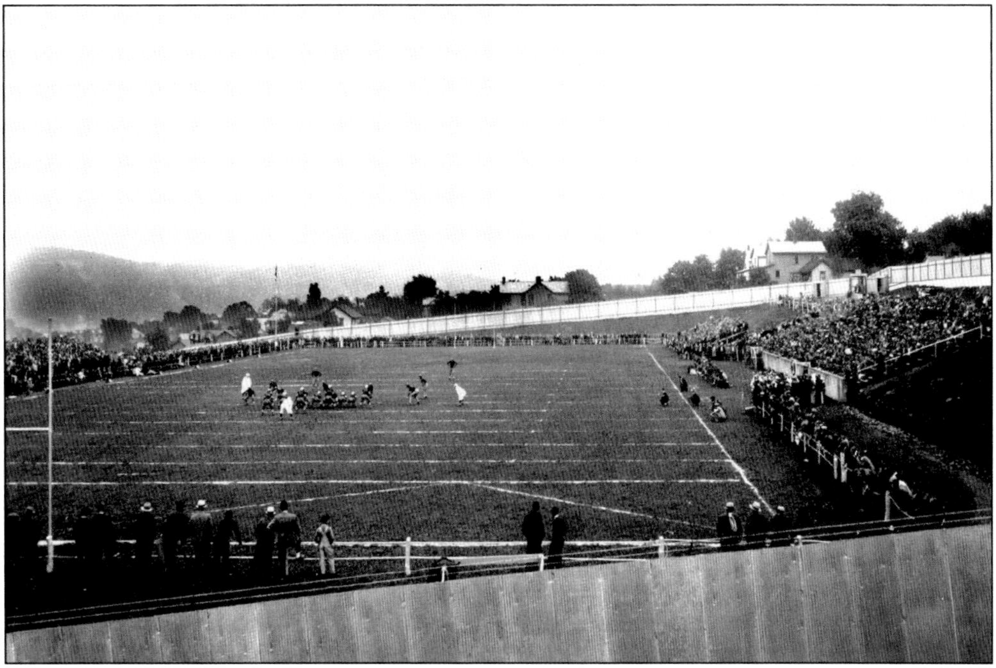

THE FOOTBALL FIELD. The California High School Cubs football team played their games only by day on the field on Pennsylvania Avenue until 1947. To get to the field, one climbed the stairs at the end of Fifth Street. Today, the field is used by Little League baseball teams.

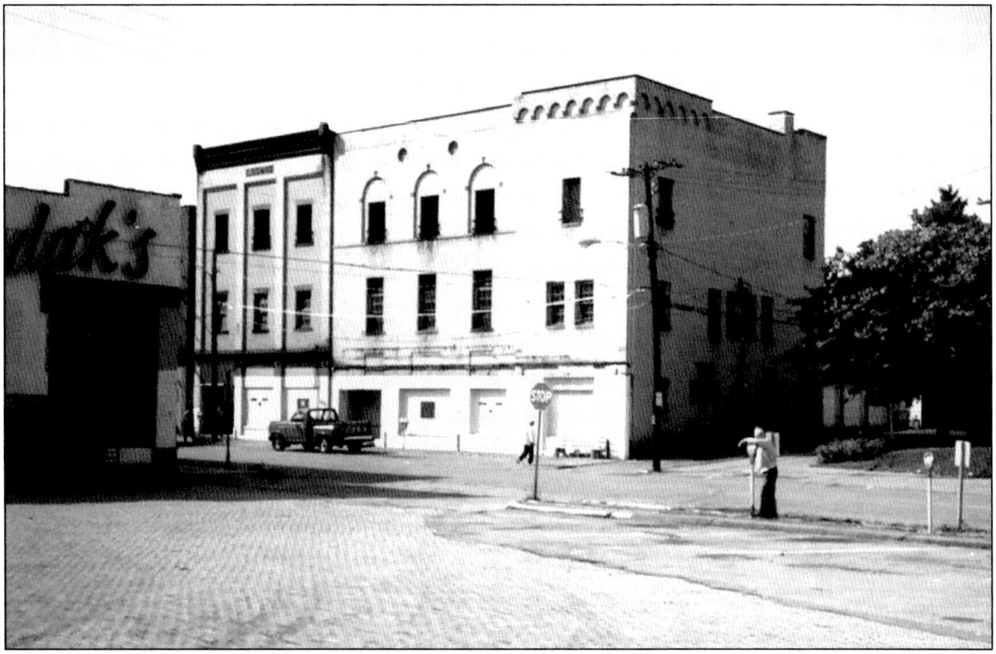

THE LOYAL ORDER OF THE MOOSE. In the 1930s, this yellow-brick building was the home of the Loyal Order of the Moose. Other organizations held meetings on the top floors. In the 1960s, the building housed Johnny Tchinski's Thorofare market, known as Johnny's Market.

THE FRATERNAL ORDER OF THE EAGLES. The Fraternal Order of the Eagles was located on the corner of Second and Union Streets in the early 1900s. Aerie No. 1881 had 59 charter members. (Courtesy Barry Niccolai.)

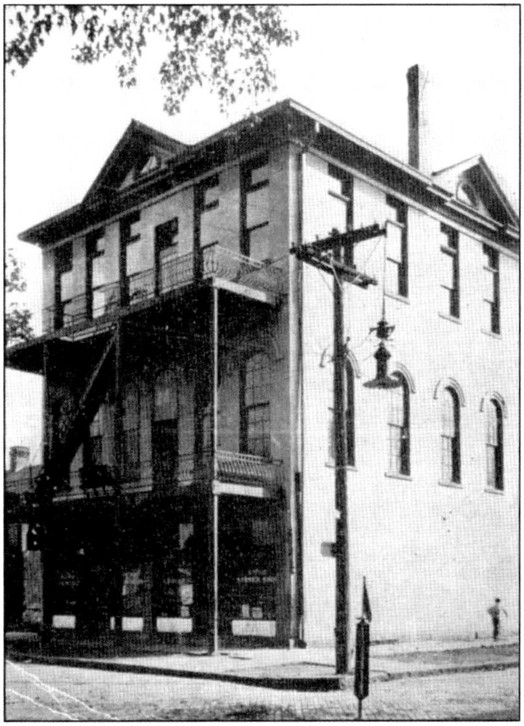

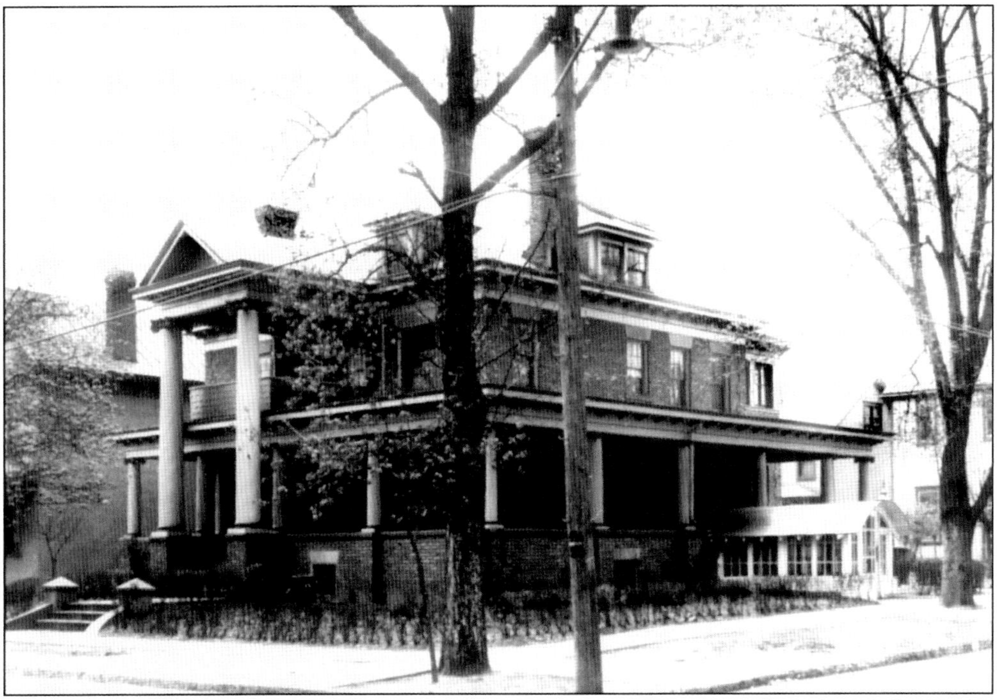

THE FRATERNAL ORDER OF THE EAGLES LODGE. In 1937, the Fraternal Order of the Eagles (FOE) Lodge, on Second and Liberty Streets, featured a downstairs ballroom accessible through the side covered entrance. The charter of the local FOE Aerie was revoked on June 6, 1989. (Courtesy Roger Sealy.)

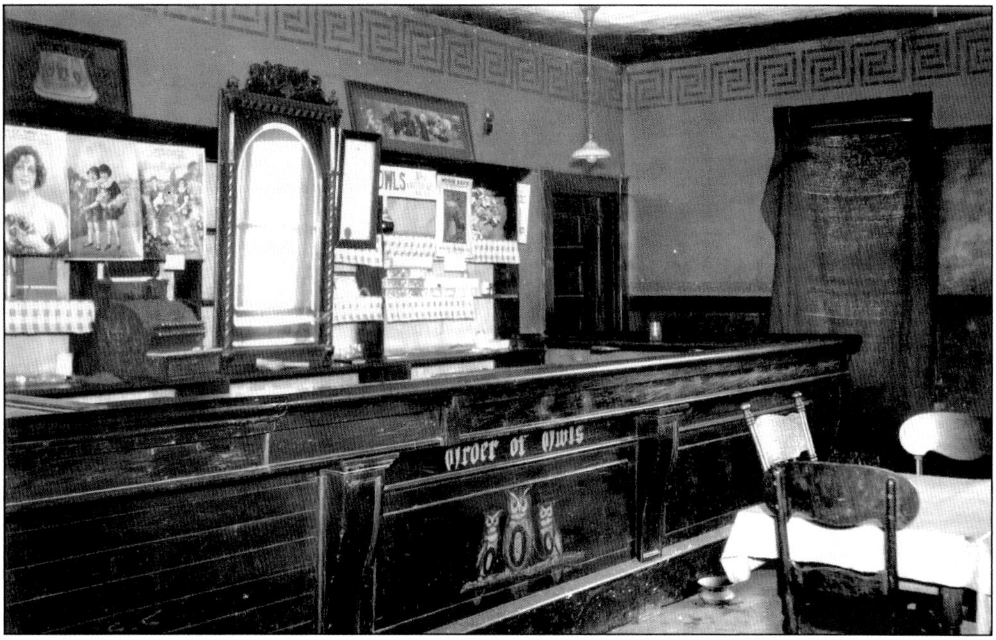

The Order of Owls. The Owls Social Club of Daisytown was in existence from 1904 to 1934. Behind the bar are advertisements for Timko Funeral Home, Zanetta Groceries, and Moose Brewery Company.

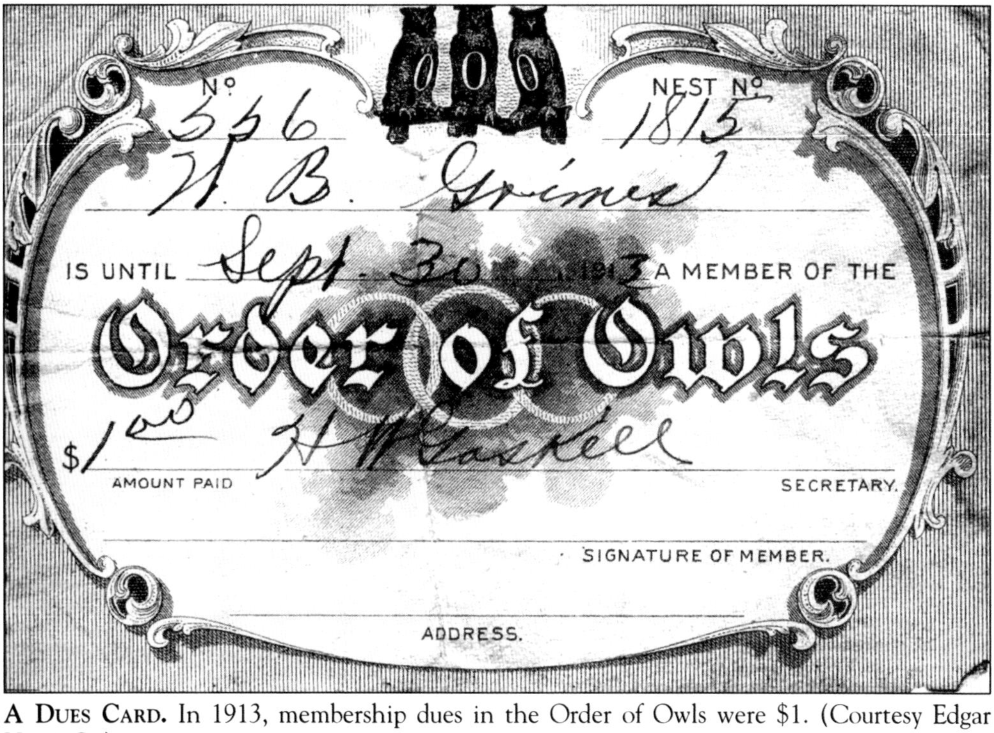

A Dues Card. In 1913, membership dues in the Order of Owls were $1. (Courtesy Edgar Harris Sr.)

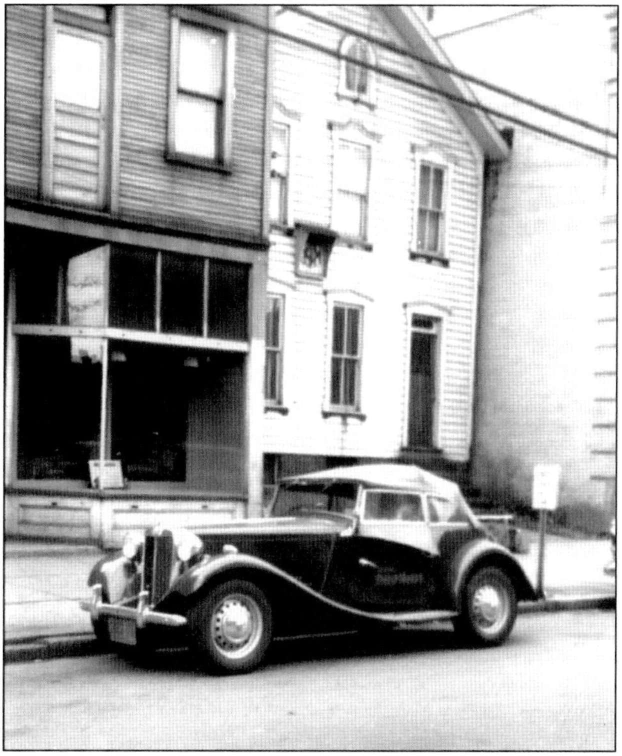

Junior Order United American Mechanics. In the early 1900s, 32 California men, pledging themselves to the ideals of building finer American citizens and a stronger America, organized the Colonel A.L. Hawkins Council No. 334, Junior Mechanics. By 1949, the council had grown to 100 members and boasted a new home, shown in the center of this photograph. (Courtesy Helen Rapp.)

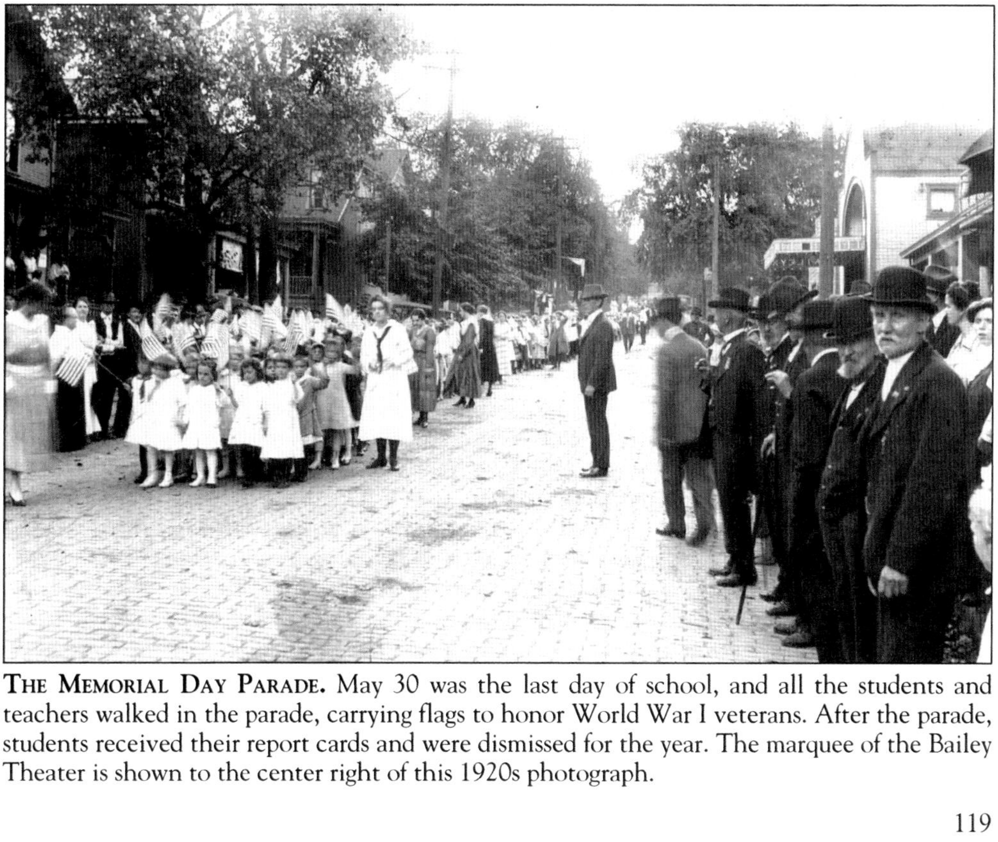

The Memorial Day Parade. May 30 was the last day of school, and all the students and teachers walked in the parade, carrying flags to honor World War I veterans. After the parade, students received their report cards and were dismissed for the year. The marquee of the Bailey Theater is shown to the center right of this 1920s photograph.

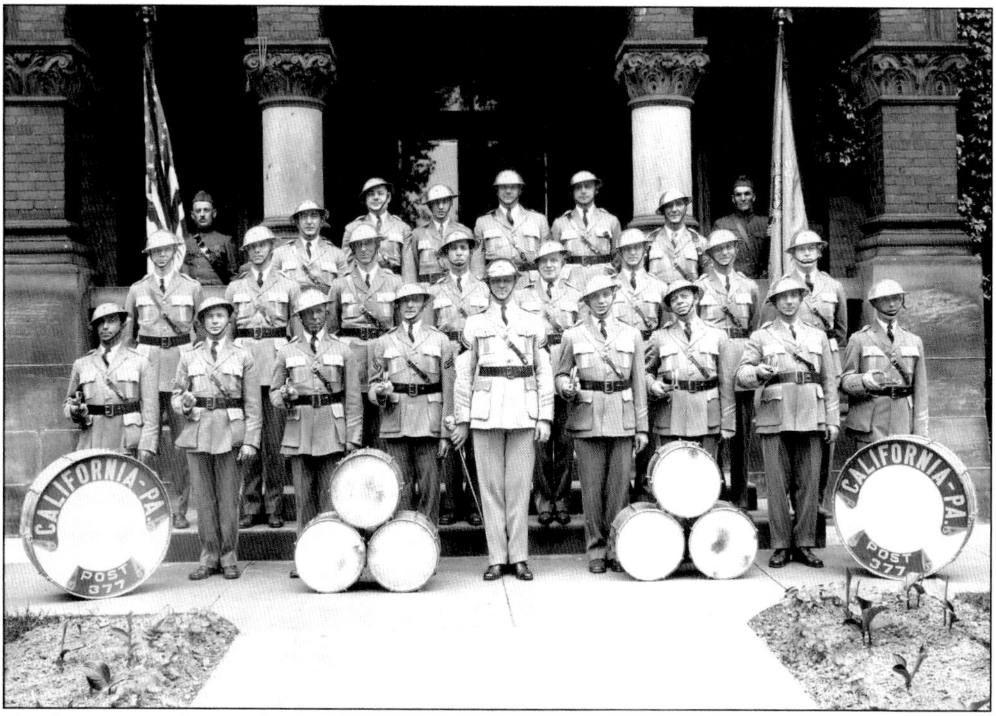

The Drum and Bugle Corps. American Legion Post No. 377 sponsored the Drum and Bugle Corps. Under the direction of Tony Mariscotti in the 1930s, the corps won several competitions and was a feature attraction at community parades and events. (Courtesy John Mariscotti.)

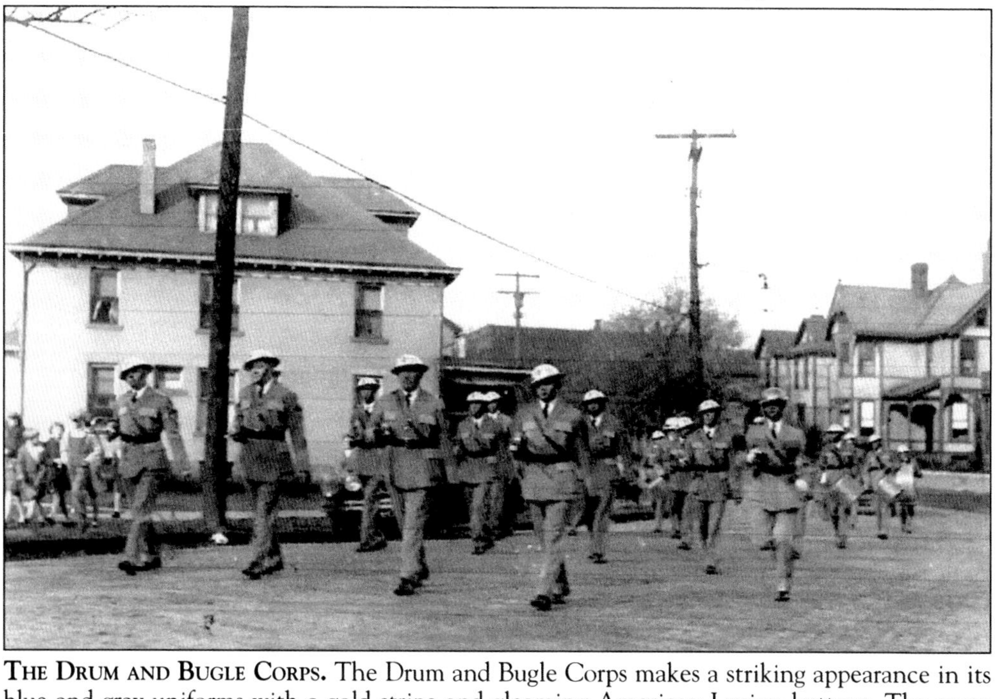

The Drum and Bugle Corps. The Drum and Bugle Corps makes a striking appearance in its blue and gray uniforms with a gold stripe and gleaming American Legion buttons. The corps disbanded sometime after World War II. (Courtesy Gerald and Patricia Cowen.)

Seven

Prologue to the Future

Farming, coal mining, and education best describe the past, present, and future of California, Pennsylvania. The student in cap and gown as well as the miner with pick and shovel were common sights on the town streets in the last century. Today the value of farming and coal mining has lessened, and education remains a high priority. Today's California community is also embracing the ingenuity and imagination of its forefathers. It is developing industrial parks, building new roads, and looking to future opportunities that will promote its continued expansion. California is saying, "It is true that education is currently the basis of our community, but let us look ahead and keep California, Pennsylvania, growing." California's first 150 years serves as prologue to the challenges of the future. The next decades will be no less critical.

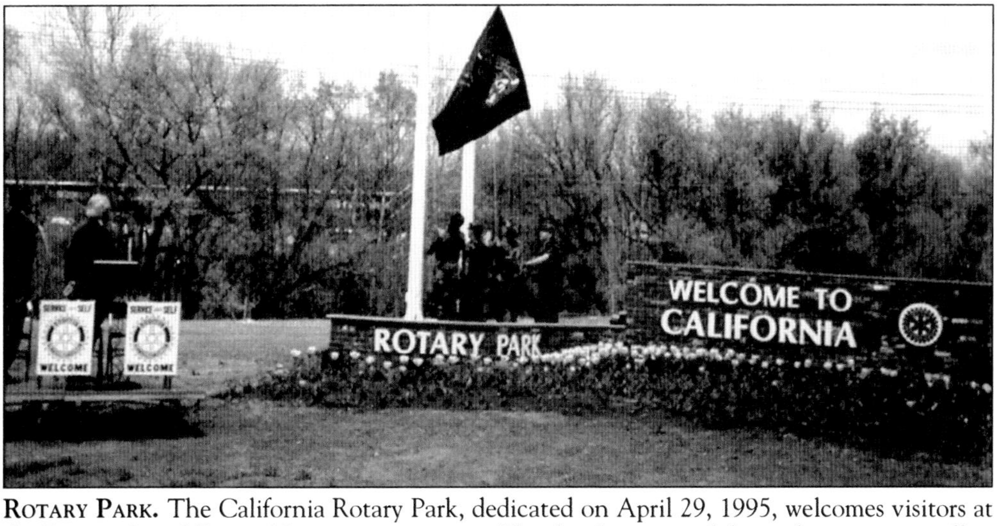

Rotary Park. The California Rotary Park, dedicated on April 29, 1995, welcomes visitors at the Route 43 and Route 88 entrance to town. The development of the park was a joint effort between the California Rotary Club and the California Borough Council. Once a flood-prone land, this grassy area is now a useful community park with attractive landscaping and a paved walking track.

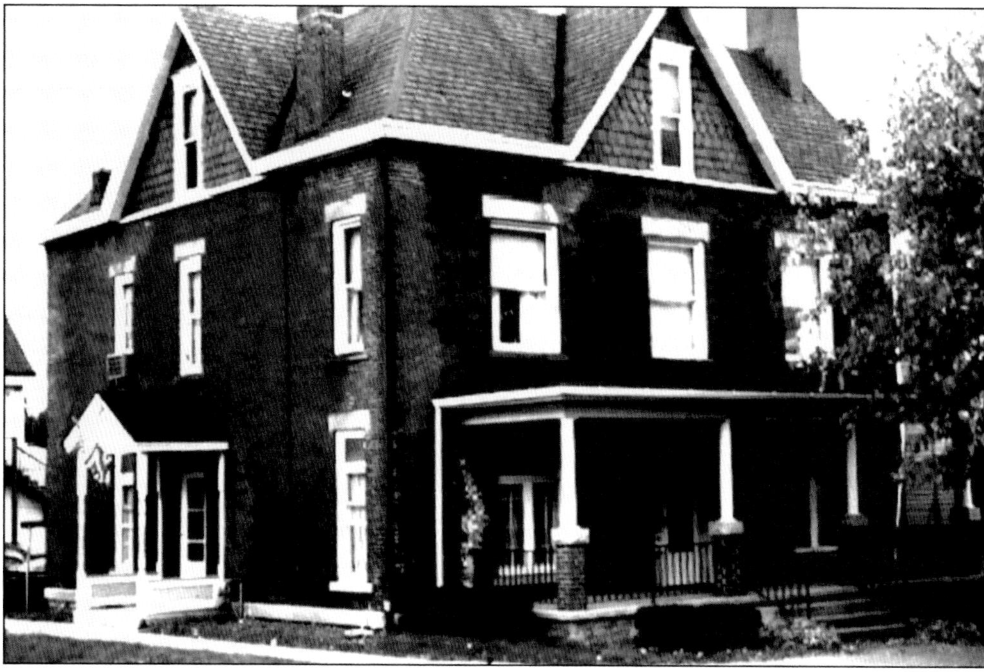

THE GALLAGHER HOUSE. One of California's finest examples of an early-20th-century Colonial Revival house is the Gallagher House, located at 429 Wood Street. Built in 1903 by Jonathan Winnett Jennings (a Methodist minister in the Monongahela Valley area), the house was listed on the National Register of Historic Places in March 1996 and is dedicated as the site of the California Area Historical Society.

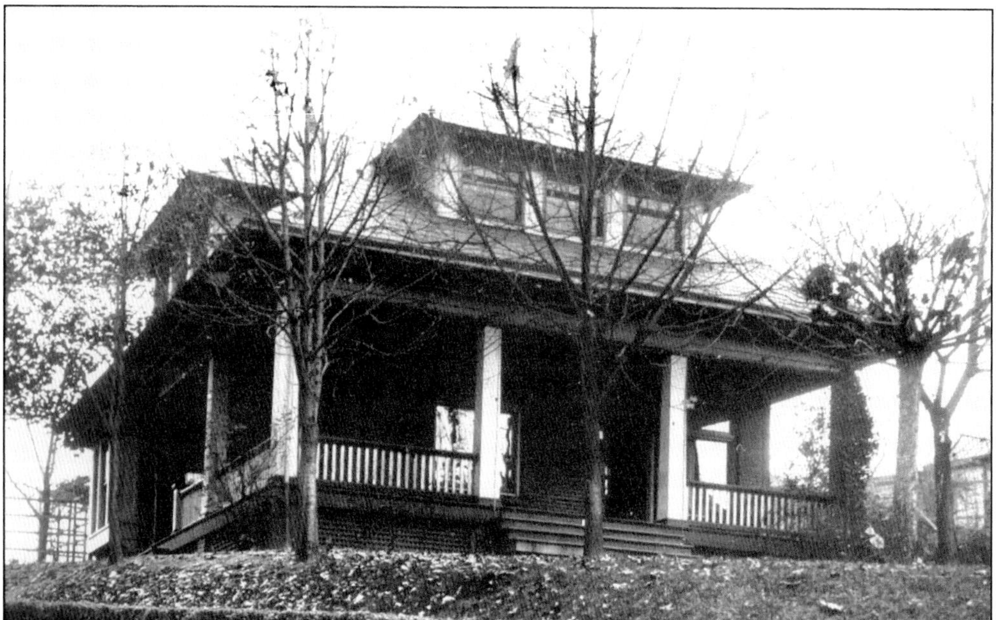

THE MOLLY FLEMING HOUSE. Recognized for its combined Arts and Crafts and Colonial Revival architecture, the Molly Fleming House, built in 1912, was placed on the National Register of Historic Places on May 30, 1997. It is located at 616 Wood Street. (Courtesy Barry Niccolai.)

THE HONOR ROLL DEDICATION. Paying homage to World War II veterans, the East Pike Honor Roll on Pennsylvania Avenue was dedicated in 1944. State senator Albert J. Reed and California State Teachers College president Michael Duda were speakers. The main attraction was the new honor roll.

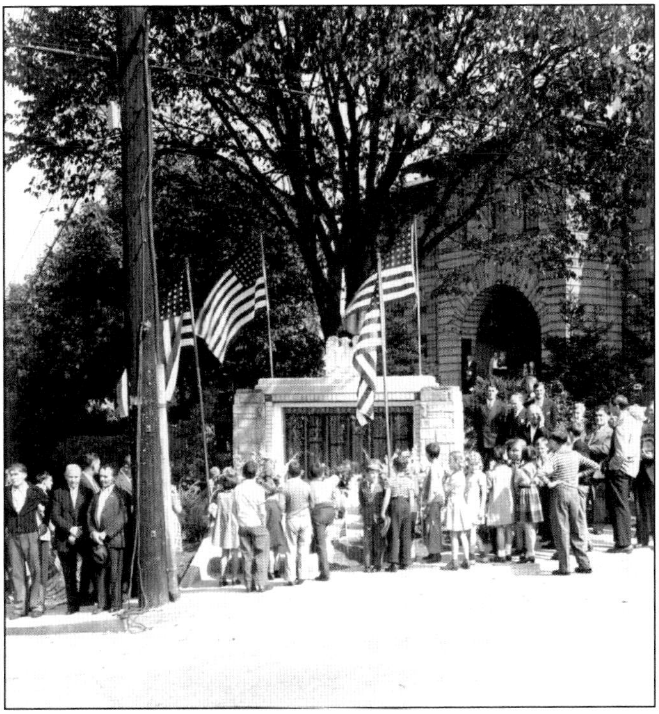

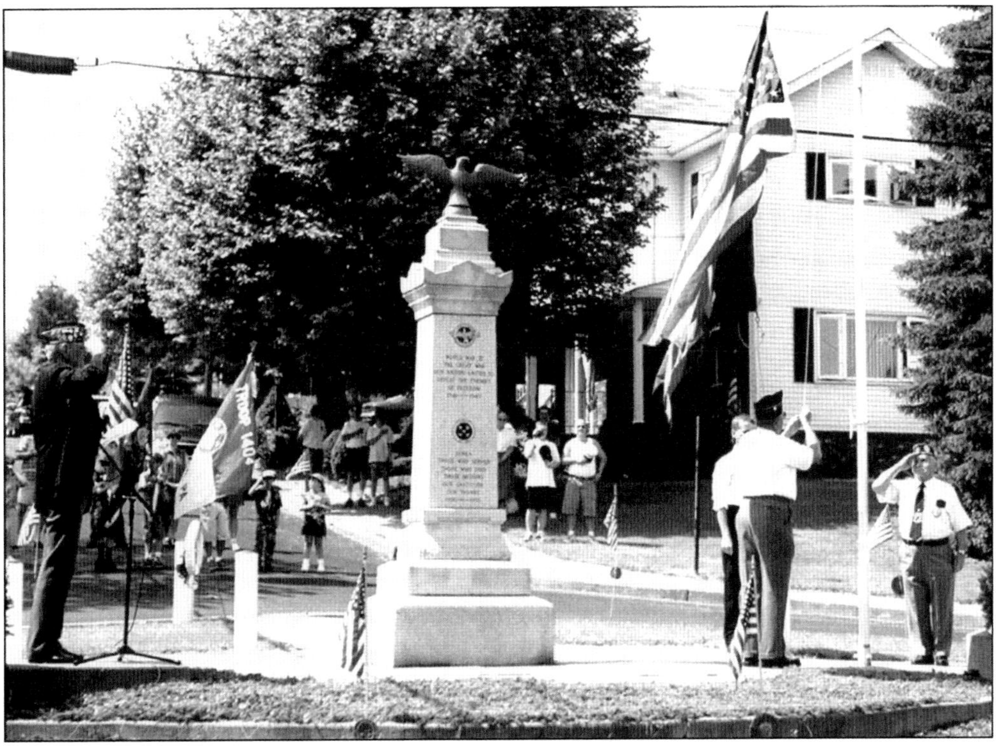

THE MEMORIAL DAY CELEBRATION. Memorial Day celebrations sponsored by the California American Legion Post No. 377 are annual ceremonies at Taylor Square. (Courtesy CAL 150 Sesquicentennial Committee.)

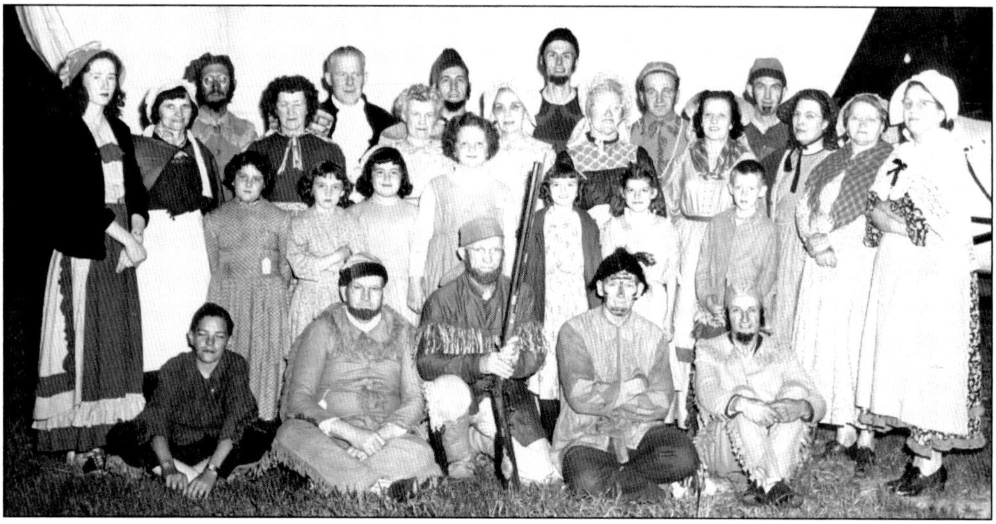

A CENTENNIAL DRAMATIZATION. The history of California has been told in many ways. At the centennial celebration during the week of June 6, 1949, history was presented in a dramatization on the high-school athletic field. *Mon Yough Trails* featured the townspeople playing the roles of everyone from Indian Peter to the pioneers going west in Conestoga wagons.

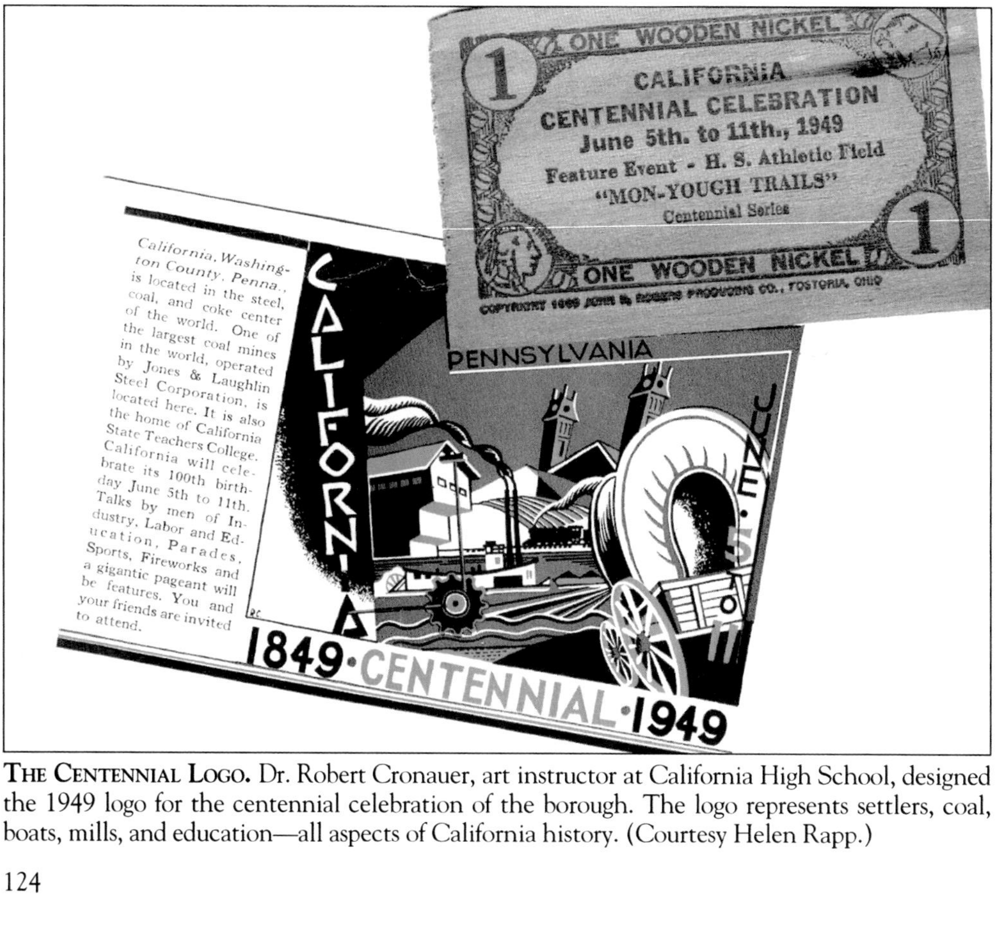

THE CENTENNIAL LOGO. Dr. Robert Cronauer, art instructor at California High School, designed the 1949 logo for the centennial celebration of the borough. The logo represents settlers, coal, boats, mills, and education—all aspects of California history. (Courtesy Helen Rapp.)

THE SESQUICENTENNIAL LOGO. Designed by Jacque Dwyer, the logo used for the sesquicentennial celebration of California was selected to represent the year-long commemoration of the 150th anniversary of the town.

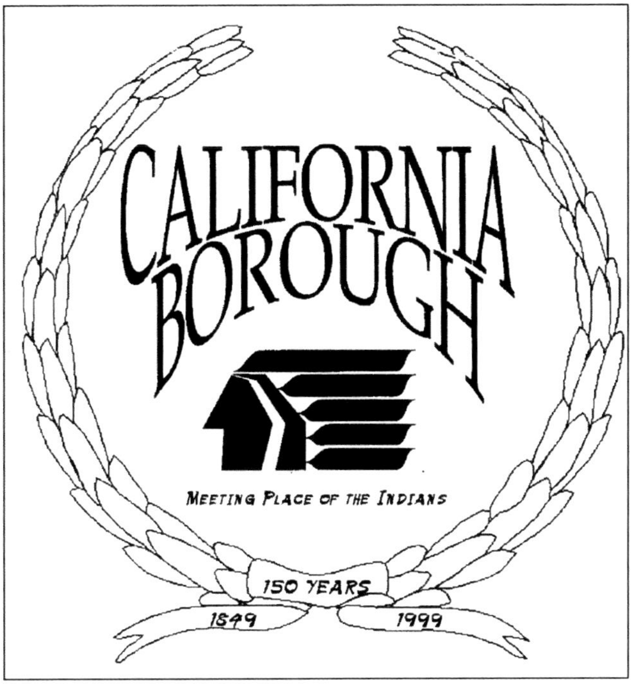

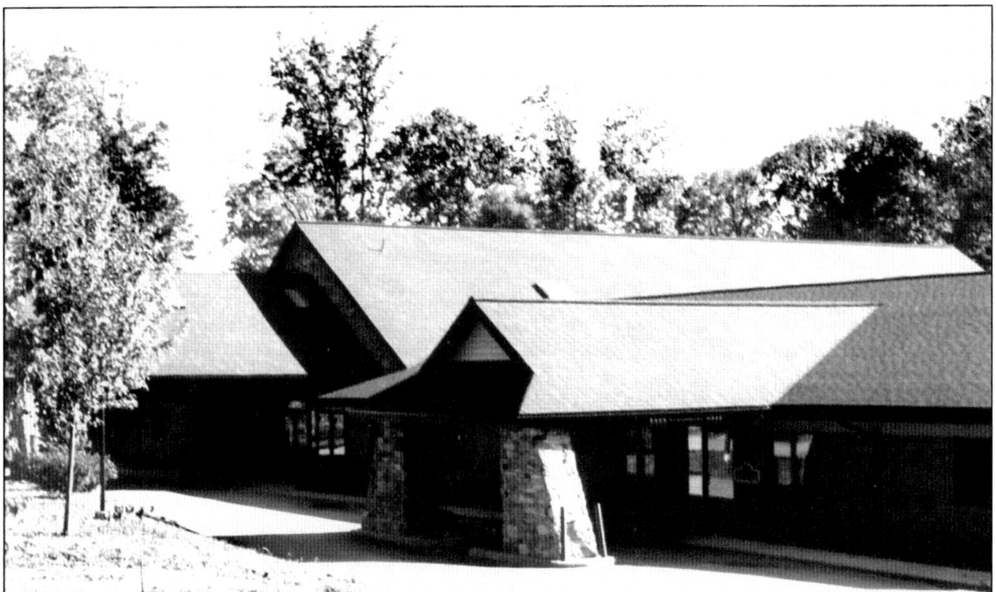

THE CENTER IN THE WOODS. On May 1992, ground was broken for a new senior citizen center on Route 88. The Center in the Woods addresses the needs of the older citizens in California and surrounding communities.

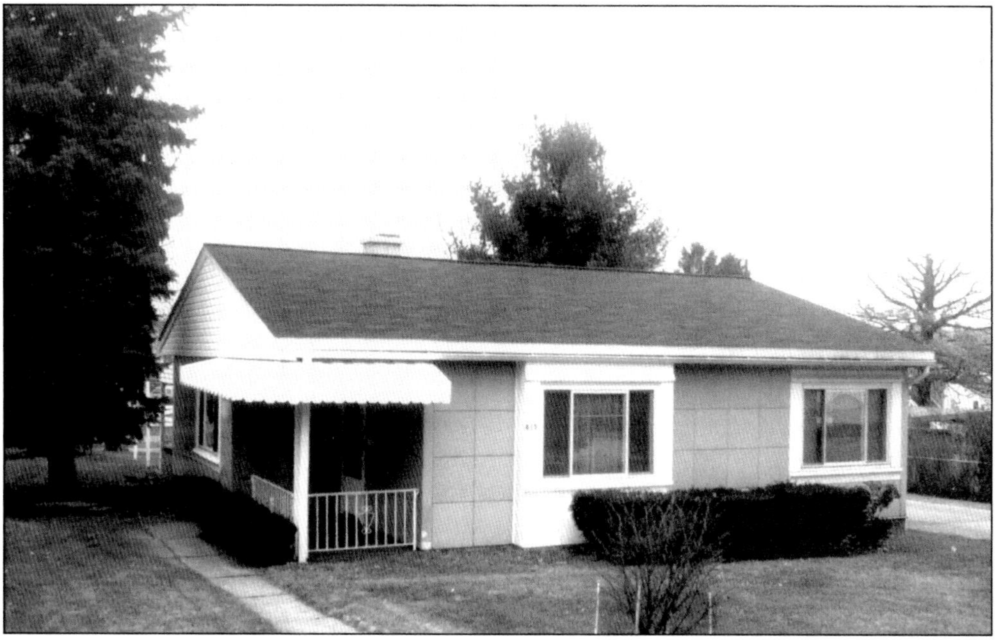

The Lustron Home. The Lustron Home, made of porcelain steel construction, represented a "modern" concept of home building in the 1940s. Three were built in California. The home shown here was built on Shutterly Avenue for the Cox family. The other Lustron Homes are located on Fifth Street and on Beazell Street.

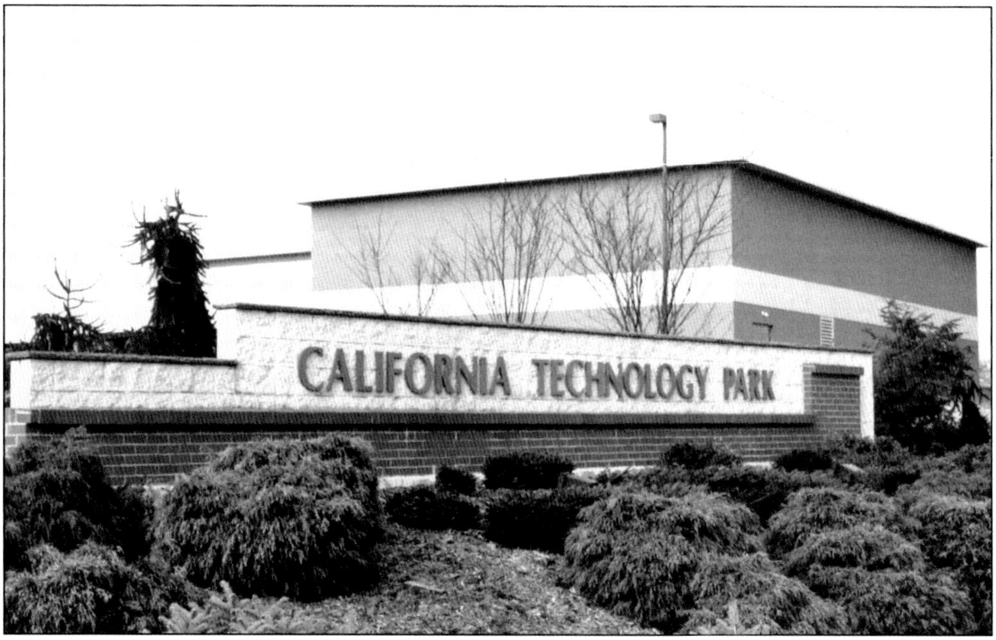

The California Technology Park. The Washington County Redevelopment Authority and Industrial Development Agency administers the California Technology Park to provide employment opportunities for residents of the Monongahela Valley. Located on Technology Drive with easy access to Route 43, the 120-acre park has attracted five industries to its complex since opening in 1991. (Courtesy Betty Carson.)

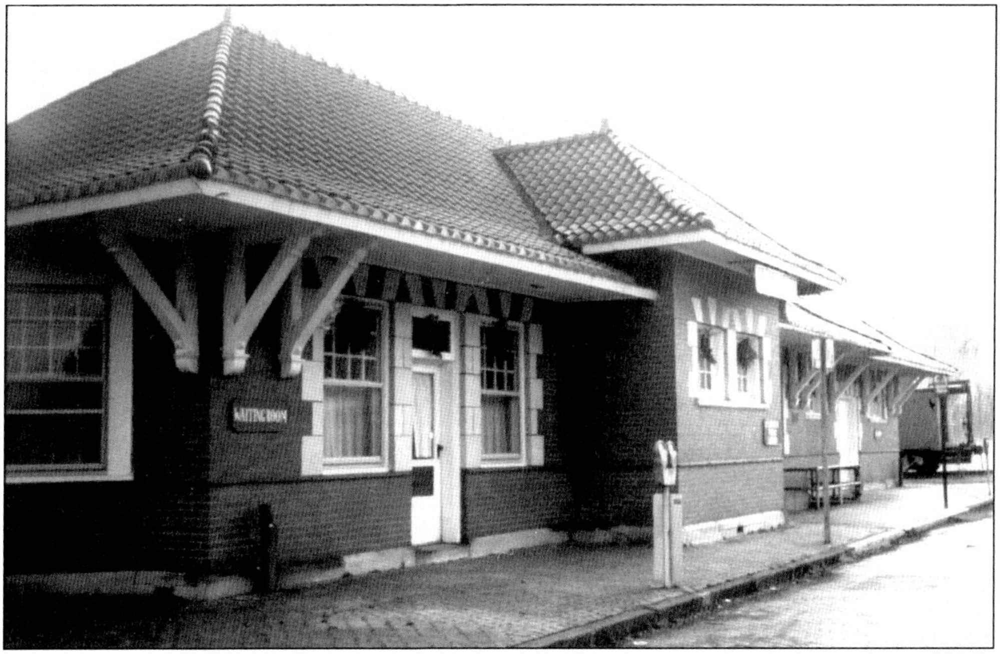

The California Public Library. Once a Pennsylvania Railroad station and depot, this building is the home of the California Public Library at Wood and Water Streets. The structure was placed on the National Register of Historic Places in June 1984. (Courtesy Barbara Rankin.)

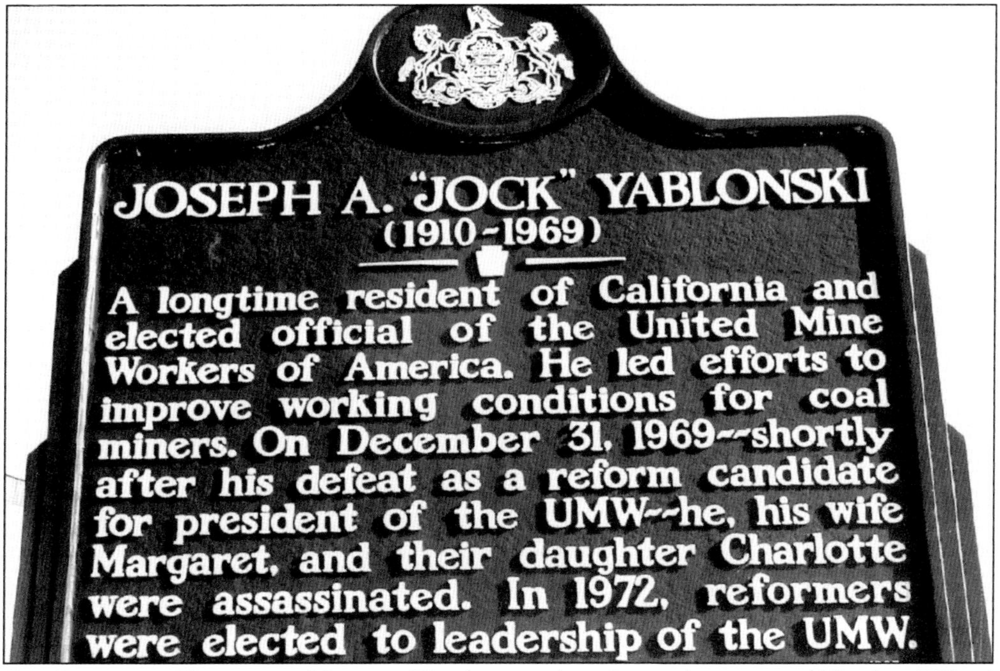

The Yablonski Historical Marker. This historical marker at the corner of Third and Wood Streets honors Joseph Yablonski for his efforts to improve working conditions for coal miners. Dedicated on November 4, 1994, the marker was sponsored by the California Area Historical Society. (Courtesy Edgar A. Harris Sr.)

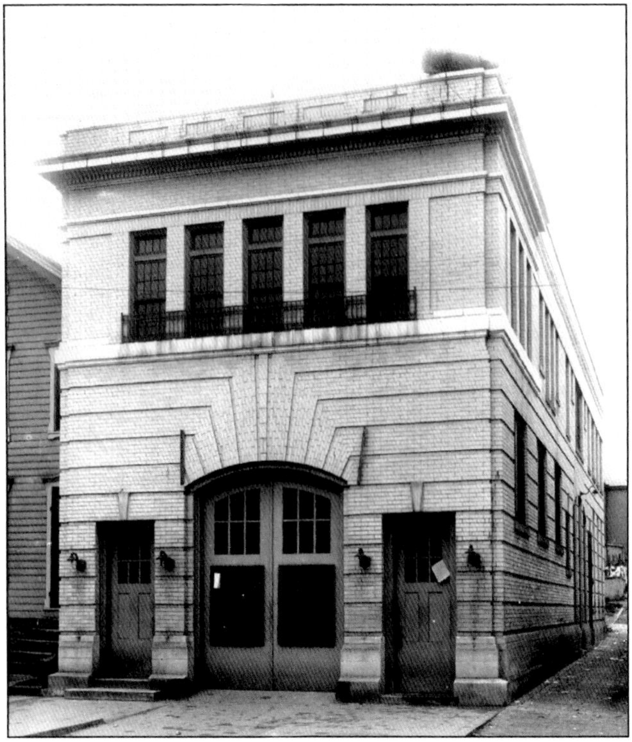

The Municipal Building. California's former municipal building, located on Third Street, was built in 1914. Borough meetings were held in the second-story boardroom. The fire department had its fire truck and equipment on the first floor, and the jail entrance was on the rear alley side. This building was razed in 1996.

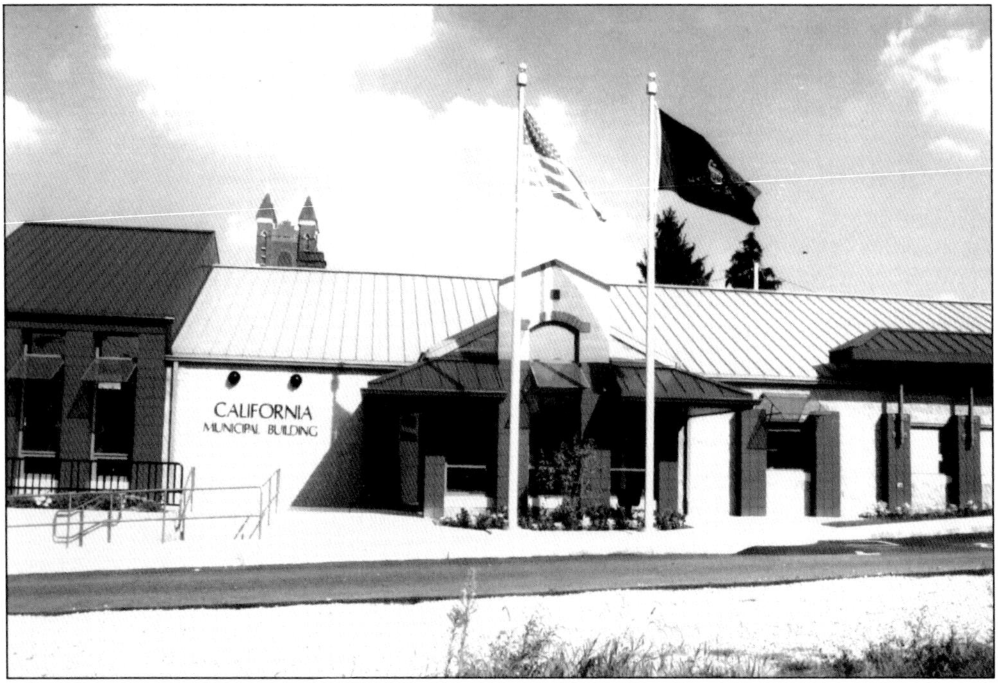

The Municipal Building. Pride in the progress of the community is shown in the new California Municipal Building, dedicated on September 20, 1997. The facility houses the borough meeting and conference rooms, the zoning office, and the police department. It is located on Third Street, the main thoroughfare through town. (Courtesy Joseph Dochinez.)